Interfacing to the
IBM Personal Computer

Lewis C. Eggebrecht is Technical Director for Franklin Computer Corporation, a manufacturer of personal and small business computer systems, in Cherry Hill, New Jersey. He served as architecture consultant on many IBM low-end products including terminal and word processing products. While employed by IBM, Mr. Eggebrecht was the system architect and design team leader for two of IBM's low cost systems, the System 23, or Datamaster, and the IBM Personal Computer. In his experience in manufacturing engineering, Mr. Eggebrecht has specialized in high performance test and process control applications. He is an avid microcomputer hobbyist with special interest in high-performance graphic systems. He is a graduate of Michigan Technological University with a Bachelor of Science degree in electrical engineering.

Interfacing to the IBM Personal Computer

by

Lewis C. Eggebrecht

Howard W. Sams & Co., Inc.
4300 WEST 62ND ST. INDIANAPOLIS, INDIANA 46268 USA

International Standard Book Number: 0-672-22027-X
Library of Congress Catalog Card Number: 83-61065

Edited by: *Welborn Associates*

Printed in the United States of America.

PREFACE

The IBM Personal Computer, hereafter called the PC, has proven to be a popular and versatile system that can be used in many applications—at home, at work, in the classroom, or the lab. Its powerful 16-bit architecture, with a capability of addressing large amounts of memory, has opened whole new horizons for the use of the personal computer. The system has the additional attribute of being an "open" design. That is, it is designed and documented such that interfaces and devices can easily be attached to the system. This book describes the PC's interfaces, resources, and functions which can be used to implement those projects that require such capabilities as those of the PC. The intent, here, is to provide sufficient information and detail so that engineers, scientists, hobbyists, and others, with a moderate computer and electronic background, can effectively interface their own devices and experiments to the PC.

This book does not present specific interface designs or projects, but it does provide information and techniques that can be used in many different projects. The major emphasis in the book is describing the capabilities and resources that are available in the PC and in its interfaces that can aid in the implementation of a specific design project or experiment. This task is accomplished by first presenting an overview of the PC system and then following that with more detailed descriptions of its electronics, its functions, and its interfaces. A review of the Intel 8088 microprocessor is also presented.

Since most interfacing applications will attach and communicate through the system's bus, this area is also covered, from both a theoretical and a practical point of view. Special emphasis is placed on the system's interrupts, direct-memory access, timing and counting, and its programmed I/O capabilities. These functions are nearly always used in interfacing projects and they must be well understood for efficient and reliable design implementations.

Finally, two design projects are presented that will be of interest to all. The first project is a PC bus extender. This feature can be used to extend the PC bus outside of the system unit box, and thus provide more feature card slots. The second project is a simple bus analyzer card extender. It can be used to help with the debugging of design projects.

The IBM Personal Computer is easy to set up, easy to learn, and easy to use. It is an affordable, easily expandable system. Hopefully, in this book, I have smoothed your pathway in the discovery and use of the PC's many advanced design features.

LEWIS C. EGGEBRECHT

CONTENTS

CHAPTER 1

OVERVIEW OF THE IBM PERSONAL COMPUTER SYSTEM

INTRODUCTION

The basic components of the IBM Personal Computer consist of the System Unit, the Keyboard, the optional IBM Monochrome Display, and the IBM Graphics Printer. They can be quickly connected and ready to use in a matter of minutes. Fig. 1-1 illustrates the major elements of a PC system. The System Unit contains the 16-bit microprocessor, the memory, and one or two diskette drives housed in a single table-top unit. This unit is

Fig. 1-1. A typical IBM Personal Computer system.

approximately $5\frac{1}{2}$ inches high, $19\frac{1}{2}$ inches wide, and 16 inches deep. The System Unit is powered from a standard 110-volt ac grounded wall outlet. Attached to the System Unit through a 6-foot, coiled, telephone-like cable is the PC keyboard. The keyboard is not rigidly attached to the system but can be moved about to the extent of the attaching cable. Pictured on top of the System Unit in Fig. 1-1 is the PC monochrome display. This unit attaches to the System Unit via two cables—a power cable and a signal cable. The last element of a typical system is the printer. The IBM printer attaches to the System Unit via signal cable but obtains its power from a standard 110-volt ac wall outlet.

THE SYSTEM UNIT

The System Unit contains the 16-bit microprocessor, the read-only memory, the user or random-access memory (RAM), the power supply, and a speaker for audio and music applications, plus five expansion slots to allow easy expansion of the system. The unit also contains an interface for attaching a cassette recorder/player for recording information on tape and playing programs stored on audio cassette tape. One or two diskette drives can also be mounted in the System Unit. Fig. 1-2 is a picture of the System Unit with the cover removed.

The Processor Board

The heart of the System Unit is the processor board which fits horizontally in the base of the System Unit. The processor board contains much of the essential electronics of the system, including the 8088 microprocessor, up to 64KB (kilobytes) of random-access memory (RAM), 40KB of read-only memory (ROM), and I/O adapters for the keyboard, tape cassette, and audio speaker. The most important features of the processor board are the 5 system-bus slots that allow additional features and interface devices to be added to the System Unit. Much of this book will be devoted to describing the functions that are available at the system bus in these 5 card slots.

In Fig. 1-2, all of the feature cards have been removed so that the processor board is visible with its 5 system-bus card slots shown empty.

The Power Supply

The power supply is housed in the System Unit. It is shown at the top right corner in Fig. 1-2. This power supply provides direct current (dc) power to the elements of the System Unit. The power supply also provides ac power to the monochrome display. This power supply provides four dc power levels—$\pm$ 5 volts and $\pm$ 12 volts. These power levels are

Fig. 1-2. The System Unit.

available at the 5 system-bus slots and can be used by feature cards. A total of 63.5 watts of dc power is available to the system and its features.

The Diskette Drives

The System Unit can house up to two 5¼-inch floppy diskette drives. At this time, two capacity sizes are offered by IBM. One is a single-sided drive with approximately 160KB of storage and the other is a double-sided drive with approximately 320KB of storage. Thus, if two double-sided drives were installed in the System Unit, a total of 640 kilobytes of storage is available within the unit. To attach the two diskette drives, a diskette adapter must be installed in one of the 5 system-bus slots. The IBM diskette-drive adapter has an external port that provides the signals for attaching two drives outside of the System Unit. These drives must, however, provide their own power.

The Speaker

Housed near the front left corner of the System Unit is a small audio speaker. The speaker is under program control and, typically, it is used as an alarm or as an output device for games and application programs that require an audio output.

THE SYSTEM KEYBOARD

The PC's keyboard is an 83-key full-function keyboard with a central body similar to that of a standard typewriter keyboard. There are extra keys on each side of the standard typewriter section, however. On the left, there are two columns of 5 keys that are program function keys. The key functions are defined by the system or application program being executed in the system. On the right side of the keyboard, an array of keys are available that are used to perform the dual functions of numeric data entry and cursor control. Fig. 1-3 is a picture of the system keyboard that clearly illustrates its layout. The keyboard interfaces to the System Unit via a four-wire interface that contains both signal and power leads. The keyboard sends a unique 8-bit scan code on both a key depression and on a key release. If a key is held down, the keyboard sends a scan code on the depression, pauses, and then sends the same scan code at a fixed typomatic rate until the key is released. Upon release of the key, a different scan code is sent. This function allows applications to define the mode of operation of the keyboard and, also, define the shift states and the typomatic functions of each key on the keyboard.

THE SYSTEM PRINTER

The system printer presently provided by IBM for the PC is an 80–character-per-second wire-matrix printer. The printer attaches to the System Unit through a 6-foot signal cable. The interface is a parallel Centronix printer interface and it is capable of attaching any printer that supports a similar interface. Printing is done using a 9-wire print head and characters are formed in a 9 × 9 matrix. Printing is done bidirectional with logic seeking. This means that the printing is accomplished using the least movement of the head across the paper. There are 12 character styles, up to 132 characters per line, and the line spacing is programmable in $\frac{1}{6}$-inch increments.

Printing Modes Supported

Through programming of special escape characters and sequences, it is possible to direct the printer to operate in a variety of modes and fonts. In normal mode, the printer prints 10 characters per inch with 80 characters per line. In enlarged mode, the printer prints 5 characters per inch and 40 characters per line. In condensed mode, the printing is done at 16.5 characters per inch and 132 characters per line. There is also a special con-

Fig. 1-3. The PC keyboard.

densed/enlarged mode where the printing is done at 8.25 characters per inch and with 66 characters per line.

Printer Character Set

The printer supports the standard 96-character set of ASCII and 9 international characters or symbols. These are selected by switch settings in the printer. The printer character set is a subset of the 256 characters that are supported by the PC display adapters. Thus, there is a large set of characters that cannot be printed but can be displayed. The printer does support a special 64-character set that contains block graphic characters. This character set can be used to print low-resolution graphic images on the printer.

Special Features

The IBM printer is nearly identical to the Epson MX-80 printer and, thus, if graphics functions and pressure-paper feed functions are desired, it is possible to substitute other models of the MX-80 printers that have these features.

THE MONOCHROME DISPLAY

At present, the only display offered by IBM for the PC is a high-resolution monochrome device. This display device attaches to the "monochrome display and printer" port adapter card that fits in one of the 5 system-bus

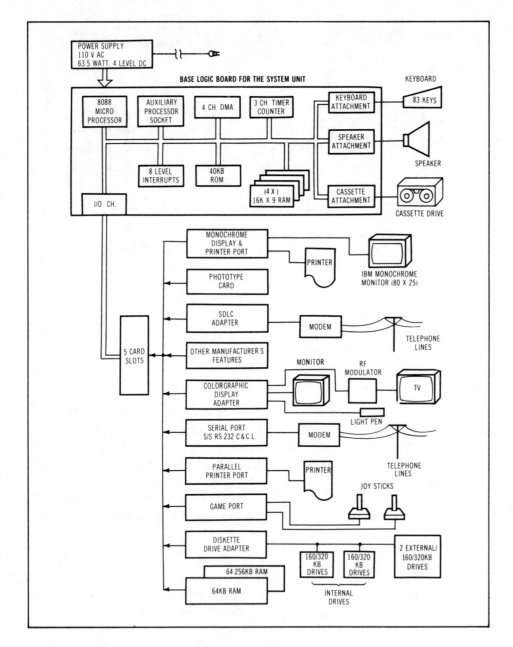

Fig. 1-4. Block diagram of the PC and its features.

card slots in the System Unit. The display obtains its power from the System Unit via a very short cable that is designed to only be attached to the System Unit. The signal interface to the display is a direct-drive interface with horizontal drive, vertical drive, video, and intensity signal lines. The display unit is a green phosphor monitor with a horizontal resolution of 720 dots and a vertical resolution of 350 dots. The screen size is approximately 11.5 inches when measured diagonally. The screen is refreshed at a 50-hertz rate; the scan frequency is approximately 17 kHz. Video data are shifted out at a 16.257 MHz rate. When the display is attached to the IBM "monochrome display and printer" port adapter, characters are formed in a 9 × 14 boxed area.

It should be noted that other displays and monitors, including tv sets, can be attached to the PC using the color graphics display adapter that is available from IBM.

THE FEATURE CARDS

IBM presently offers a set of feature cards that fit into the 5 system-bus slots to provide memory expansion, device attachment, and standard interfaces for a variety of devices and purposes.

Diskette Drive Attachment Adapter Card

This feature card allows the attachment of two 5¼-inch diskette drives internal to the System Unit and two external drives. It takes one slot in the System Unit. The card is capable of supporting both single- and double-sided diskettes in double-density format.

Parallel Printer Port Attachment Card

This card allows the attachment of most printers that use the industry-standard Centronix parallel interface. It is capable of supporting both programmed data transfer and interrupt-driven data transfer. The attachment card fits in one of the 5 system-bus card slots.

Serial Port Attachment Card

This card has a single ASYNC serial port with an RS-232-C electrical interface that allows attachment to a modem for data transmission over telephone lines. It has a programmable baud rate from 50 to 9600 baud and a programmable data frame size of 5, 6, 7, or 8 bits. The number of stop bits is also programmable from 1, to 1½, to 2. Parity can be selected as being even, odd, or not generated. The card also has a jumper-selectable current-loop electrical interface for local attachment to current-loop attached devices. This card fits into the System Unit and takes one system-bus card slot.

Game Control Adapter Card

This adapter card allows the attachment of joysticks and paddles to the IBM PC in support of game programs. It contains four inputs that sense resistive values from a joystick or a paddle and four inputs that are used to sense a switch closure from the button or triggers on joysticks or paddles. This feature fits in the System Unit and takes one system-bus card slot.

Color Graphics Display Adapter Card

This card provides the ability to attach a variety of tv-frequency monitors and displays. It supports both monochrome and color in both text and graphic modes. In text mode, it supports either a 40×25 or an 80×25 display format. Also, in text mode, each character is formed in an 8×8 character box. Characters can be monochrome or they can be displayed in color with 8 background colors and 16 foreground colors. Each character in text mode can also be made to blink. Multiple pages of text may also be stored in the adapter, as four 80×25 screens or eight 40×25 screens.

The adapter card has two graphics modes—a 320×200 four-color mode and a 640×200 monochrome mode. In the 320×200 mode, each dot on the screen can be programmed with one of four colors. Two sets of four colors are available. The 640×200 mode is only supported in monochrome since all of the 16KB on-card memory is used to represent the on or off state of the dots, leaving no memory to represent color information.

The graphics display adapter can support three different display interfaces—a direct drive, a composite video, and an rf modulator. The rf modulator interface allows, through the use of an external rf modulator device, attachment to a standard home tv set. The adapter will also support a light pen input device.

The display adapter card contains a ROM character generator that provides 256 characters for display on the screen. In addition to the standard 96 ASCII characters, there are special characters for supporting games and text processing, plus international characters and symbols, line graphics, and scientific notation and Greek characters.

The color graphics adapter card fits in the System Unit and takes one of the system-bus card slots.

Monochrome Display Adapter and Parallel Printer Port Adapter Card

This card is a combination adapter supporting two functions, that of attachment of the IBM monochrome display and that of providing a parallel printer port. The display adapter portion of this card supports a text-only 80 × 25 screen format on the IBM monchrome display. The character set is the same character set that is used on the color graphic adapter card but it is styled in a larger font to take advantage of the higher performance of the monochrome display. Characters are formed in a 9 × 14 character box and each character can be highlighted, underlined, blinked, and reversed from green-on-black to black-on-green. This card does not support a light pen and it can only be used to attach to the IBM monochrome display. The parallel printer port portion of this card is identical to that of the parallel printer port attachment card described elsewhere in this chapter. This adapter card fits in the System Unit and uses one of the 5 system-bus card slots.

Prototyping Card

This is a card design that allows the prototyping of user-defined adapters and interfaces to the IBM system bus. It is a nearly blank card with wiring on it that allows interfacing to the system-bus interface lines. It is wired such that the system bus can be buffered and an address can easily be decoded by just adding a few components. The majority of the card is simply an array of holes that allow the insertion of components and provides for the custom wiring of your design.

SDLC Adapter Card

This is another new communications card that has just been announced by IBM. It is typically used to attach the terminal and computer together over telephone lines. The letters SDLC stand for Synchronous Data Line Control and indicate a special protocol that is used in data communications. This card also requires a special synchronous modem in order to be used on the telephone lines.

Memory Expansion Cards

IBM presently offers two memory expansion cards, a 64KB card and a 64 to 256KB memory card. Both cards fit in the System Unit and they take one of the 5 system-bus I/O slots. The 64KB card cannot be extended in size by adding a memory chip. However, the 64–256KB card can be purchased with only 64KB of memory and it can later be upgraded in 64KB increments to a maximum size of 256KB. Each card has dip switches on it which can be set to position the card in the memory-address space on any 64KB boundary.

Other Adapters and Devices

The adapters, interfaces, and devices available on the PC are not limited to those offered by IBM. A large number of companies are manufacturing and offering for sale a variety of adapter cards and devices for the IBM PC. Before you embark on an adapter design, it would pay to do a little research to see if the design is not already available in the industry. A good place to look is in the many excellent personal computing magazines that are now being published. These magazines not only contain many advertisements but they often contain a directory of the manufacturers of adapter devices for many popular personal computers.

Fig. 1-4 is a block diagram of the IBM PC and the features and adapters presently being offered by IBM.

CHAPTER 2

THE SYSTEM UNIT PROCESSOR BOARD

INTRODUCTION

The system board is the heart of the electronics in the PC. An understanding of its contents and functions is necessary since most of the interfacing problems encountered will be solved by using many of the capabilities that are present on this board. Fig. 2-1 is a photograph of a system board that has been removed from the System Unit and Fig. 2-2 gives a detailed block diagram of the functional elements on the system board.

SYSTEM BOARD FUNCTIONS

This chapter is a brief summary of the functions and capabilities of the system board. Many of these functions are very relevant to the task of interfacing to the PC and they will be covered in much greater detail in later chapters.

The 8088 Microprocessor

If the system board is the heart of the PC electronics, the 8088 microprocessor is the heartbeat of the system. The 8088 is a 16-bit microprocessor with an 8-bit memory bus. Its instructions can manipulate 16-bit data, but the data and instructions are fetched and written to memory 8 bits at a time. The 8088 has the ability to address up to 1 megabytes of memory, which can contain either data or programs.

The 8088 will also support the functions of interrupts and direct-memory access. These are of particular value when interfacing to the PC. These functions are covered in detail in later chapters.

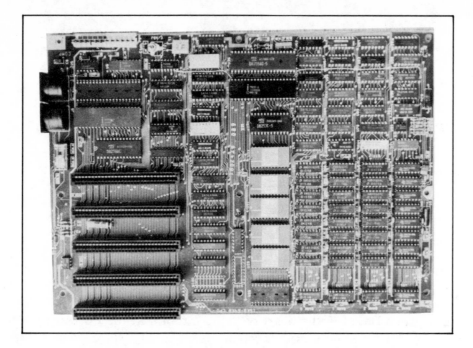

Fig. 2-1. The base logic processor board.

The Clock Circuits

In the PC implementation, the 8088 is run at a clock rate of 4.77 MHz. This results in a system clock time of approximately 210 nanoseconds. Since most bus cycles are 4 clock cycles long, a typical memory cycle in the PC is 840 nanoseconds long.

The 8088 microprocessor and many of the processor board functions derive their timing information and signals from the base system oscillator. The oscillator circuit is driven from a 14.31818-MHz crystal. The 8284A clock chip divides this base frequency by three to derive the 4.77-MHz signal for the 8088 microprocessor. Both the 14.31818-MHz and the 4.77-MHz signals are also available on the system-bus card slots. The 4.77-MHz signal is further divided by a factor of four to give a 1.19-MHz signal that is used to drive the clock inputs on the system board's timer counters.

System Board Bus

The major functional components of the system board are tied to the 8088 microprocessor by the system bus. This bus is made up of several types of signal lines—data bus, address bus, control, timing, interrupt requests, and direct-memory access (DMA) control. The bus starts at the

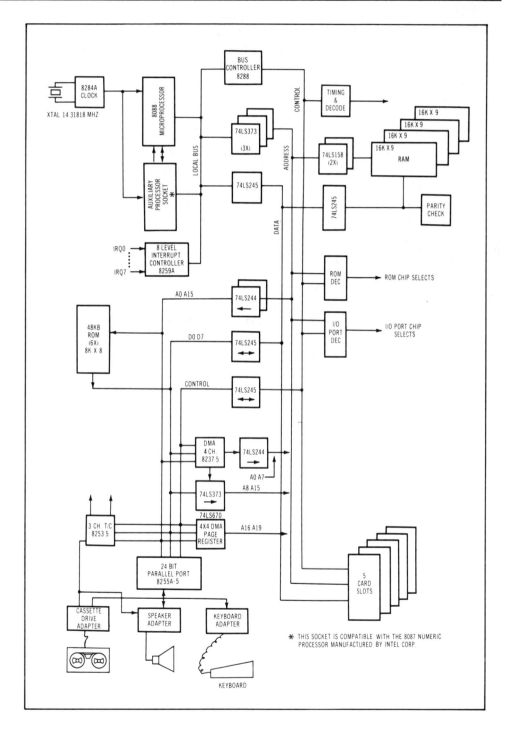

Fig. 2-2. Block diagram of system board.

pin of the 8088 microprocessor. This interface is a highly encoded and multiplexed interface and it is commonly referred to as the local bus. Attached to the local bus are: (1) an auxiliary processor socket that is capable of accepting the Intel 8087 numerical processor, (2) an 8-level 8259A interrupt controller, (3) the 8288 bus controller, and (4) bus repowering and demultiplexing circuits. The outputs of the bus controller and the local bus demultiplexing and repowering circuits form the basic signals that represent the system bus. Attached to the system bus on the processor board are: (1) processor support circuits (including DMA channels and timer counters), (2) I/O port and memory address decode logic, (3) ROM, (4) RAM, (5) feature-installed sense switches, (6) integrated I/O adapters, and (7) the system board's 5 feature card slots.

System Board ROM

Attached to the system board's bus is 40KB of read-only memory (ROM). The ROM is decoded in such a manner that it resides in the uppermost 40K of address space in the 1-megabyte address space of the 8080 microprocessor. The ROM starts at hex address F6000 and extends to hex address FFFFF. At present, there is an empty module socket on the system that could accept one additional 8KB ROM or EPROM chip. This empty socket is decoded such that it resides in the system memory address space that starts at hex address F4000 and extends to hex address F5FFF. The system board is designed so that there is a 16KB region of the 8088's address space that is nonusable. The region from hex address F0000 to hex address F3FFF has no sockets on the processor board and, thus, cannot exist on the system-bus card slots, since the processor bus is not enabled for this memory decode.

The 40KB of ROM on the system board contains microcode supporting the following functions of the system.

—System initialization.
—Power-on diagnostics and system checkout.
—System configuration determination.
—I/O device drivers that are commonly called BIOS (Basic Input/Output System).
—Diskette bootstrap loader.
—Font bit patterns for the first 128 characters of the system's 256 character set. This takes 1024 bytes of ROM space.

All of the above functions reside in one of the 8KB ROM chips. This ROM chip resides in the address space beginning at hex address FE000 and going to FFFFF. The program listings for these functions are documented in the IBM Technical Reference Manual.

The remaining 32KB of ROM (in the other four 8KB ROM chips) contains the Microsoft BASIC Interpreter.

System Board RAM

The system board is designed so that from 16KB to 64KB of random-access memory (RAM), in 16KB increments, can be installed. The first 16KB is soldered into the system board and the remaining 48KB is placed on sockets. The system board's RAM resides in the 8088's address space beginning at hex address 00000; it extends to hex address 0FFFF, assuming that all 64KB of memory is installed. It should be noted that if less than the full 64KB of memory is installed, additional remaining memory cannot be installed in the system board's card slots. This is because the system bus to the card slots is not enabled for any memory addresses below 64K. This means that memory expansion beyond 64KB, using the system board's card slots, should only be done after all 64KB of system board memory is installed. If this is not done, the installed memory will be noncontiguous or it will have a hole. Most of the PC's software requires a contiguous memory space.

The system board's memory is actually 9 bits wide; the ninth bit is a parity bit. Parity is generated on every memory write cycle and stored in the ninth bit. On every memory read cycle, parity is regenerated from the 8 data bits and compared to the parity bit that was previously stored on the last write cycle. If the parity is the same, the data are assumed to be good. If the parity bits do not compare, a parity check is generated and is reported to the system by generating an interrupt to the 8088 microprocessor. The system software will then attempt to write a message to the system's display device and, then, halt the processor.

The system board uses $16K \times 1$ dynamic memory chips with an access time of 250 nanoseconds. These chips require three power levels to operate—+5 volts, −5 volts, and +12 volts.

System Board Timer/Counter

To support the system timing and counting function, an 8253-5 timer/counter chip with three 16-bit timer counters is attached to the system bus. The clock input on all three channels is driven by a free-running 1.19-MHz clock signal. The output from timer Channel 0 is tied to the system interrupt level 0 and is programmed to generate an interrupt every 54.925 milliseconds (or approximately 18.2 times per second). This timer is used by the system I/O routines and by the system's time-of-day clock. The output of timer Channel 1 is used to generate a DMA request on DMA Channel 0. This is used to refresh the system's dynamic memory by creating a dummy memory-read cycle every 72 processor clocks or every 15.12 microseconds. Thus, timer Channel 1 is programmed to generate a DMA request every 15.12 microseconds. The output from timer Channel 2 is used to drive the system's audio speaker and to transmit data to the audio cassette port on the system board.

System Board DMA

Some I/O devices, such as the PC's diskette drives, transmit data faster than the processor can handle under program control. To handle this problem, the system board has a facility that allows data to be transmitted directly between an adapter or a device and memory without the involvement of the 8088 processor. This function is accomplished in the PC (and on the system board) through the use of a chip called a DMA controller. The specific device used in the PC is an 8237-5 DMA controller chip. This device supports data transfers from or to the four adapters and memory. When an adapter or device wants to transfer information, it requests the 8237-5 to perform the function. The DMA controller requests the 8088 to leave the system bus and, then, the controller takes over the system bus and performs the actual data transfer. The DMA controller can only address 64K of memory, thus extra circuits are added to provide the extra addressing bits needed to address the full 1 megabyte of the system memory. The extra addressing bits are added from four 4-bit page registers. There is one 4-bit page register for each DMA channel. The 4 bits from the page register are used as the high-order memory address bits during DMA cycles.

Channel 0 of the four DMA channels is used on the system board to perform system dynamic memory refresh. The other three channels are available on the system bus in the 5 card slots located on the system board.

System Board Interrupts

The 8088 microprocessor supports two interrupt input sources—a maskable and a nonmaskable input. Since more interrupt levels are desirable, an 8259A interrupt controller chip is added. This expands the maskable interrupt input on the 8088 processor to eight levels. This chip is not attached to the system bus but to the local bus on the 8088 microprocessor. Of the eight levels available, two are used on the system board and the remaining six are made available on the system bus; they are present in the system board card slots. Level 0 is used on the system board to accept interrupts from the timer/counter Channel 0 output. Level 1 is used on the system board to accept interrupts from the PC keyboard.

System Board Integrated I/O Adapters

The system board has integrated on it the adapters for the keyboard, the audio speaker, and an audio cassette port. These devices are primarily interfaced to the system bus through the use of a parallel register chip. The specific chip used in the PC design is an 8255A-5 device. This device supports 24 bits of programmable input/output lines.

One 8-bit port of the 8255A-5 is used to create a sub-bus, which is used to either read data from the system's configuration dip switches or to read the scan code from the keyboard input shift register. Other bits in this device are used to drive the audio speaker cone, read serial data from the audio cassette, control the motor in an audio cassette machine, modulate the clock input on timer counter Channel 2, sense check the latches and configuration dip switches, and interface to the keyboard serial interface.

Details of these interfaces will be covered in more depth in later chapters since these adapters can be used to attach to various other interfaces and devices.

The circuit schematic of the system board is published in the IBM Technical Reference Manual.

CHAPTER 3

THE 8088 MICROPROCESSOR

INTRODUCTION

An understanding of the capabilities and functions of the PC's microprocessor, the Intel 8088, is essential to designing and attaching interfaces
and devices to the Personal Computer. This chapter covers the more sali-
ent points of the 8088 and stresses those areas that are of particular interest in implementing an interface design project.

The 8088 microprocessor is a derivation of the Intel 8086 microprocessor, with the major difference being the data bus width. The 8086 has both
an internal data path of 16 bits and an external memory data-bus width of
16 bits, whereas, the 8088 has an internal data-path width of 16 bits but
its memory interface is only 8 bits. It should be noted that code written for
either processor will execute on the other processor with no changes. This,
however, does not mean that code written on a different 8088- or 8086-
based system will run without change. This is because the code may be
dependent on other system resources or functions other than those of the
processor. The difference in bus width between the 8086 and 8088 could
lead you to conclude that the 8086 is twice as fast as the 8088 processor.
This, in general, is not true. Since the 8088 executes its instructions off of
an internal queue that is filled as soon as there is an empty location, it is
possible to overlap execution cycles and instruction-fetch bus cycles. As
long as the instructions are executed off of the internal queue and do not
have to wait for a bus cycle, they execute just as fast as they would on an
8086 processor. However, if data cycles are 16 bits long, they will take two
memory cycles, whereas, in an 8086 microprocessor, it would take only
one cycle. Thus, if an application is heavily byte-data-oriented, it will perform nearly as well on an 8088 microprocessor as it will on an 8086 proc-

essor. If the application is 16-bit in nature, it will perform less well on the 8088 device, but it is not likely to be at half speed.

The following is a quick summary of the highlights of the 8088 microprocessor, all of which are described in greater detail later in this chapter.

—16-bit internal architecture.
—Supports 1 megabyte of attached memory.
—8- and 16-bit signed and unsigned arithmetic in both binary and decimal notation, including multiply and divide.
—14 words of 16-bit registers.
—Maskable and nonmaskable interrupt capability.
—24-operand addressing modes.
—Direct-memory access capability.
—Supports on local bus co-processors.
—Supports both memory-mapped I/O and I/O-mapped I/O.
—String operations.

INTERFACE SIGNAL PINS

A good way to learn about the 8088 microprocessor is to describe the functions of its interface signal pins. Fig. 3-1A shows a functional block diagram of the 8088 CPU. Fig. 3-1B is a pin-definition diagram of the 8088's signals. Note that some pins have two definitions. The 8088 processor has two modes of operation that are selected by strapping pin 33 (MN/MX). When this pin is held high, the 8088 is in the minimum mode and its interface pins are compatible with those of an 8085 microprocessor. It can be directly attached to any of the 8085 family of support devices. When in the minimum mode, a bus controller chip is not needed since the bus commands are decoded and available from the 8088. In the minimum mode, the request/grant interface is not supported and, thus, it is not possible to attach co-processors, such as the 8087 math co-processor. In the PC design, pin 33 is strapped low so that it operates in the maximum mode. Therefore, only the maximum mode pin definitions will be described here.

AD0-AD7 Definition

These eight signal pins (pins 9 through 16) are used to transmit memory and I/O address information on each bus cycle. These signals, however, are multiplexed; they present address bits A0–A7 at the beginning of the bus cycle and, later in the cycle, are used as the processor's data bus. In

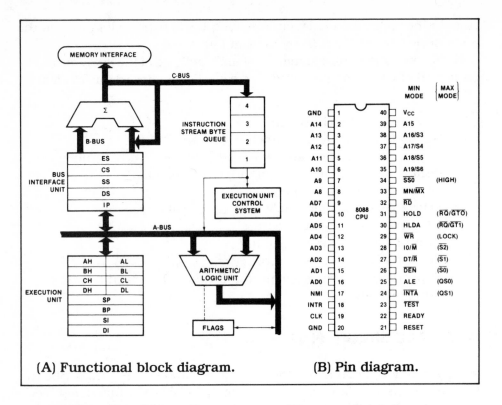

(A) Functional block diagram. (B) Pin diagram.

Fig. 3-1. The 8088 microprocessor (Courtesy Intel Corp.).

the PC design, the address information on A0–A7 is latched off from this bus. It is then repowered and becomes the system-bus address bits A0–A7. These lines are also repowered and become the system's data bus D0–D7.

A8-A15 Definition

These eight signal lines (pins 2 through 8, and pin 39) output memory and I/O address bits A8–A15 on each bus cycle. These lines are not multiplexed and they remain stable throughout the bus cycle. In the PC design, these lines are latched and repowered and, then, become the system-bus address bits A8–A15.

A16/S3-A19/S6 Definitions

At the begining of each memory bus cycle, these lines (pins 35 through 38) provide memory address bits A16–A19. During the remainder of the cycle, these bits present the 8088 internal status. When S6 is set low, S5 gives the status of the interrupt enable flag, and S4 and S3 are encoded to tell which segment register is being used for the bus cycle.

S4	S3	Segment
0	0	Alternate data segment
0	1	Stack segment
1	0	Code segment
1	1	Data segment

The PC design does not use this status information. These lines are latched and repowered and they become the system-bus address bits A16–A19.

CLK Definition

This input line (pin 19) provides the basic timing information for the 8088 microprocessor. In the PC design, this line comes from the 8284A clock chip and is a 4.77-MHz signal with a $\frac{1}{3}$ duty cycle.

RQ/GT0 Definition

This is a bidirectional signal used by other local bus masters to request the use of the local bus. In the PC design, this line (pin 31) is tied to the RQ/GT0 line on the auxiliary processor socket. This socket is compatible with the 8087 numeric processor manufactured by Intel Corp. The RQ/GT0 signals allow the auxiliary processor to take over the local bus and, thus, the system, to perform its functions.

RQ/GT1 Definition

This line (pin 30) is used to perform the same function as the RG/GT0 line, but it is on a lower-priority level. In the PC design, this line is not used and tied up.

LOCK Definition

This line (pin 29) is activated by a lock instruction prefix and remains active until the end of the next instruction. It is used to indicate to other bus masters that they should not attempt to gain control of the bus. The PC design is not a multi-master bus design and this line is not used.

NMI Definition

This input line (pin 17) is used to generate a nonmaskable interrupt to the 8088 microprocessor. In the PC design, it is masked outside the processor with a programmable port bit. Also in the PC design, this interrupt request input is used to report parity errors in the system board memory, accept interrupt requests from the auxiliary processor socket, and accept interrupt requests from devices on the system bus.

INTR Definition

This input signal (pin 18) is the maskable interrupt input to the 8088 processor. In the PC design, it is attached to the 8259A interrupt controller which expands this input to 8 system interrupt inputs.

READY Definition

This input line (pin 22) is used to insert "wait" states in the 8088 microprocessor bus cycles and, thus, extend the length of a cycle. This signal is used to slow down the 8088 processor when it is accessing an I/O port or a memory that is too slow for a normal 8088 bus cycle. In the PC design, this line comes from the 8284A clock chip which synchronizes it with the system clock. The PC uses the Ready function to insert one wait state in all I/O port accesses, insert one wait state in all DMA cycles, and provide a wait state generation function on the system bus.

RESET Definition

This signal (pin 21) is used to halt the microprocessor. In the PC design, this signal comes from the 8284A clock chip which receives its input from the system's power supply. The system power supply generates a signal called "power good," which indicates that the power levels are at their proper levels and Reset can be removed from the 8088 processor.

QS0 and QS1 Definitions

These two output lines (pins 24 and 25) give the status of the 8088's internal instruction queue. In the PC design, these lines are wired to the auxiliary processor socket in such a manner that it can track the status of the 8088's queue.

TEST Definition

This input pin (pin 23) is tested by the "wait for test" instruction. If TEST is low, execution continues; if TEST is high, the 8088 waits in an idle state until the pin goes low. In the PC design, the test input is wired to the busy output pin of the 8087 co-processor socket.

$\overline{S0}$, $\overline{S1}$, and $\overline{S2}$ Definitions

These output pins (pins 26 through 28) present status information that pertains to the type of bus cycle that is to be performed. This status is valid at the beginning of each bus cycle. In the PC design, these bits are wired to the 8288 bus controller chip where they are decoded. The 8088 decoded output signals become the control lines on the system bus. The following signals are generated from the status lines by the 8288 bus controller and are present on the system bus: IOR, IOW, MEMR, MEMW, and ALE.

The following defines the decode of the $\overline{S0}$, $\overline{S1}$, and $\overline{S2}$ status output lines.

$\overline{S2}$	$\overline{S1}$	$\overline{S2}$	Bus Cycle Type
0	0	0	Interrupt acknowledge
0	0	1	I/O port read
0	1	0	I/O port write
0	1	1	Halt
1	0	0	Code access
1	0	1	Memory read
1	1	0	Memory write
1	1	1	Passive

MEMORY ADDRESSING

One of the unique characteristics of the 8088 microprocessor is its ability to address the more than 65,536 bytes of data that are specified by a 16-bit address field. The 8088 has a 20-bit address capability that allows a physical memory size of 1,048,576 bytes. Since most of the 8088's memory reference instructions only permitthe specification and manipulation of a 16-bit address field, it would appear as though, at most, only 65,536 bytes of memory can be used. This is partially true; at any instance, the programmer's view of storage is limited to a 65,536-byte region. But, he has the capability of moving this 65,536-byte region to any 16-byte boundary in the 1,048,576-byte space. This is done by manipulating the contents of a special register called a *segment register*. The value loaded into the segment register is used to locate, in the 1-megabyte space, the 64K region that the 8088's instructions operate on. Since this register is also only 16 bits in length, it cannot by itself specify any boundary in the 1-megabyte space. To solve this problem, the 16-bit segment register only specifies on 16-byte boundaries. Thus, the 16-bit register can now specify 65,536 different 65,536-regions, in the 1 megabyte, on any 16-byte boundary. Thus, the physical memory address is formed by shifting the contents of the segment register left 4 bits and adding it to the instruction-generated 16-bit address. Fig. 3-2 illustrates the physical address generation.

In reality, there are four segment registers. One is used to address code, one is used to address data referenced by code, one is used to address data references in code via the stack, and one is an extra segment. The extra segment is typically used in data move operations where the operation is to take place between two different 64K regions and there is a requirement for both a source segment and a destination segment register. These four segment registers can all point to different 64K regions in the 1-megabyte space. Thus, once the segment registers are set, the program instructions view a 64K code space, a 64K data space, a 64K extra data space, and a 64K stack space. Any time that the program needs to reference outside of these spaces, it must first manipulate the appropriate segment register. It should be noted that the segments can either overlap or all point to the same 64K space.

The segment's value is often referred to as the base address and an address within a segment is called an offset. Thus, any address in the 1-megabyte address space can be identified by specifying a base and an off-

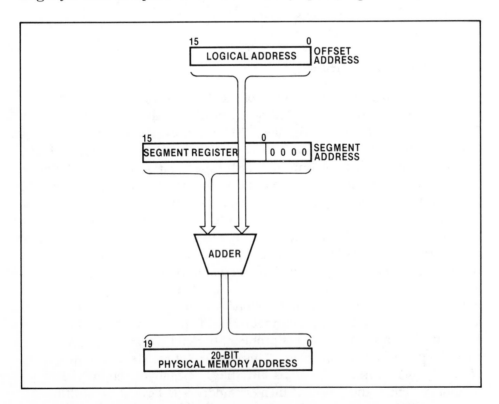

Fig. 3-2. 8088 memory address generation (Courtesy Intel Corp.).

set. Note that many different base and offset combinations can be used to specify a memory address.

Before we investigate addressing within a 64K segment (the offset), it is best to cover in detail the register set of the 8088 microprocessor.

8088 REGISTERS

As pointed out earlier, the 8088 has fourteen 16-bit registers. These registers can be further classified as follows: a data group of 4 registers, a pointer and an index group of 4 registers, 4 segment registers, an instruction pointer register, and a flag register. Fig. 3-3 is a diagram of the 8088 register facilities.

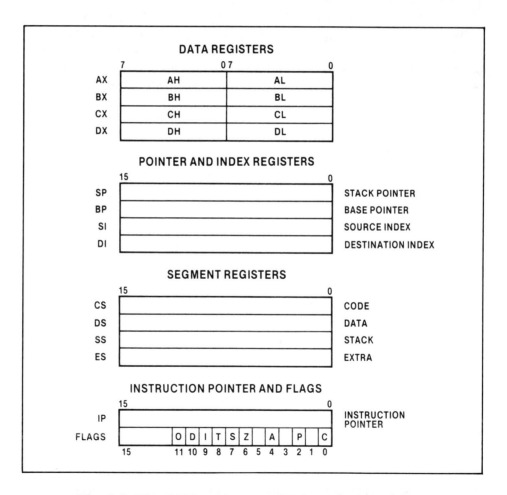

Fig. 3-3. The 8088 register set (Courtesy Intel Corp.).

Data Group Registers

These are four general-purpose 16-bit registers that are normally used by the instructions set to perform arithmetic and logical operations. These registers can also be addressed as eight 8-bit registers for byte operations of the instruction set.

The Pointer and Index Group

This set of four 16-bit registers is typically used to generate effective memory addresses or the offset portion of the physical address. These registers are only addressable as 16-bit values. These registers can also be used by the instructions set to perform arithmetic and logical operation in addition to generating effective memory addresses.

In the 8088's instruction set, not all registers are specifiable in each instruction. In many cases, an instruction can use only a specific register or register set to perform its function. For certain 8088 instructions performing specific operations, the registers have an implied usage. Table 3-1 lists those instruction operations which imply a specific usage of the registers.

Table 3-1. Implicit Use of the 8088 Registers

Register	Operations
AX	Word Multiply, Word Divide, Word I/O
AL	Byte Multiply, Byte Divide, Byte I/O, Translate, Decimal Arithmetic
AH	Byte Multiply, Byte Divide
BX	Translate
CX	String Operations, Loops
CL	Variable Shift and Rotate
DX	Word Multiply, Word Divide, Indirect I/O
SP	Stack Operations
SI	String Operations
DI	String Operations

(Courtesy Intel Corp.)

Segment Registers

These four 16-bit registers are used as previously discussed, to place the 64K segments in the 1-megabyte address space. The segment register that is used with a specific memory reference is defined in Table 3-2. Note that a default segment register is selected by the 8088 microprocessor hardware. Further, in some cases, it is possible for the programmer to override the default value and, by using a segment prefix instruction, specify a different segment register. See the earlier section on memory addressing in this chapter for a description of the functions of these registers.

Table 3-2. Segment Register Use

Type of Memory Reference	Default Segment Base	Alternate Segment Base	Offset
Instruction Fetch	CS	NONE	IP
Stack Operation	SS	NONE	SP
Variable (except following)	DS	CS,ES,SS	Effective Address
String Source	DS	CS,ES,SS	SI
String Destination	ES	NONE	DI
BP Used as Base Register	SS	CS,DS,ES	Effective Address

(Courtesy Intel Corp.)

The Instruction Pointer Register

This register contains the offset address, of the next instruction, from the current code-segment base value.

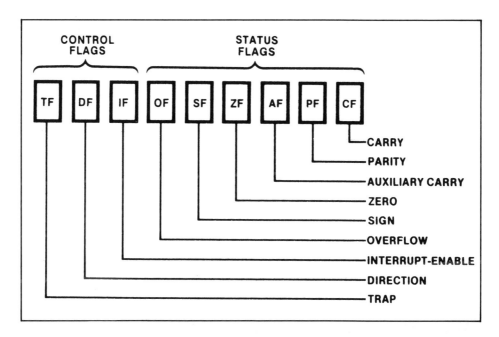

Fig. 3-4. The 8088 flag bits (Courtesy Intel Corp.).

The Flag Register

This is a 16-bit register, but only nine of its bits are used. Six of these bits are status bits which reflect the results of the instruction arithmetic and the logical operations. The other three bits are control bits. Fig. 3-4 is a diagram that defines the flag bits. The following is a brief description of each flag.

AF—This bit is the auxiliary carry flag. It is set when there has been a carry out, a borrow from, or a borrow to a nibble in the decimal arithmetic instructions.

CF—This bit is set if there has been a carry out or a borrow into the high-order bit as a result of an arithmetic operation.

OF—This bit is set if an arithmetic overflow has occurred and it indicates that the results are too large for the destination field.

SF—This bit indicates that the high-order bit of the results is set to a 1 and, thus, is a negative number.

PF—This bit is set when the results contain an even number of bits.

ZF—This bit is set when the results are zero.

DF—This bit is a control bit and, when set, causes string operations to be auto-decremented or processed from the high address to the low address. If this bit is set to zero, the string is processed in an auto-increment mode.

IF— This bit is a control bit and, when set, allows the 8088 processor to recognize external maskable interrupts.

TF—This bit is also a control bit and, when set, puts the 8088 microprocessor in a single-step mode. After each instruction, an interrupt is automatically generated.

EFFECTIVE MEMORY ADDRESS GENERATION

Now that we have a good understanding of the 8088's resources, we can investigate how the instructions set addresses the memory within a segment. As previously pointed out, a 20-bit address is physically made up of two parts—a segment or base value and an offset or effective-address value. The effective address is the sum of a displacement in the instruction, the contents of a base register, and the contents of an index register. An 8088 instruction can specify any combination of the above to create an effective address. Table 3-3 summarizes these addressing modes and the registers that are available in each mode.

Table 3-3. Effective Addressing Modes

EA Components	
Displacement Only	
Base or Index Only	(BX,BP,SI,DI)
Displacement + Base or Index	(BX,BP,SI,DI)
Base + Index	BP + DI, BX + SI
	BP + SI, BX + DI
Displacement + Base + Index	BP + DI + DISP
	BX + SI + DISP
	BP + SI + DISP
	BX + DI + DISP

(Courtesy Intel Corp.)

8088 INSTRUCTION SET

The instruction set of the 8088 microprocessor is very large and could be the subject of a book by itself. Thus, it will only be summarized here. It is suggested that if detailed descriptions and timing information on the 8088 instruction set is required, that you obtain one of the following books.

The iAPX 88 BOOK, published by Intel Corp.

iAPX 86,88 USER'S MANUAL, published by Intel Corp.

MACRO ASSEMBLE, published by IBM.

Tables 3-4 and 3-5 summarize the 8088's instruction set.

Table 3-4. 8088 Instruction Set Summary

DATA TRANSFER

MOV · Move:

7 6 5 4 3 2 1 0   7 6 5 4 3 2 1 0   7 6 5 4 3 2 1 0   7 6 5 4 3 2 1 0

Register/memory to/from register	1 0 0 0 1 0 d w	mod reg r/m		
Immediate to register/memory	1 1 0 0 0 1 1 w	mod 0 0 0 r/m	data	data if w 1
Immediate to register	1 0 1 1 w reg	data	data if w 1	
Memory to accumulator	1 0 1 0 0 0 0 w	addr-low	addr-high	
Accumulator to memory	1 0 1 0 0 0 1 w	addr-low	addr-high	
Register/memory to segment register	1 0 0 0 1 1 1 0	mod 0 reg r/m		
Segment register to register/memory	1 0 0 0 1 1 0 0	mod 0 reg r/m		

PUSH · Push:

Register/memory	1 1 1 1 1 1 1 1	mod 1 1 0 r/m
Register	0 1 0 1 0 reg
Segment register	0 0 0 reg 1 1 0

POP · Pop:

Register/memory	1 0 0 0 1 1 1 1	mod 0 0 0 r/m
Register	0 1 0 1 1 reg
Segment register	0 0 0 reg 1 1 1

XCHG · Exchange:

| Register/memory with register | 1 0 0 0 0 1 1 w | mod reg r/m |
| Register with accumulator | 1 0 0 1 0 reg |

IN=Input from:

| Fixed port | 1 1 1 0 0 1 0 w | port |
| Variable port | 1 1 1 0 1 1 0 w |

OUT = Output to:

Fixed port	1 1 1 0 0 1 1 w	port
Variable port	1 1 1 0 1 1 1 w
XLAT=Translate byte to AL	1 1 0 1 0 1 1 1
LEA=Load EA to register	1 0 0 0 1 1 0 1	mod reg r/m
LDS=Load pointer to DS	1 1 0 0 0 1 0 1	mod reg r/m
LES=Load pointer to ES	1 1 0 0 0 1 0 0	mod reg r/m
LAHF=Load AH with flags	1 0 0 1 1 1 1 1
SAHF=Store AH into flags	1 0 0 1 1 1 1 0
PUSHF=Push flags	1 0 0 1 1 1 0 0
POPF=Pop flags	1 0 0 1 1 1 0 1

ARITHMETIC

ADD · Add:

Reg/memory with register to either	0 0 0 0 0 0 d w	mod reg r/m		
Immediate to register/memory	1 0 0 0 0 0 s w	mod 0 0 0 r/m	data	data if s w 01
Immediate to accumulator	0 0 0 0 0 1 0 w	data	data if w 1	

ADC · Add with carry:

Reg/memory with register to either	0 0 0 1 0 0 d w	mod reg r/m		
Immediate to register/memory	1 0 0 0 0 0 s w	mod 0 1 0 r/m	data	data if s w 01
Immediate to accumulator	0 0 0 1 0 1 0 w	data	data if w 1	

INC · Increment:

Register/memory	1 1 1 1 1 1 1 w	mod 0 0 0 r/m
Register	0 1 0 0 0 reg
AAA=ASCII adjust for add	0 0 1 1 0 1 1 1
DAA=Decimal adjust for add	0 0 1 0 0 1 1 1

SUB · Subtract:

Reg/memory and register to either	0 0 1 0 1 0 d w	mod reg r/m		
Immediate from register/memory	1 0 0 0 0 0 s w	mod 1 0 1 r/m	data	data if s w 01
Immediate from accumulator	0 0 1 0 1 1 0 w	data	data if w 1	

SBB · Subtract with borrow

Reg/memory and register to either	0 0 0 1 1 0 d w	mod reg r/m		
Immediate from register/memory	1 0 0 0 0 0 s w	mod 0 1 1 r/m	data	data if s w 01
Immediate from accumulator	0 0 0 1 1 1 0 w	data	data if w 1	

DEC · Decrement:

7 6 5 4 3 2 1 0   7 6 5 4 3 2 1 0   7 6 5 4 3 2 1 0   7 6 5 4 3 2 1 0

Register/memory	1 1 1 1 1 1 1 w	mod 0 0 1 r/m
Register	0 1 0 0 1 reg
NEG Change sign	1 1 1 1 0 1 1 w	mod 0 1 1 r/m

CMP · Compare:

Register/memory and register	0 0 1 1 1 0 d w	mod reg r/m		
Immediate with register/memory	1 0 0 0 0 0 s w	mod 1 1 1 r/m	data	data if s w 01
Immediate with accumulator	0 0 1 1 1 1 0 w	data	data if w 1	
AAS ASCII adjust for subtract	0 0 1 1 1 1 1 1
DAS Decimal adjust for subtract	0 0 1 0 1 1 1 1
MUL Multiply (unsigned)	1 1 1 1 0 1 1 w	mod 1 0 0 r/m
IMUL Integer multiply (signed)	1 1 1 1 0 1 1 w	mod 1 0 1 r/m
AAM ASCII adjust for multiply	1 1 0 1 0 1 0 0	0 0 0 0 1 0 1 0
DIV Divide (unsigned)	1 1 1 1 0 1 1 w	mod 1 1 0 r/m
IDIV Integer divide (signed)	1 1 1 1 0 1 1 w	mod 1 1 1 r/m
AAD ASCII adjust for divide	1 1 0 1 0 1 0 1	0 0 0 0 1 0 1 0
CBW Convert byte to word	1 0 0 1 1 0 0 0
CWD Convert word to double word	1 0 0 1 1 0 0 1

LOGIC

NOT Invert	1 1 1 1 0 1 1 w	mod 0 1 0 r/m
SHL/SAL Shift logical/arithmetic left	1 1 0 1 0 0 v w	mod 1 0 0 r/m
SHR Shift logical right	1 1 0 1 0 0 v w	mod 1 0 1 r/m
SAR Shift arithmetic right	1 1 0 1 0 0 v w	mod 1 1 1 r/m
ROL Rotate left	1 1 0 1 0 0 v w	mod 0 0 0 r/m
ROR Rotate right	1 1 0 1 0 0 v w	mod 0 0 1 r/m
RCL Rotate through carry flag left	1 1 0 1 0 0 v w	mod 0 1 0 r/m
RCR Rotate through carry right	1 1 0 1 0 0 v w	mod 0 1 1 r/m

AND · And:

Reg/memory and register to either	0 0 1 0 0 0 d w	mod reg r/m		
Immediate to register/memory	1 0 0 0 0 0 0 w	mod 1 0 0 r/m	data	data if w 1
Immediate to accumulator	0 0 1 0 0 1 0 w	data	data if w 1	

TEST · And function to flags, no result:

Register/memory and register	1 0 0 0 0 1 0 w	mod reg r/m		
Immediate data and register/memory	1 1 1 1 0 1 1 w	mod 0 0 0 r/m	data	data if w 1
Immediate data and accumulator	1 0 1 0 1 0 0 w	data	data if w 1	

OR · Or:

Reg/memory and register to either	0 0 0 0 1 0 d w	mod reg r/m		
Immediate to register/memory	1 0 0 0 0 0 0 w	mod 0 0 1 r/m	data	data if w 1
Immediate to accumulator	0 0 0 0 1 1 0 w	data	data if w 1	

XOR · Exclusive or:

Reg/memory and register to either	0 0 1 1 0 0 d w	mod reg r/m		
Immediate to register/memory	1 0 0 0 0 0 0 w	mod 1 1 0 r/m	data	data if w 1
Immediate to accumulator	0 0 1 1 0 1 0 w	data	data if w 1	

STRING MANIPULATION

REP=Repeat	1 1 1 1 0 0 1 z
MOVS=Move byte/word	1 0 1 0 0 1 0 w
CMPS=Compare byte/word	1 0 1 0 0 1 1 w
SCAS=Scan byte/word	1 0 1 0 1 1 1 w
LODS=Load byte/wd to AL/AX	1 0 1 0 1 1 0 w
STOS=Stor byte/wd from AL/A	1 0 1 0 1 0 1 w

Courtesy Intel Corp.

Table 3-5. 8088 Instruction Set Summary

CONTROL TRANSFER

CALL = Call:

	7 6 5 4 3 2 1 0	7 6 5 4 3 2 1 0	7 6 5 4 3 2 1 0
Direct within segment	1 1 1 0 1 0 0 0	disp-low	disp-high
Indirect within segment	1 1 1 1 1 1 1 1	mod 0 1 0 r/m	
Direct intersegment	1 0 0 1 1 0 1 0	offset-low	offset-high
		seg-low	seg-high
Indirect intersegment	1 1 1 1 1 1 1 1	mod 0 1 1 r/m	

JMP = Unconditional Jump:

Direct within segment	1 1 1 0 1 0 0 1	disp-low	disp-high
Direct within segment-short	1 1 1 0 1 0 1 1	disp	
Indirect within segment	1 1 1 1 1 1 1 1	mod 1 0 0 r/m	
Direct intersegment	1 1 1 0 1 0 1 0	offset-low	offset-high
		seg-low	seg-high
Indirect intersegment	1 1 1 1 1 1 1 1	mod 1 0 1 r/m	

RET = Return from CALL:

Within segment	1 1 0 0 0 0 1 1		
Within seg adding immed to SP	1 1 0 0 0 0 1 0	data-low	data-high
Intersegment	1 1 0 0 1 0 1 1		
Intersegment adding immediate to SP	1 1 0 0 1 0 1 0	data-low	data-high
JE/JZ=Jump on equal/zero	0 1 1 1 0 1 0 0	disp	
JL/JNGE=Jump on less/not greater or equal	0 1 1 1 1 1 0 0	disp	
JLE/JNG=Jump on less or equal/not greater	0 1 1 1 1 1 1 0	disp	
JB/JNAE=Jump on below/not above or equal	0 1 1 1 0 0 1 0	disp	
JBE/JNA=Jump on below or equal/not above	0 1 1 1 0 1 1 0	disp	
JP/JPE=Jump on parity/parity even	0 1 1 1 1 0 1 0	disp	
JO=Jump on overflow	0 1 1 1 0 0 0 0	disp	
JS=Jump on sign	0 1 1 1 1 0 0 0	disp	
JNE/JNZ=Jump on not equal/not zero	0 1 1 1 0 1 0 1	disp	
JNL/JGE=Jump on not less/greater or equal	0 1 1 1 1 1 0 1	disp	
JNLE/JG=Jump on not less or equal/greater	0 1 1 1 1 1 1 1	disp	

	7 6 5 4 3 2 1 0	7 6 5 4 3 2 1 0
JNB/JAE Jump on not below/above or equal	0 1 1 1 0 0 1 1	disp
JNBE/JA Jump on not below or equal/above	0 1 1 1 0 1 1 1	disp
JNP/JPO Jump on not par/par odd	0 1 1 1 1 0 1 1	disp
JNO Jump on not overflow	0 1 1 1 0 0 0 1	disp
JNS Jump on not sign	0 1 1 1 1 0 0 1	disp
LOOP Loop CX times	1 1 1 0 0 0 1 0	disp
LOOPZ/LOOPE Loop while zero/equal	1 1 1 0 0 0 0 1	disp
LOOPNZ/LOOPNE Loop while not zero/equal	1 1 1 0 0 0 0 0	disp
JCXZ Jump on CX zero	1 1 1 0 0 0 1 1	disp

INT Interrupt

	7 6 5 4 3 2 1 0	7 6 5 4 3 2 1 0
Type specified	1 1 0 0 1 1 0 1	type
Type 3	1 1 0 0 1 1 0 0	
INTO Interrupt on overflow	1 1 0 0 1 1 1 0	
IRET Interrupt return	1 1 0 0 1 1 1 1	

PROCESSOR CONTROL

	7 6 5 4 3 2 1 0	7 6 5 4 3 2 1 0
CLC Clear carry	1 1 1 1 1 0 0 0	
CMC Complement carry	1 1 1 1 0 1 0 1	
STC Set carry	1 1 1 1 1 0 0 1	
CLD Clear direction	1 1 1 1 1 1 0 0	
STD Set direction	1 1 1 1 1 1 0 1	
CLI Clear interrupt	1 1 1 1 1 0 1 0	
STI Set interrupt	1 1 1 1 1 0 1 1	
HLT Halt	1 1 1 1 0 1 0 0	
WAIT Wait	1 0 0 1 1 0 1 1	
ESC Escape (to external device)	1 1 0 1 1 x x x	mod x x x r/m
LOCK Bus lock prefix	1 1 1 1 0 0 0 0	

Footnotes:

AL = 8-bit accumulator
AX = 16-bit accumulator
CX = Count register
DS = Data segment
ES = Extra segment
Above/below refers to unsigned value.
Greater = more positive;
Less = less positive (more negative) signed values
if d = 1 then "to" reg; if d = 0 then "from" reg
if w = 1 then word instruction; if w = 0 then byte instruction

if mod = 11 then r/m is treated as a REG field
if mod = 00 then DISP = 0*, disp-low and disp-high are absent
if mod = 01 then DISP = disp-low sign-extended to 16-bits, disp-high is absent
if mod = 10 then DISP = disp-high: disp-low

if r/m = 000 then EA = (BX) + (SI) + DISP
if r/m = 001 then EA = (BX) + (DI) + DISP
if r/m = 010 then EA = (BP) + (SI) + DISP
if r/m = 011 then EA = (BP) + (DI) + DISP
if r/m = 100 then EA = (SI) + DISP
if r/m = 101 then EA = (DI) + DISP
if r/m = 110 then EA = (BP) + DISP*
if r/m = 111 then EA = (BX) + DISP
DISP follows 2nd byte of instruction (before data if required)

*except if mod = 00 and r/m = 110 then EA = disp-high: disp-low

if s:w = 01 then 16 bits of immediate data form the operand.
if s:w = 11 then an immediate data byte is sign extended to form the 16-bit operand.
if v = 0 then "count" = 1; if v = 1 then "count" in (CL)
x = don't care
z is used for string primitives for comparison with ZF FLAG

SEGMENT OVERRIDE PREFIX

0 0 1 reg 1 1 0

REG is assigned according to the following table

16-Bit (w = 1)	8-Bit (w = 0)	Segment
000 AX	000 AL	00 ES
001 CX	001 CL	01 CS
010 DX	010 DL	10 SS
011 BX	011 BL	11 DS
100 SP	100 AH	
101 BP	101 CH	
110 SI	110 DH	
111 DI	111 BH	

Instructions which reference the flag register file as a 16-bit object use the symbol FLAGS represent the file:

FLAGS = X:X:X:X:(OF):(DF):(IF):(TF):(SF):(ZF):X:(AF):X:(PF):X:(CF)

CHAPTER 4

SYSTEM UNIT BUS OPERATIONS

INTRODUCTION

Most interfacing applications will attach to the PC through one of the five system-bus card slots. On the system bus, data are transferred during what is called a bus cycle. This chapter describes the types of bus cycles that are possible and how they are used to transfer information between memory, I/O, and the 8088 microprocessor.

There are two general classifications of bus cycles: 8088-driven and DMA-driven bus cycles. When the 8088 microprocessor generates a bus cycle, it drives the system bus with an address of a memory location or an I/O port, controls the direction of data flow, and is either the source or sink for the data. When the 8088 drives the bus, there are five different kinds of bus cycles generated. The first type is a memory-read bus cycle. The second is a memory-write bus cycle. The third type is an I/O port read bus cycle. The fourth type is an I/O port write bus cycle. The fifth is an interrupt-acknowledge bus cycle. The interrupt-acknowledge bus cycle is not covered here since it only occurs on the local bus of the system and is not present on the system bus.

The second general classification of bus cycles are those that are driven by the DMA controller (the 8237-5 chip). During direct-memory access (DMA) operations, the 8088 microprocessor is removed from the system bus and the 8237-5 DMA controller drives the bus cycles. The DMA controller drives a memory address onto the bus and controls the flow of data between an interface adapter and memory. Note that in DMA bus cycles, the DMA controller does not source or sink the data. Data are transferred directly between the interface adapter and memory. When the DMA controller drives the system bus, there are two types of bus cycles generated. The first type is a cycle that reads from an interface adapter and writes the data into a memory location that is specified by the address from the DMA controller. The second type of bus cycle is one which reads data from a memory location specified by the DMA controller and, then, writes that data into an interface adapter.

Table 4-1 gives a summary of the types of bus cycles that are generated on the system unit's bus. The remainder of this chapter will describe, in detail, the operations of each of these types of bus cycles.

Table 4-1. Summary of Bus Cycle Types

Type of Bus Cycle	Purpose	Direction of Data Flow
Memory read	8088 data or an instruction fetch	Memory to 8088
Memory write	8088 data write	8088 to memory
I/O port read	8088 data fetch from I/O	I/O port to 8088
I/O port write	8088 sends data to I/O	8088 to I/O port
Interrupt acknowledge	Send interrupt data to 8088	8259A-5 to 8088
DMA write I/O	Send data from memory to an I/O interface adapter	Memory to I/O
DMA read I/O	Send data from an I/O interface adapter to memory	I/O to memory

MEMORY-READ BUS CYCLE

The memory-read bus cycle is used to fetch instructions and data for the system's memory. This memory may be on the system board, in the system-bus card slots, ROM, or RAM. This cycle is driven from the 8088 microprocessor. All bus cycles are made up of a minimum of four processor clocks. Each clock is approximately 210 nanoseconds in length. Thus, a minimum length for a memory-read bus cycle is approximately 840 nanoseconds. The bus cycle's length can be extended by a memory device in the system-bus card slots by lowering a bus interface line called READY. The memory device must perform this action, otherwise the bus cycle will be four clocks in length. The exact timing and control of the READY signal will be covered in a later chapter. Those bus signals that are active are driven from the 8088 microprocessor and its signal-buffering circuits. The one exception is the data bus, which will be driven with the data from the address' memory location. Fig. 4-1 illustrates the basic timing and signals used on the system bus to execute a memory-read bus cycle.

The memory-read cycle begins during the T1 clock with the ALE signal going active. The back edge of this signal indicates that the address bus contains a valid memory address. Next, the MEMR bus signal is activated at approximately T2 time. This indicates to the devices attached to the bus that the cycle is a memory-read cycle. It also indicates that if the device contains memory with an address that corresponds to the one that is on the address bus, it should drive the data bus with its contents. All memory devices must decode the address on the bus and, thus, determine if it is the device that should respond. The 8088 microprocessor captures the data from the data bus at the beginning of the T4 clock. Shortly after the beginning of the T4 clock, the MEMR bus signal is deactivated and the bus cycle ends at the end of the T4 clock.

MEMORY-WRITE BUS CYCLE

The memory-write bus cycle is used any time an instruction in an 8088 program writes data to a memory location. As in the memory-read bus cycle, the 8088 and its bus buffers drive an address onto the system bus, indicating the address of the memory location that should accept the data from the 8088 microprocessor. In addition to driving the address bus and the control signals, the 8088 also drives the data bus with the data that is to be written in the selected memory location. Fig. 4-2 illustrates the basic timing of the memory-write bus cycle.

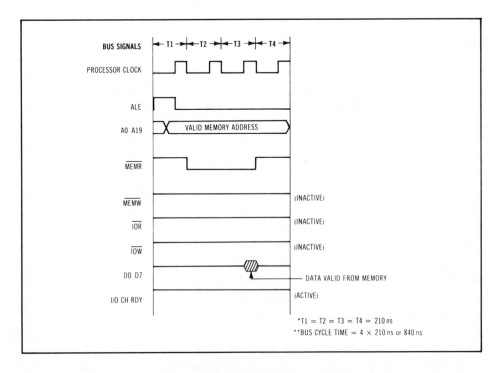

Fig. 4-1. Memory-read bus cycle.

The ALE bus signal is activated during clock time T1, indicating that the address bus contains a valid memory address. Next, the $\overline{\text{MEMW}}$ bus signal is activated indicating that the bus cycle is a memory-write cycle. The $\overline{\text{MEMW}}$ signal is activated at approximately time T2. Shortly after $\overline{\text{MEMW}}$ is activated, the 8088 processor drives the system data bus with the data that are to be written into the selected memory location. At time T4, the $\overline{\text{MEMW}}$ bus signal is deactivated and the bus cycle is completed at the end of clock time T4.

I/O PORT READ BUS CYCLE

This bus cycle is initiated each time an 8088 microprocessor IN instruction is executed. This bus cycle is similar to the memory-read bus cycle. Its purpose is to fetch data from one of the I/O port addresses in the I/O port address space. In the PC design, the bus cycle is always a minimum of five clocks, or approximately 1.05 microseconds, in length. A specific I/O port device may further extend the length of the bus cycle by deactivating the READY bus signal. During an I/O port read bus cycle, the 8088 microprocessor drives a 16-bit port address onto the system address bus. Note that during this bus cycle, the high-order 4 bits of the address bus are never

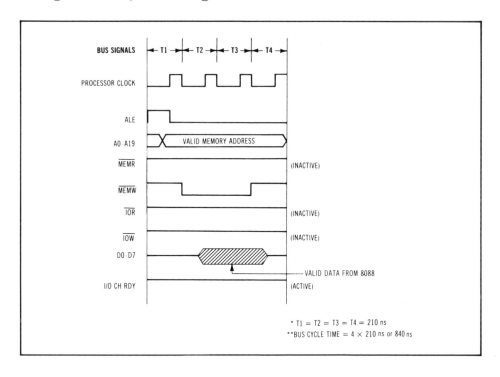

Fig. 4-2. Memory-write bus cycle.

activated. Fig. 4-3 illustrates the basic timing of an I/O port read bus cycle.

During clock time T1, the ALE bus signal is activated indicating that address bus bits 0–15 contain a valid I/O port address. At clock time T2, the bus control signal, $\overline{\text{IOR}}$, is activated, indicating both that the bus cycle is an I/O port read cycle and that the addressed port should respond by driving the data bus with its contents. At the beginning of clock time T4, the processor samples the data on the data bus and the $\overline{\text{IOR}}$ bus signal is deactivated. The bus cycle is completed at the end of the T4 clock time. It should be noted that a normal I/O port read bus cycle is four clock times, but, in the PC design, one extra clock time, called a TW clock, is automatically inserted in every cycle.

I/O PORT WRITE BUS CYCLE

An I/O port write bus cycle is initiated each time an 8088 microprocessor OUT instruction is executed. This bus cycle writes data from the 8088 to a specific I/O port address in the I/O address space of the 8088 micro-

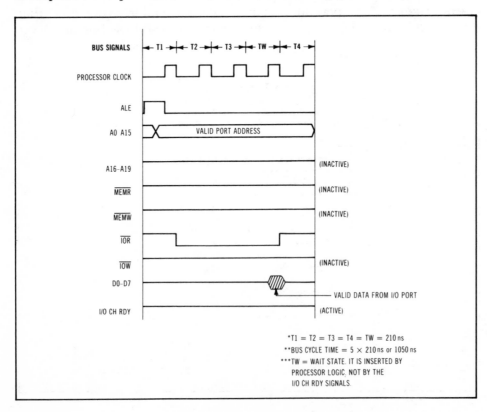

Fig. 4-3. I/O port read bus cycle.

processor. This bus cycle is normally four clocks in length, but the PC design automatically inserts an extra TW clock. Thus, in the PC, all I/O port write bus cycles are a minimum of five clocks, or approximately 1.05 microseconds, in length. The bus cycle can be further extended through the use of the READY signal on the system bus. It should be noted now that only bits 0–15 of the address bus are used to address I/O ports. Thus, address bits 16–19 are not activated during this bus cycle. Fig. 4-4 illustrates the basic timing of an I/O port write bus cycle.

As with the other bus cycles, the ALE bus signal is activated during the T1 clock time and it indicates that the address bus contains a valid port address. Next, the bus control signal $\overline{\text{IOW}}$ is activated at clock time T2, indicating that the bus cycle is an I/O port write cycle and that the selected port address should take data from the data bus. Shortly after the T2 clock time, the 8088 microprocessor drives the data bus with the data for the port address. At the beginning of the T4 clock time, the $\overline{\text{IOW}}$ bus control signal is deactivated. The bus cycle is completed at the end of T4 clock.

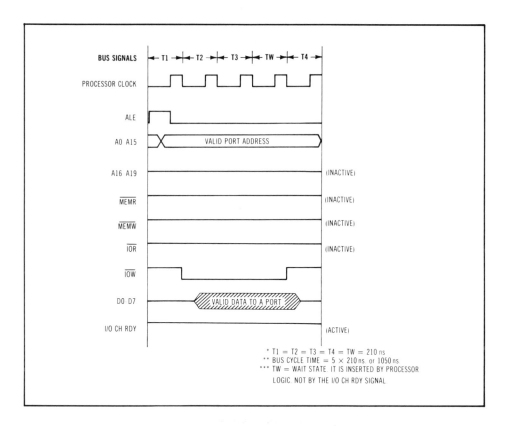

Fig. 4-4. I/O port write bus cycle.

DMA BUS CYCLE

The DMA bus cycles are a little more complicated, since both a read and a write function are performed in the same cycle. In addition, the bus is not driven from the 8088 microprocessor but from the DMA controller and its support circuits. The cycles are not initiated by either the 8088 microprocessor or the DMA controller, but are initiated by a request from an interface adapter. A whole set of bus activities precedes the actual DMA bus cycle. This activity will not be covered here, but it can be studied in Chapter 10, which covers the DMA capabilities of the PC in detail. A DMA bus cycle can be initiated from the system bus by raising any of the three system-bus signal lines, DRQ1, DRQ2, or DRQ3. The first indication on the system bus that a request has been granted and that a DMA bus cycle has started is when the bus is signaled by the activation of a bus signal called AEN. Shortly after the AEN signal is activated, one of four signals, DACK0, DACK1, DACK2, or DACK3, is activated. These signals indicate to the interface adapter which DMA request or channel is being serviced by this DMA bus cycle.

A normal DMA bus cycle will take five processor clock times to execute. In the PC design, an extra clock time is added, lengthening the DMA cycle to six clocks, or approximately 1.26 microseconds. When the DMA controller has control of the system bus, its timing signals will be generated from the same clock signal that the 8088 processor uses. Since the DMA controller generates slightly different bus timings, the DMA clocks are called "S" clocks. The "S" clock times indicate the state of the DMA controller just as the "T" clocks indicate the state of the 8088 microprocessor. When the DMA controller is not executing a DMA cycle, it is in what is called an *idle state*, continually executing an "SI" clock state while looking for DMA requests from the system. When a request is detected, the controller sends a signal to the 8088 processor telling it to get off the bus at the next convenient time. The controller also goes to the "S0" clock state, which continually looks for a response from the 8088 microprocessor that will tell it that the bus has been given up and that it is free to begin a DMA cycle. When the controller receives the HLDA signal from the 8088 processor, it enters the S1 clock state, signaling the beginning of the DMA cycle. The DMA controller then proceeds through the six clock states of the bus cycle. Fig. 4-5 illustrates the bus timing of these six clock states for a DMA cycle that reads data from the requesting interface adapter and then writes the data into the memory location specified by the DMA controller.

DMA Memory-Write Cycle

The purpose of a DMA write bus cycle is to fetch data from an interface adapter and write that data into the memory location that is specified by the DMA controller. After a DMA cycle is initiated on the bus, the controller and its support circuits drive the system address bus with the address of the target memory location. Next, the IOR bus signal is activated indicating that the interface adapter that requested the DMA cycle should drive the system data bus with its data. Next, the $\overline{\text{MEMW}}$ bus signal is activated, indicating to the memory, which was addressed earlier in the cycle, that it should take the interface adapter's data and write them into memory. Note that the data from the interface adapter are not buffered anywhere. It is the responsibility of the interface adapter to maintain valid data until the memory can perform the write operation. Fig. 4-5 illustrates the basic bus signal timing used to perform this bus cycle.

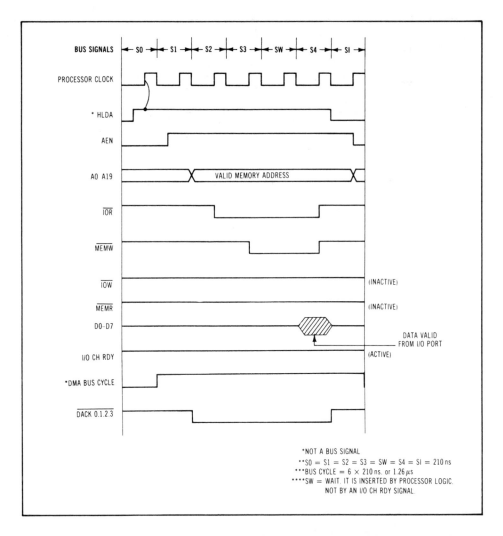

Fig. 4-5. DMA memory write bus cycle.

DMA Memory-Read Cycle

This bus cycle is used to transfer data from system memory to an interface adapter. After a DMA cycle has been initiated on the system bus, the DMA controller and its support circuits drive the system address bus with a memory address. Next, the controller activates the $\overline{\text{MEMR}}$ bus signal, thereby indicating to the memory that it should drive the system data bus with its contents. Next, the controller activates the $\overline{\text{IOW}}$ bus signal. This indicates to the interface adapter that it should take the data from the memory. Fig. 4-6 illustrates the basic signal and bus timings used in a DMA memory-read cycle.

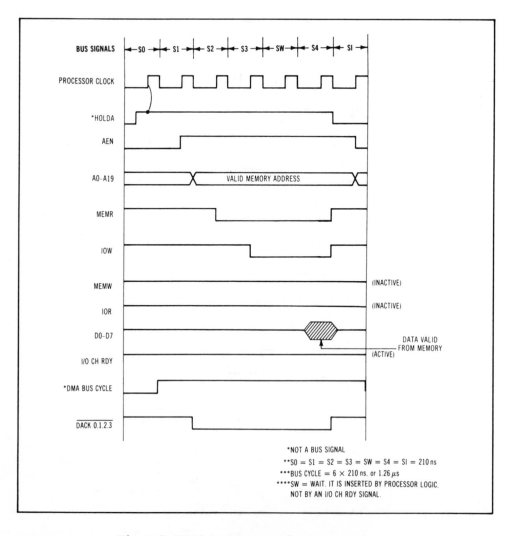

Fig. 4-6. DMA I/O port write bus cycle.

Memory-Refresh DMA Cycle

DMA memory-read bus cycles are used by the system to refresh the dynamic memory of the system. The system hardware automatically generates a dummy DMA memory-read bus cycle every 72 processor clocks, or approximately every 15.12 microseconds. The DMA controller is programmed to continuously increment the memory address with each cycle, thus providing the refresh address required by the dynamic memory. Since the data read during these cycles are not used, the DMA cycle is shortened such that the bus bandwidth used to refresh memory is reduced. These DMA cycles occur on DMA Channel 0 only and are five clocks in length. Thus, out of every 72 processor or bus clocks, five are used to support the refresh function in the system. This indicates that the system bus is used 7% of the time for memory refresh.

CHAPTER 5

SYSTEM-BUS SIGNAL DESCRIPTIONS

INTRODUCTION

The PC system bus is available for the attachment of interfacing projects at five different 62-pin card slots on the processor card. All the card slots are bused with identical signals on each pin. All the signals are at TTL-logic levels, except for those of the power and ground buses that are provided in the connectors. The bus is a demultiplexed and repowered superset of the 8088 microprocessor bus. The 8088 bus signals are augmented by the addition of signals to support direct-memory access, interrupts, timing and control of the I/O and memory read and write, wait-state generation, memory refresh, and error detection. The following series of definitions is a detailed functional description of all the 62-pin signals. Timing and loading information is discussed later in Chapters 6 and 7.

SIGNAL DEFINITIONS

OSC (oscillator)

This signal is an output-only signal with a frequency of 14.31818 MHz and a period of approximately 70 ns. It has a duty cycle of approximately 50%. This signal is the highest frequency signal on the bus and all other timing signals are generated from this signal. The frequency of this signal can be adjusted and trimmed with the adjustment of a trimming capacitor that is located on the base processor card. This signal can be divided by four to give the 3.58-MHz frequency required for color-tv color burst information. Care should be taken when this signal is used to clock other bus signals, since bus delay effectively desynchronizes this signal with respect to other bus signals. Thus, specific timing relationship cannot be guaranteed.

CLK (clock)

This signal is derived from the OSC signal previously described. It is also an output-only signal. This signal is obtained by dividing the OSC signal by three, which gives a frequency of 4.77 MHz. This signal is not symmetric but has a one-third/two-thirds duty cycle. Its period is 210 ns with a high time of 70 ns and a low time of 140 ns. This signal is well synchronized with respect to the memory-read and memory-write controls and it can be used to generate system-bus wait states. A typical bus cycle is four clock periods, or approximately 840 ns.

RESET DRV (reset driver)

This output-only signal is held active high during system power-on sequences. It remains active until all levels have reached their specified operating range and, then, it goes inactive. In addition, if any power level falls outside its specified operating range after power-on, this line is brought active high. This signal is generally used to provide a power-on reset to bus-attached interface logic or I/O devices to bring them to a known state before operation by the system. This signal is set active and inactive on the falling edge of the OSC signal. Due to logic delays, this synchronization should not be relied upon for any attachment design.

A0 Through A19

Address bits A0 through A19 are output-only signals that are used to address system-bus attached memory and I/O. (A0 is the least-significant and A19 is the most-significant bit.) These 20 signal lines are driven by the 8088 microprocessor during system-bus cycles for memory and I/O read and write. They are driven by the direct-memory access logic feature during DMA cycles. With 20 address lines, it is possible to address one megabyte of system memory, but not all address space is available in the system bus. Base system memory (RAM 0 to 64K) resides on the base board and this address space cannot be addressed on the system bus. Similarly, the base processor board contains address space for 48KB of ROM, which resides at the top of the 1 megabyte address space. This, again, cannot be addressed on the system bus. The processor, through the use of the IN and OUT instructions, can address up to 64K I/O port addresses. These port addresses are also carried on the address bus on lines A0 through A15. Lines A16 through A19 are not used and are held inactive during I/O port bus cycles. However, on the Personal Computer, only address lines A0 through A9 are used for addressing I/O ports. In addition, only I/O port addresses in the range 0200 HEX to 03FF HEX are valid on the system bus. There are some exceptions to this rule. These are explained in Chapter 12.

D0 Through D7

These eight lines are bidirectional data lines used to transmit data between the 8088 microprocessor, memory and I/O, and I/O ports. (D0 is the least-significant and D7 is the most-significant bit. During 8088-initiated write bus cycles, data are presented on the bus for writing into memory or I/O ports. Data are valid slightly before the back rising edge of the IOW or MEMW control signals. The rising edges of these signals are usually used to clock the data on the data bus into memory or I/O port registers. During 8088-initiated read bus cycles, the addressed memory or I/O port register must place their data on the data bus before the rising edge of the I/O or MEMR control signals. During direct-memory access cycles, the data bus is used to transfer data directly between an I/O port and memory without the intervention of the microprocessor. During DMA cycles, the processor is disconnected from the bus and the direct-memory access control device, 8237-5, controls the bus transfer.

ALE (address latch enable)

This is an output-only signal driven from the 8288 bus controller. It is used to indicate that the address bus is now valid for the beginning of a bus cycle. This signal goes "active high" just prior to the address bus being valid and falls to "inactive low" just after the address bus is valid. This signal is used to latch the address information from the local address/data bus of the 8088 microprocessor. It should be noted that the system's data bus does not contain address information and, thus, ALE cannot be used to demultiplex addresses from the data bus. The ALE signal is a good sync point when looking at 8088-initiated bus cycles, since it starts at the beginning of each bus cycle. ALE is not active during direct-memory access cycles.

I/O CH CK (I/O channel check)

This is a low-level input-only signal used to report error conditions on the bus-attached interface cards. This signal, when set low, will generate a nonmaskable interrupt (NMI) to the 8088 microprocessor. The NMI is actually masked by an I/O register port bit and must be enabled before the interrupt can be received by the 8088 processor. The I/O CH CK is also masked off by an I/O register port bit and must be enabled before it can cause an NMI. In addition, if the line is not masked off, its state can be read in an I/O register port bit. Since there is more than one source for an NMI, the software must determine the actual source by checking the status of the I/O CH CK line in the I/O port register status bit. See Chapter 12 for a discussion of I/O port address and bit assignments. In the system, this line is used to report parity error conditions on bus-attached memory cards.

I/O CH RDY (I/O channel ready)

This is an input-only signal that is used to extend the length of bus cycles, so that memory or I/O ports that are not fast enough to respond to a normal bus cycle of four clocks (840 ns) can still be attached to the system bus. If a memory or an I/O port wants to extend the bus cycle, it will force the I/O CH RDY line low when it decodes its address and receives a MEMR, MEMW, IOR, or IOW command. This signal should be carefully controlled so that only the additional wait states that are required are added to the bus cycle. By holding this line inactive, additional wait states can extend the bus cycle in increments of 210 ns up to a maximum of 10 clocks, or 2100 ns (2.1 μs). Chapters 6 and 13 give detailed timing information that tells how to control the I/O CH RDY line. This signal should be driven with an open-collector driver since it is wired ''ORed'' with other I/O CH RDY signals from other bus-attached interface cards.

IRQ2 Through IRQ7 (interrupt requests 2 through 7)

These six input-only signals are used to generate interrupt requests to the 8088 microprocessor from the system bus. These signals go directly to the 8259A interrupt controller of the processor card. The BIOS programs of the ROM initalize the 8259A controller such that IRQ2 is the highest-priority signal and IRQ7 the lowest. If the level is not masked, a rising-edge signal will generate an interrupt request to the 8088 microprocessor. Once a rising-edge request occurs, it must remain active until the 8088 processor issues an INTA (interrupt acknowledge) signal. The INTA signal is not present on the system bus, thus the request is usually reset with an I/O register port bit using the OUT command issued in the interrupt-service routine. If the interrupt request is not held active until the INTA signal time, a level-7 interrupt is generated regardless of the priority level of the level presented. It should be noted that the character of these lines can be changed by reprogramming the initialization parameter in the 8259A controller. Chapter 9 describes the 8259A controller programming procedure.

IOR (I/O read)

This signal is an output-only signal from the 8288 bus controller. It is used to indicate to the I/O ports that the present 8088-initiated bus cycle is an I/O port read cycle and that the address on the address bus is an I/O port address. The I/O port address should respond by placing its read data on the system data bus. This signal is active low so the I/O port should place its data on the bus approximately 30 nanoseconds prior to the rising edge of the IOR to ensure that the processor gets valid data. When a direct-access cycle occurs, the IOR signal is driven from the direct-memory access (DMA) controller on the processor board, an 8237-5 device. In this case, the address bus does not contain an I/O port address but, instead, contains the memory address where the port's read data will be written. The I/O port is selected not by an address but by the active DACK signal from the 8237-5 DMA controller.

IOW (I/O write)

This signal is a low-level active output-only signal. It is driven from the 8288 bus controller during 8088-initiated bus cycles and indicates the address bus that contains an I/O port address and that data bus that contains data to be written into the I/O port. When the signal goes active low, the data bus may not be valid, thus, port data should be clocked or latched using the rising edge of this signal. When a DMA bus cycle occurs, this signal is driven from the 8237-5 DMA controller. The IOW signal is then used to write data from memory, which is now on the data bus, to the DACK-selected I/O port. Again, data may not be valid on the leading active low edge of this signal and should be clocked into the port using the rising edge of this signal.

MEMW (memory write)

This is a low-level active signal used to write data from the system bus into memory. This signal is driven from the 8288 bus controller during 8088-initiated bus signals and indicates that the address bus contains an address of a memory location to which the data on the data bus are to be written. Data may not be valid on the data bus when MEMW first goes active low, but are valid prior to the rising edge of the signal. During DMA cycles, this signal is driven from the 8237-5 DMA controller and is used to write data on the bus from an I/O port into memory. Particular care should be used when this signal is used to initiate a dynamic memory-write cycle, since the write data may not be valid as it goes active. This may require that dynamic RAM memories will have to be designed to use the "late write, or CAS write" feature.

MEMR (memory read)

This signal is a low-level output-only signal used to request read data from memory. This signal is driven from the 8288 bus controller on 8088-

initiated bus cycles. It indicates that the address bus contains a valid memory-read address and that the specified memory location should drive the system data bus with its read data. As with the IOR signal, the memory must drive valid data onto the data bus approximately 30 nanoseconds prior to the rising edge of the MEMR signal to ensure that the processor receives valid data. During DMA cycles, this signal is driven from the 8237-5 DMA controller and indicates that the address' memory location should respond by driving the data bus with its read data so that it can be written into the DACK-selected I/O port.

DRQ1 Through DRQ3 (direct-memory access request 1 through 3)

These three lines are active-high input-only lines used by the interface to request DMA cycles. If a device or interface logic wants to transfer data between itself and memory without the intervention of the 8088 microprocessor, the request is initiated by raising a DRQ line. These lines go directly to the 8237-5 DMA controller on the processor system card where they are prioritized with other DMA requests before the DMA cycle is granted. The ROM BIOS of the Personal Computer initializes the DMA controller such that DRQ1 is the highest priority and DRQ3 is the lowest. DRQ0 is actually the highest priority, but it is not available on the system bus. It is used on the processor card to refresh the system's dynamic memory. Depending on the mode programmed in the DMA controller, care must be taken in the control of the DRQ lines, since if the DRQ is held active-high too long, more than one cycle may be taken. Typically, the DRQ is reset by its corresponding DACK signal. See Chapter 10 for a detailed discussion of the direct-memory access function.

DACK0 Through DACK3 (direct-memory access acknowledge 0 through 3)

These four signals are low-level active output-only signals issued by the 8237-5 DMA controller to indicate that the corresponding DRQ has been honored and the DMA controller will take the bus and proceed with the requested DMA cycle. There is no corresponding DRQ0 on the system bus; thus, DACK0 is sent only to indicate that the present DMA cycle is a dummy read cycle which can be used to refresh system dynamic memory. During DACK0 memory read cycles, the address bus contains valid incrementing refresh addresses. DACK0 refresh cycles occur every 72 clocks, or 15.12 μs.

AEN (address enable)

This signal is an output-only active-high signal issued by the DMA control logic. It indicates that a DMA bus cycle is in progress. On the processor card, this signal is used to disable the 8088 microprocessor address, data, and control buses from the system bus and enable the address and control bus from the DMA controller. On the system bus, its purpose is to disable I/O port address decodes during DMA cycles so that DMA memory addresses are not used as I/O port addresses during DMA cycles. This is possible since IOW and IOR may be active with memory addresses on the address bus during DMA cycles.

TC (terminal count)

This signal is an output-only active-high signal issued by the 8237-5 DMA controller. It indicates that one of the DMA channels has reached its preprogrammed number of transfer cycles. This signal is typically used to terminate a DMA block data transfer. Since it is issued when any of the four DMA channels reach their terminal counts, it is necessary to condition this signal with the appropriate DACK signal. Thus, the interface logic should AND the TC with the DACK to get the TC for that specific channel. A TC signal can be used as an interface timing signal, since it comes every 990.804 ms. This is how long it takes the refresh cycles to address the first 65,536 memory addresses before TC is reached and the cycle is restarted.

BUS POWER AND GROUND

Fig. 5-1 illustrates the signals present on the system bus. In addition to the previously discussed signals, the system contains the following power levels.

+5 V DC (5-volts direct current)

The +5-volt dc power level is available on two pins of the card edge connectors on the bus and it is regulated to $\pm5\%$ (+4.75 to +5.25 volts dc).

+12 V DC (12-volts direct current)

The +12-volt dc power level is available at one pin of the card edge connectors on the bus and it is regulated to $\pm5\%$ (+11.4 to +12.6 volts dc).

−5 V DC (5-volts direct current)

The −5-volt dc power level is available on one pin of the card edge connectors on the bus and is regulated to $\pm10\%$ (−4.5 to −5.5 volts dc).

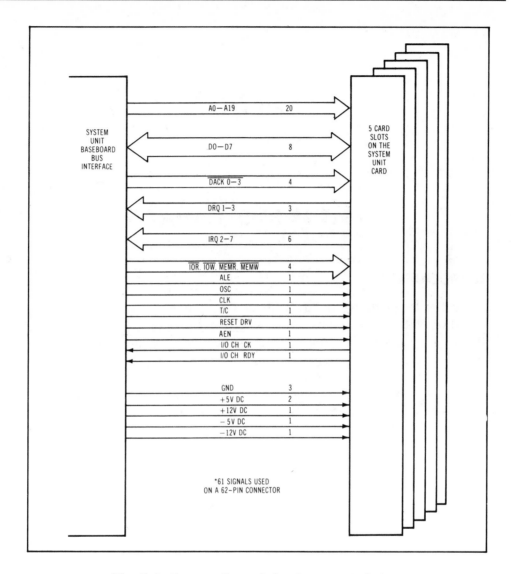

**Fig. 5-1. Connection of the System Unit bus
to five feature card slots.**

− 12 V DC (12-volts direct current)

The − 12-volt dc power level is available on one pin of the card edge connectors on the bus and is regulated to ±10% (− 10.8 to − 13.2 volts dc).

GND (ground)

System dc and frame ground is provided at three pins on the card edge connectors of the bus.

CHAPTER 6

SYSTEM-BUS TIMINGS

INTRODUCTION

The key to the design of any system-bus attached interface is an understanding of its timing compatibility with the system bus. As an example, it is necessary to know how fast data must be presented after a memory or a register is accessed by the 8088 microprocessor. This chapter presents detailed timing information on each type of bus cycle that exists on the system bus. Timing information is presented as *maximum worst case* and *minimum worst case* data. This means that the timing information is valid for all conditions of bus loading and power levels that are within their specified limits. When ''worst-case'' minimum delays are of interest and none are given for a device, one-half of the typical specification is used. This will, in general, provide a sufficient design margin. No typical timing information is used in maximum worst case delay-timing calculations. This ensures that designs that are based on this data will have no difficulty operating on the system bus. This data are based on timing information taken from the 1982 *Intel Component Data Catalog* and the Texas Instruments 1981 *TTL Data Book for Design Engineers*. Also, the data discussed here represent timings of the system bus, as it appears at the five card slots on the system board, and as defined by the PC System Unit board logic schematics, published in the *IBM Technical Reference Manual*. Except for data taken from the *IBM Technical Reference Manual*, timing data presented here does not necessarily represent information that is endorsed or supported by IBM.

TIMING DIAGRAMS AND TABLES

Separate timing charts and tables are provided for each of the following types of bus cycles.

8088-Initiated Memory-Read Bus Cycle

Fig. 6-1 illustrates the signal timing relationships of the memory-read bus cycle and Table 6-1 contains the timing data relative to the timing chart.

8088-Initiated Memory-Write Bus Cycle

Fig. 6-2 illustrates the signal timing relationships of the memory-write bus cycle and Table 6-2 contains the timing data relative to the timing chart.

8088-Initiated I/O Port Read Bus Cycle

Fig. 6-3 illustrates the signal timing relationships of the I/O port read bus cycle and Table 6-3 contains the timing data relative to the timing chart.

8088-Initiated I/O Port Write Bus Cycle

Fig. 6-4 illustrates the signal timing relationships of the I/O port write bus cycle and Table 6-4 contains the timing data relative to the timing chart.

DMA-Initiated Read-From-Memory, Write-To-I/O Bus Cycle

Fig. 6-5 illustrates the signal timing relationships of this DMA-initiated bus cycle and Table 6-5 contains the timing data relative to the timing chart.

DMA-Initiated Read-From-I/O, Write-To-Memory Bus Cycle

Fig. 6-6 illustrates the signal timing relationships of this DMA-initiated bus cycle and Table 6-6 contains the timing data relative to the timing chart.

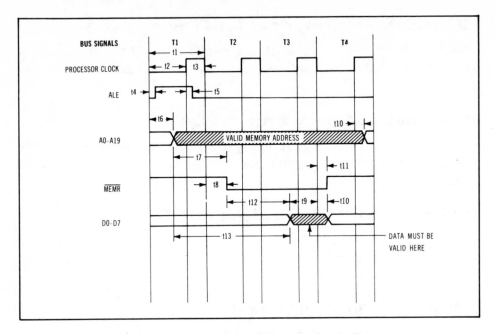

Fig. 6-1. Memory-read bus cycle timings.

Table 6-1. Memory-Read Bus Cycle Timings

Symbol	Max	Min
t1	—	209.5
t2	—	124.5
t3	—	71.8
t4	15	—
t5	15	—
t6	128	16
t7	—	91.5
t8	35	10
t9	—	42
t10	—	10
t11	35	10
t12	—	342
t13	—	458.5

*All times are in nanoseconds.

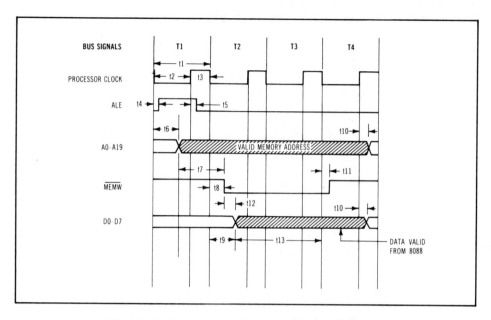

Fig. 6-2. Memory-write bus cycle timings.

Table 6-2. Memory-Write Bus Cycle Timings

Symbol	Max	Min
t1	—	209.5
t2	—	124.5
t3	—	71.8
t4	15	—
t5	15	—
t6	128	16
t7	—	91.5
t8	35	10
t9	122	14
t10	—	10
t11	35	10
t12	112	—
t13	—	297

*All timings are in nanoseconds.

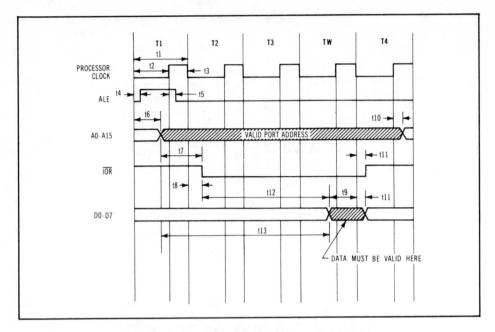

Fig. 6-3. I/O port read bus cycle timings.

Table 6-3.   I/O Port Read Bus Cycle Timings

Symbol	Max	Min
t1	—	209.5
t2	—	124.5
t3	—	71.8
t4	15	—
t5	15	—
t6	128	16
t7	—	91.5
t8	35	10
t9	—	42
t10	—	10
t11	35	10
t12	—	551.5
t13	—	668

*All times are in nanoseconds.

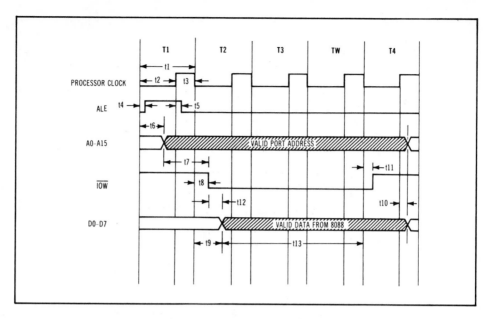

Fig. 6-4. I/O port write bus cycle timings.

Table 6-4.   I/O Port Write Bus Cycle Timings

Symbol	Max	Min
t1	—	209.5
t2	—	124.5
t3	—	71.8
t4	15	—
t5	15	—
t6	128	16
t7	—	91.5
t8	35	10
t9	122	14
t10	—	10
t11	35	10
t12	112	—
t13	—	506.5

*All times are in nanoseconds.

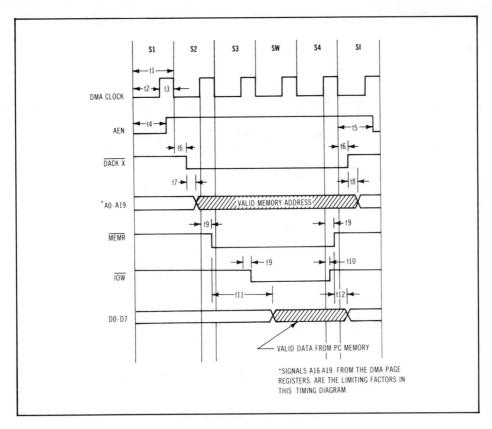

Fig. 6-5. DMA-initiated read-from-memory bus cycle timings.

Table 6-5. DMA Bus Cycle Timings

Symbol	Max	Min
t1	—	209.5
t2	—	119
t3	—	79
t4	183	132
t5	183	130
t6	170	—
t7	45	—
t8	—	11
t9	202	—
t10	142	—
t11	333	—
t12	—	4

*All times are in nanoseconds.

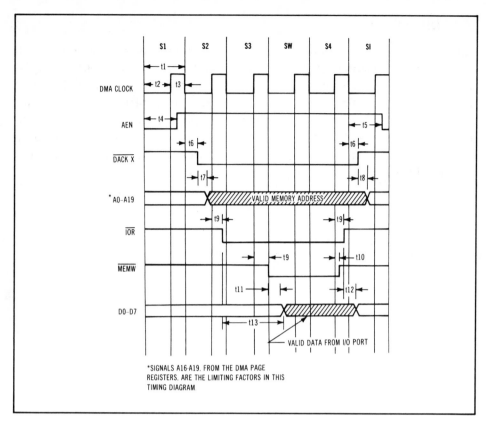

Fig. 6-6. DMA-initiated read-from-I/O bus cycle timings.

Table 6-6.   More Bus Cycle Timings

Symbol	Max	Min
t1	—	209.5
t2	—	119
t3	—	79
t4	183	132
t5	183	130
t6	170	—
t7	45	—
t8	—	11
t9	202	—
t10	142	—
t11	30	—
t12	—	4
t13	240	—

*All times are in nanoseconds.

SUMMARY

It is likely that the actual timings of the system bus will be better than those values presented in the tables. A design should not count on this, though, since worst case conditions can and will occur, and will create problems on a specific system. In many cases, the problem will be intermittent and very difficult to diagnose. It should be further noted that the timing information will be affected by improper power levels and grounding and by very high capacitive or dc loads. Chapter 7 discusses bus loading and the driving capabilities of the system bus.

CHAPTER 7

SYSTEM-BUS LOADING AND DRIVING CAPABILITIES

INTRODUCTION

One of the more important considerations, when attaching a design to the system bus, is that of the bus signal-driving capability and bus loading. For bus output signals, you will have to determine if there is sufficient signal drive to support your design. If not, signal repowering will be needed. For input bus signals, you will need to determine if your design has sufficient drive capability to drive the system bus.

The bus loading and driving specifications presented here were derived from an inspection of the logic schematics for the PC system that were published in the *IBM Technical Reference Manual* and from data in the *1982 Component Data Catalog* and Texas Instruments' *1981 TTL Data Book for Design Engineers*.

SYSTEM-BUS DRIVE CAPABILITY

There are two specifications on the bus output signals that are of interest, IOL and IOH. IOL refers to the maximum current that can be sinked into the output driver at the low logic level. IOH is the maximum current that can be sourced from the driver at the high logic level. Table 7-1 lists the capability of the output drivers as they exist in the five I/O card slots. Note that some bus signals are used on the system board before being driven to the card slots. Table 7-1 takes into account the use of these loads and, thus, reflects the true drive available in the five I/O system-bus card slots. The actual drive left for a specific design, in a card slot, is the difference between the values given in the table and the values taken by the other cards in the remaining card slots. Tables 7-2 through 7-7 reflect the output drive loads taken by the most popular IBM PC cards. Thus, to determine the load available, sum the values in the tables for the cards that are in your system and subtract that value from the values in Table 7-1.

SYSTEM-BUS LOAD PRESENTED IN CARD SLOTS

The system-bus input signal presents a load to the cards in the five card slots. This load is the input low-level current required from the driver to establish a good low-level logic signal. This load is called IIL or low-level input current. The driving circuit must also provide current in the upper level to the bus receiving circuit. This is called the high-level input current, or IIH. The IIL and IIH load values for the bus input signal are listed in Table 7-8.

Table 7-1.   System-Bus Drive Capability

Bus Output Signal	IOL	IOH
D0–D7	23.6	−14.96
A19–A16	7.2	−2.46
A14–A15	21.2	−2.51
A13	23.2	−2.56
A0–A12	23.4	−2.56
IOR, IOW, MEMR, MEMW	23.8	−4.98
CLK	23.2	−14.96
AEN	24.0	−15.00
DACK0	24.0	−15.00
DACK1	3.2	−0.20
DACK2, DACK3	2.8	−0.18
ALE	14.8	−0.94
RESET DRV	8.0	−0.40
T/C	8.0	−0.40
OSC	5.0	−1.00

Note 1: All current values are in milliamperes.

Note 2: Table values are adjusted for loads taken on the system board.

Note 3: Values are "worst case" instances of either the 8088 bus drive or the DMA bus drive.

Table 7-2. Bus Loading From IBM Monochrome Display and Parallel Printer Adapter

Bus Signal	Load Taken From	
	IOL	IOH
D0–D7	−0.2	0.020
A0–A3	−0.2	0.020
A4–A9	−0.8	0.040
A10–A19	−0.4	0.020
AEN	−0.4	0.020
MEMW	−0.8	0.040
IOR	−0.4	0.020
IOW	−0.4	0.020
MEMR	−0.4	0.020
RESET DRV	−0.4	0.020
CLK	−2.0	0.050

All values are in milliamperes.

Table 7-3. Bus Loading From IBM Color Graphics Monitor Adapter

Bus Signal	Load Taken From	
	IOL	IOH
D0–D7	−0.2	0.020
OSC	−0.4	0.020
RESET DRV	−0.8	0.040
CLK	−0.4	0.020
AEN	−0.8	0.040
MEMR	−0.8	0.040
MEMW	−0.8	0.040
IOR	−0.8	0.040
IOW	−0.41	0.050
A0	−0.2	0.020
A1, A2	−0.8	0.040
A3	−1.2	0.060
A4–A9	−0.8	0.040
A10–A19	−0.4	0.020

All values are in milliamperes.

Table 7-4. Bus Loading From IBM Parallel Printer Adapter

Bus Signal	Load Taken From	
	IOL	IOH
D0–D7	−0.2	0.020
A3–A7 and A9	−0.4	0.020
A8	−0.8	0.040
AEN	−0.4	0.020
RESET DRV	−0.4	0.020
IOR	−0.4	0.020
IOW	−0.4	0.020

All values are in milliamperes.

Table 7-5. Bus Loading From IBM Diskette Drive Adapter

Bus Signal	Load Taken From	
	IOL	IOH
D0–D7	−0.2	0.020
A0–A9	−0.4	0.020
AEN	−0.4	0.020
IOR	−0.4	0.020
IOW	−0.4	0.020
DACK2	−0.4	0.020
RESET DRV	−0.4	0.020

All values are in milliamperes.

Table 7-6. Bus Loading From IBM 64KB RAM Card

Bus Signal	Load Taken From	
	IOL	IOH
D0–D7	−0.2	0.020
A0–A13	−0.4	0.020
A14	−4.0	0.100
A15	−2.4	0.070
A16–A19	−6.0	0.150
DACK0	−0.8	0.040
MEMR	−2.4	0.070
MEMW	−2.4	0.070

All values are in milliamperes.

Table 7-7. Bus Loading From IBM Game Control Adapter

Bus Signal	Load Taken From	
	IOL	IOH
D0–D7	−0.2	0.020
A0–A9	−0.4	0.020
AEN	−0.4	0.020
IOR	−0.4	0.020
IOW	−0.4	0.020

All values are in milliamperes.

Table 7-8. Load Presented to Bus Input Signals

Bus Signal	Load	
	IIL	IIH
D0–D7	−0.4	0.040
I/O CH CK	−0.4	0.020
I/O CH RDY	−0.4	0.020
IRQ2–IRQ7	−0.010	0.010
DRQ1–DRQ3	−0.010	0.010

All values are in milliamperes.

CAPACITIVE BUS LOADING

Another concern, when designing to the system bus, is that of capacitive loading on the output bus signals. As each load is added, the capacitance that the driver circuit sees is increased. As the capacitance increases, the signal becomes distorted and delayed. Each load adds from 10 to 20 picofarads of capacitance to the bus. Thus, with 10 loads, the capacitance is from 100 to 200 picofarads. Signal capacitance values of greater than 200 picofarads will, in general, affect the bus signals to the extent that unreliable operation may occur.

GENERAL RULES OF THUMB

In general, a loading calculation will not be required if a few simple rules are followed. First, do not attach an NMOS LSI device directly to the system bus. Typically, these devices have a very low drive capability and are not tolerant to negative undershoot that may exist on the system bus. Secondly, do not present more than two LS device loads to any bus signal. Third, decouple bus drivers and transceivers with a 0.01-μF capacitor between the +5 volt and ground leads. Last, do not run the bus signal for long distances on the attachment card. This will add excessive capacitance and will distort and delay the bus signal. Signal buffer circuits should be placed near the bus connector. If these simple rules are followed, you should not have to go through a detailed bus loading calculation.

CHAPTER 8

SYSTEM-BUS MECHANICAL AND POWER CHARACTERISTICS

INTRODUCTION

Most interface designs will be done on cards that must fit in one of the System Unit's card slots. This chapter provides information relative to the mechanical aspects of the System Unit and to the card size that will fit in the card slots. Also, the power-supply capabilities of the System Unit are covered in this chapter. This will provide the interface designer with needed information on the levels, power, and the tolerances of power that are available to implement a design.

SYSTEM-BUS CARD SLOTS

Fig. 8-1 is a photograph of the System Unit card-connector area. As can be seen, there is space and connectors for up to five cards. The connectors are capable of supporting 62 signal connectors to a card, 31 on each side of the card. The connection tabs are spaced on 100-mil centers, or one-tenth of an inch apart. Each card slot is capable of accepting a card, with components and wiring area, of approximately 4.1 inches by 13 inches (10.42 cm × 33.02 cm). Slot 2 is capable of accepting a slightly larger card. This is possible because the System Unit's base board has no components under this card and it may extend lower. The card slots are spaced 1 inch apart. Cards are retained by attaching an ''L'' bracket to the back end of the card which, in turn, attaches to the top of the back bulkhead of the System Unit. Cables may be attached to the rear of the card and can extend through the L bracket and through the slots cut in the rear bulkhead of the System Unit. This scheme allows cards to be nearly any length or height, up to the maximum size specified earlier. In addition, a connector may be

Fig. 8-1. Card slot area in the Personal Computer.

attached to the rear of the card and extended through the bulkhead slots, thus, eliminating the need for an internal cable from the card to the bulkhead. Fig. 8-2 is a drawing defining the signal and slot labeling convention. Fig. 8-3 shows the arrangement of the card slots on the System Unit's logic board.

PC CARD SIZE

Fig. 8-5 is a drawing of the maximum card size dimensions that will fit in a System Unit card slot. The card should be constructed of a material with a minimum thickness of 0.060 inch to ensure good contact in the connectors. In addition, the card-edge signal tabs should be plated with gold to ensure a positive, long-lasting, and reliable contact.

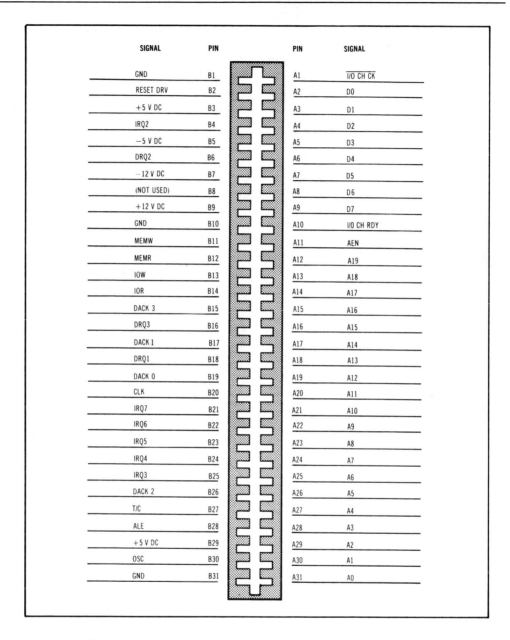

SIGNAL	PIN		PIN	SIGNAL
GND	B1		A1	I/O CH CK
RESET DRV	B2		A2	D0
+5 V DC	B3		A3	D1
IRQ2	B4		A4	D2
−5 V DC	B5		A5	D3
DRQ2	B6		A6	D4
−12 V DC	B7		A7	D5
(NOT USED)	B8		A8	D6
+12 V DC	B9		A9	D7
GND	B10		A10	I/O CH RDY
MEMW	B11		A11	AEN
MEMR	B12		A12	A19
IOW	B13		A13	A18
IOR	B14		A14	A17
DACK 3	B15		A15	A16
DRQ3	B16		A16	A15
DACK 1	B17		A17	A14
DRQ1	B18		A18	A13
DACK 0	B19		A19	A12
CLK	B20		A20	A11
IRQ7	B21		A21	A10
IRQ6	B22		A22	A9
IRQ5	B23		A23	A8
IRQ4	B24		A24	A7
IRQ3	B25		A25	A6
DACK 2	B26		A26	A5
T/C	B27		A27	A4
ALE	B28		A28	A3
+5 V DC	B29		A29	A2
OSC	B30		A30	A1
GND	B31		A31	A0

Fig. 8-2. Pin and signal definitions for the card slots.

Fig. 8-5 illustrates the available space and size of the cable-access area that is at the rear bulkhead of the machine.

Several manufacturers provide excellent prototyping cards that can be used to wire-wrap a design so that you can try it in a system. The following is a list of some manufacturers and their addresses.

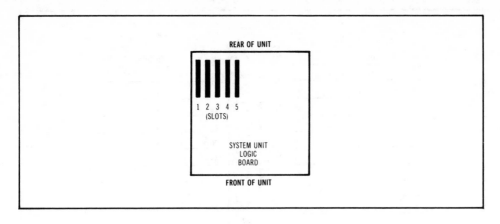

**Fig. 8-3. Arrangement and location of the card slots
in the System Unit.**

Vector Electronic Co., Inc.
12460 Gladstone Ave.
Sylmar, CA 91342

This manufacturer offers three different styles of prototyping cards plus an extender card.

Sigma Designs, Inc.
P.O. Box 3765
Santa Clara, CA 95055

Automated Business Machines, Inc.
29352 Avocet Lane
South Laguna, CA 92677

Personal Computer Products
1400 Colman Ave., Suite C-18
Santa Clara, CA 95050

Micro Match
10343 Commerce Ave.
Tujunga, CA 91042

AST Research Inc.
2691 Richter Ave., Suite 104
Irvine, CA 92714

SYSTEM UNIT POWER

There are four power levels available on the signal tabs in each card slot. Table 8-1 summarizes these levels, the total power from the power supply, its tolerances, and the total wattage. In addition, Table 8-1 approximates the power that is available in each card slot—assuming a typical system configuration. If you have an unusual system configuration, it may be necessary to measure the current drawn on each level to determine if there is sufficient power to support your design.

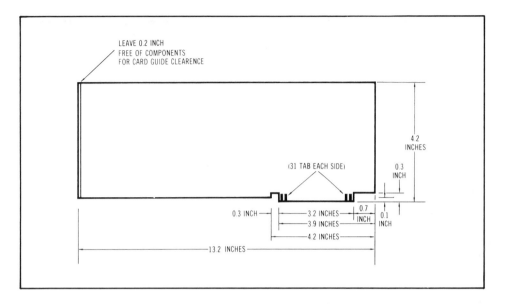

Fig. 8-4. Outline drawing showing dimensions of the PC cards.

Table 8-1.   PC Power Supply

DC Power	Max (Vdc)	Min (Vdc)	Current (Amps)	Power (Watts)	Typical Current/Slot (Amperes)
+ 5 V DC	5.25	4.80	7.0	35.0	0.7
− 5 V DC	5.50	4.60	0.3	1.5	0.03
+12 V DC	12.6	11.52	2.0	24.0	0.10
−12 V DC	13.2	10.92	0.25	3.0	0.05

Note: The ac power outlet to the monochrome display is 120 V ac and it provides a maximum
of 0.75 ampere.

POWER DECOUPLING

A common problem in circuit designs is the one of improper power distribution and decoupling. Since most electronic devices have highly variable power requirements that are often dependent on the operation that is occurring at an instant in time, they require a decoupling device. The purpose of the decoupling device is to supply the short-term power requirements of a device so that the power does not have to come directly from the system's power supply. Since the power system with its wiring and its cables add inductance to the power source, it cannot respond quickly to high, transient, power requirements. To solve this problem, decoupling capacitors are typically added at key points in the design so that transient

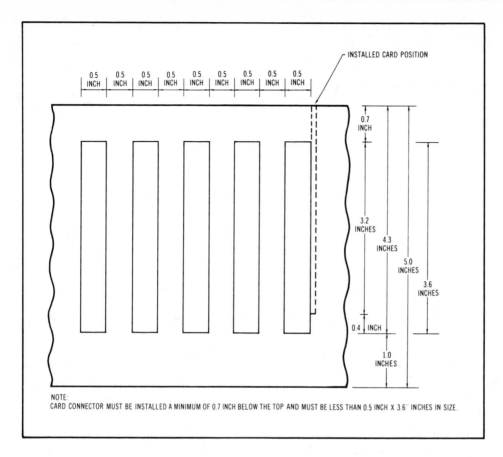

Fig. 8-5. Rear view of cable access area.

power can be drawn from them and not directly from the power supply. For large, slow, power fluctuations, a bulk capacitor is used to store the power requirements. These bulk-type decoupling capacitors are typically tantalum capacitors having capacitances of 8 to 20 microfarads. These devices should be tied across the power level and ground at the card edge connectors and at the extreme ends and tops of the card. It is particularly important to decouple the +5-volt power level since it will likely draw the most power in a typical design.

For high frequency and smaller transient power requirements, smaller high-frequency decoupling capacitors must be used. These devices are typically ceramic capacitors in the range of 0.1 to 0.01 microfarad. These devices are normally placed across the ground and power leads of high transient-current devices. Devices that will typically require a high-frequency decoupling capacitor are "S"-type TTL devices, bus drivers and transceivers, LSI devices, and any high-current high-switching-speed device.

CHAPTER 9

SYSTEM INTERRUPTS

INTRODUCTION

Interrupts can be very useful and often necessary functions when interfacing a design to a microprocessor system. Their major advantage is the ability to get the attention of the microprocessor for service of a function, without requiring the processor to be constantly polling an interface for work requests. This leaves the processor free to do other things until it is specifically required by the interface. A good example of the use of interrupts is the servicing of the keyboard on the Personal Computer. Each keystroke generates at least one interrupt to the 8088 microprocessor. As the microprocessor is executing its program, it cannot also be in a loop waiting for the user to strike a key. If this were the case, the program would never get executed since the full attention of the processor would be devoted to looking for the next keystroke. A simple solution is to have the program, that is being executed, stop periodically and look at the keyboard interface to see if a key has been struck. However, the application program must know when to look and how often. Otherwise, much of its processing time would be used in nonproductive polling of the keyboard interface. The interrupt function of the Personal Computer solves this problem by automatically stopping the program at some convenient point, i.e., the next instruction boundary, and points the processor to the program needed to service the keyboard each time a key is struck. After the completion of the program (to receive the key), the hardware automatically returns control to the program (that was executing) at the next sequential instruction.

The interrupt function is often used in interfacing applications where programs require synchronization with external events, or where error or status conditions may arise that require the processor's or the program's attention. Since many interface conditions may require service, and possibly all at the same time, the Personal Computer's interrupt functions provide nine interrupt levels or request ports. These nine request ports are prioritized such that when multiple requests are active at the same time, they are serviced in a sequential pre-described order.

PC INTERRUPT SYSTEM

The 8088 microprocessor has two interrupt input ports available: a maskable-interrupt input port and a nonmaskable-interrupt (NMI) input port. Attached to the NMI are three possible sources for the NMI: a baseboard RAM parity error, an auxiliary processor-socket interrupt request, and an I/O-channel check request. Since the NMI is not masked internally in the 8088 microprocessor, logic on the baseboard uses an I/O-register port bit to mask and unmask the NMI. On the maskable-interrupt 8088 port, an 8259A interrupt controller is attached. The 8259A controller extends the port to eight prioritized interrupt-request level ports. Thus, a total of nine interrupt level requests are available on the Personal Computer. However, not all of these levels are available for interfacing applications. Some are used by the system's integrated I/O and the system-bus attached adapters. Table 9-1 is a brief summary of the interrupt levels and their present usage.

Table 9-1. Summary of Interrupt Levels

Interrupt Level			Usage
Highest Level	NMI		Baseboard RAM parity, I/O channel check, numeric processor.
	IRQ	0	System timer output 8253-5 Channel 0.
	IRQ	1	Keyboard scan code interrupt.
Available in System Bus	IRQ	2	Not used at present.
	IRQ	3	Not used at present.
	IRQ	4	RS-232-C serial port.
	IRQ	5	Not used at present.
	IRQ	6	Diskette DRV status.
	IRQ	7	Parallel PRT port (not used in BIOS).

Fig. 9-1 is a graphic representation of the Personal Computer interrupt system.

THE INTERRUPT CONTROLLER

Fig. 9-2 is a block diagram of the key elements of an 8259A interrupt controller. The 8259A interrupt controller expands the 8088 microprocessor's maskable interrupt-input port to eight prioritized interrupt-input ports. The logic in the controller captures interrupt requests in a bank of

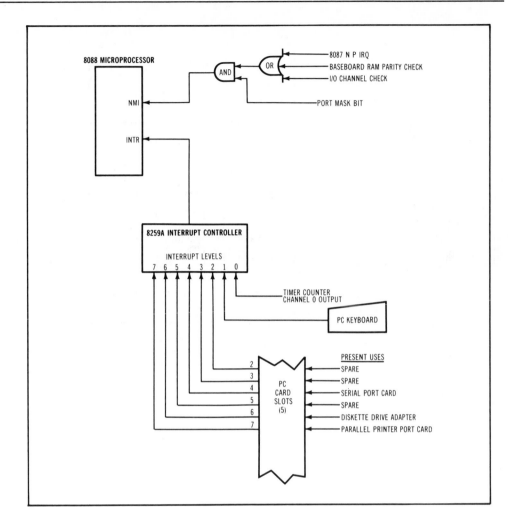

Fig. 9-1. Interrupt system block diagram.

eight latches called the interrupt request register (IRR). The IRR can be programmed to set by either an edge-sensitive signal or a level-sensitive signal. There is also an 8-bit interrupt mask register (IMR) that can be programmed to enable or disable any interrupt requests to the controller. After interrupt requests are set in the IRR, they are fed through priority-resolving logic. The results of the priority logic are then fed to another 8-bit register called an in-service register (ISR). This register reflects the level that is presently being serviced by the 8088 microprocessor. The controller can be programmed to support a variety of interrupt prioritization modes by just setting the mode bits during the controller initialization. These modes are covered in detail later in this chapter. In addition, the controller

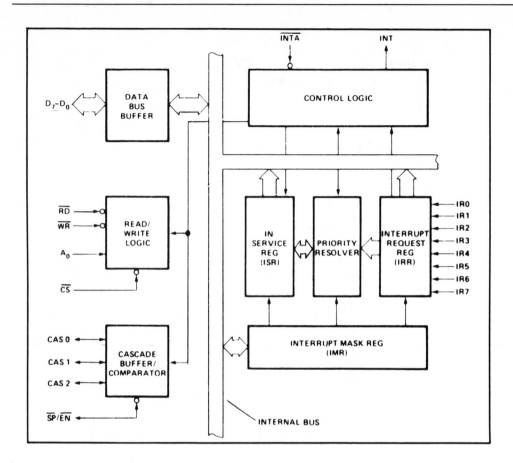

**Fig. 9-2. Block diagram of an 8259A interrupt controller
(Courtesy Intel Corp.).**

allows the masking and clearing of the interrupt request during system operation by programming a set of command control registers. During operation of the controller, it is also possible to read the status of many of the controller's internal registers.

The 8259A interrupt controller supports a cascade mode, which allows additional controllers to be added to a system and, thus, expands the number of external interrupt request ports. The PC system design does not support this mode, however, since the cascade interface lines do not exist on the system bus.

SEQUENCE OF EVENTS IN AN INTERRUPT

When an interrupt request occurs in the system, a sequence of events takes place that directs the request to the proper program needed to service the specific request. Before this sequence of events can occur, however, some system initialization is required so that the requests are properly handled when they occur. The following is the event sequence that occurs when an interrupt is activated. Let us assume that the interrupt initialization sequence has been done and that the interrupt request is not masked off.

1. The interface logic activates an interrupt request line on the system bus interface.
2. The interrupt controller (8259A) receives the request and prioritizes it with other requests that may be either coming in or pending.
3. If the request is the only one, or is the next highest level pending at the end of the higher-level service, an interrupt request is sent to the 8088 microprocessor.
4. The 8088 MPU next sends two INTA response pulses to the 8259A interrupt controller. The first freezes the priority and sets the levels in the service latch. The second INTA requests an 8-bit pointer value.
5. The 8088 processor then receives the 8-bit pointer value. It is used to index into a low memory table, which contains the IP and the offset value of the interrupt-service routine for the specific level that is being serviced.
6. Next, the 8088 microprocessor fetches the IP and code segment value, pushes its present IP, code segment, and flags onto the system stack, and, then, branches to the newly fetched IP and code segment value. The interrupt service program will not begin execution.

Fig. 9-3 gives a block diagram of the signal and data flow during a system interrupt.

INTERRUPT HOUSEKEEPING

Once the interrupt service routine is entered, there are a few housekeeping chores that need to be done before the actual routine is executed. First, if the routine used some of the 8088 register, which is highly likely, it should "push" the present register values onto the system stack so that their value will not be altered and they can be returned at the end of the routine. Secondly, you may also want to reset the interrupt request itself and reset the in-service latch by issuing an EOI (end of interrupt instruction) to the 8259A interrupt controller. This will allow additional interrupts to be received by the 8259A controller. Note that additional requests from the 8259A controller to the 8088 microprocessor are still masked off, however. This occurs automatically when the interrupt is serviced. It can be enabled by changing the status bit in the flag register or by "POPing"

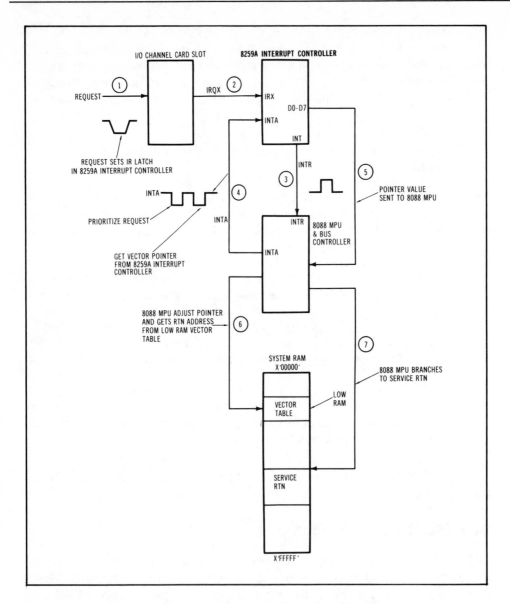

Fig. 9-3. Diagram of the interrupt signal flow.

the old status from the stack during an RTN instruction at the end of the routine. If it is enabled before the end of a routine, a higher level may interrupt the present level. This may not be bad, but the consequences must be studied carefully for your specific application.

Now, the interrupt service routine may finally be executed. Again, at the end of the routine, there is a bit more housekeeping required. First, the registers that were saved on the system stack must be restored for the program that was interrupted. This is done by POPing them back off the stack, restoring the system flags to their old value, and executing an interrupt RTN instruction, which POPs the old IP and code segment from the stack and then branches to that address.

SYSTEM INITIALIZATION FOR INTERRUPTS

The preceding descriptions have all assumed that the interrupt-controller stack pointer and interrupt vector tables have been initialized to support the desired results when an interrupt occurs. The following is a brief summary of all of the events in an interrupt sequence, including the required initialization sequence.

1. Initialize the stack pointer to the status and register-save restore area in system RAM.
2. Initialize the low RAM addresses in 8088 memory with addresses of the interrupt-service routines. The first 1024 bytes of the 8088 address space are reserved for a four-byte pointer to any of 256 possible interrupts. The four-byte value consists of an IP (instruction pointer) value and a CS (code segment) value. BIOS only does this for interrupts that it is using.
3. Initialize the 8259A-5 interrupt controller chip.
   A. Initialize the ICW 1–4 command words.
   B. Initialize the OCWs (operation control words). This means Unmask the interrupt levels.
4. Unmask the system interrupt in the 8088 MPU. (Set status bit in the flag register.)
5. The interface generates on interrupt request.
6. The 8259A interrupt controller gets requests; sets request latch.
7. The 8259A controller sets INTR request to the 8088 microprocessor.
8. The 8088 MPU responds with an INTA pulse which prioritizes the request and sets the requests in the service latch in the 8259A controller.
9. The 8088 MPU sends a second INTA pulse, which is responded to by the 8259A controller with the level's pointer value. It is used to index into the 8088 low storage to obtain the level's service address.
10. Next, the 8088 MPU masks off the interrupts, pushes its flags onto the stack, pushes the next instruction address (IP and CS values) onto the stack, fetches the new IP and CS values using the pointer value, and branches to the new IP and CS address value.
11. The interrupt service routine pushes onto the stack register that it will use and which it could destroy.

12. To allow additional interrupt levels, the interrupt routine will issue an end-of-interrupt instruction, EOI, to the 8259A controller.
13. The interrupt service routine will now be executed.
14. At completion of the service routine, the register and status are restored by POPing them from the stack.
15. Lastly, the service routine executes an interrupt-return instruction, which unmasks the interrupts, pops the old CS and IP values from the stack, and branches to these values and picks up execution from where it was interrupted.

INTERRUPT INITIALIZATION

Now that we have a good understanding of how interrupts operate in the Personal Computer, it is time to consider the details of system initialization in order to use interrupts. This initialization, as outlined in the previously detailed interrupt-sequence summary, is directed both at the memory of the 8088 microprocessor and at the 8259A-5 interrupt-controller chips. Let us first consider the initialization of the low RAM memory of the 8088 MPU, which contains the interrupt vector table.

INTERRUPT VECTOR TABLE INITIALIZATION

The first 1024 bytes of memory in an 8088 microprocessor system are devoted to the interrupt function in an 8088 processor system. The 8088 MPU architecture will support a maximum of 256 interrupts. The low RAM area is used to store the addresses of each of the 256 possible interrupt-service routines. Each address is made up of two 16-bit values, an instruction pointer (IP), and a code segment (CS) value. When one of the 256 possible interrupts occurs, this table is accessed, and the associated CS and IP values are used to branch to the correct interrupt-service routine. The interrupts of an 8088 MPU can be generated in a variety of manners, including internally, by software, and externally. Fig. 9-4 illustrates the use of the low RAM area for all types of 8088 MPU interrupts.

As previously discussed, an 8-bit pointer is passed to the 8088 processor on the second INTA pulse of an interrupt cycle. This pointer is used to develop a 10-bit address for addressing the RAM vector table in the first 1024 bytes of the 8088 memory. The 10-bit pointer has the following address value.

$$A9 \; A8 \; A7 \; A6 \; A5 \; L3 \; L2 \; L1 \; 0 \; 0$$

The two least-significant bits are set to zeros by the 8088 microprocessor. This ensures that each vector has a four-byte space reserved for the IP and the CS. The L1 L2 L3 field is added by the 8259A controller hardware

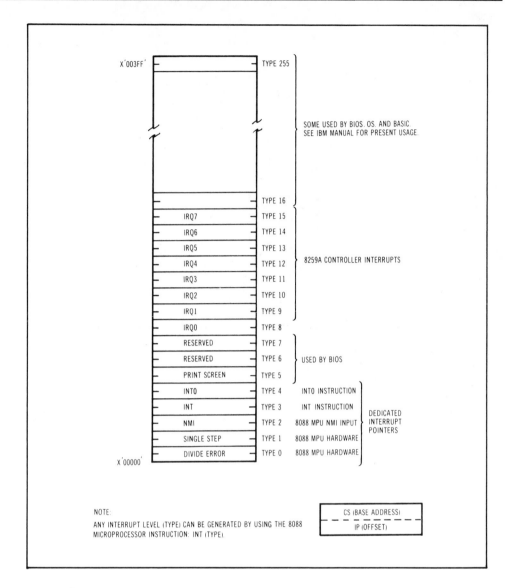

**Fig. 9-4. Vector pointers of the 8259A interrupt controller
in PC low memory.**

and represents the encoded level values that are being serviced. This value is transferred to the 8088 MPU as the three least-significant bits in the second INTA bus-cycle byte. The A5 through A9 field comes from the 8259A interrupt controller as the remaining bits of the second INTA bus-cycle byte. This field, if programmed into the 8259A controller, is initialization command word 2 (ICW2) data. This value locates the position of the 32-byte area in the low 1024 memory address space, which contains the

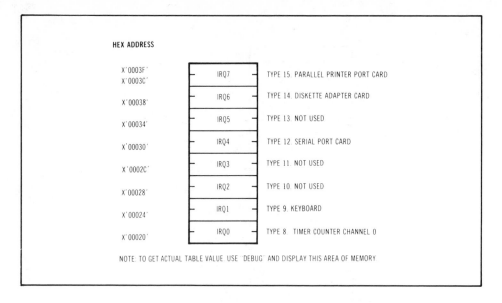

HEX ADDRESS

X'0003F'	IRQ7	TYPE 15. PARALLEL PRINTER PORT CARD
X'0003C'		
X'00038'	IRQ6	TYPE 14. DISKETTE ADAPTER CARD
X'00034'	IRQ5	TYPE 13. NOT USED
X'00030'	IRQ4	TYPE 12. SERIAL PORT CARD
X'0002C'	IRQ3	TYPE 11. NOT USED
X'00028'	IRQ2	TYPE 10. NOT USED
X'00024'	IRQ1	TYPE 9. KEYBOARD
X'00020'	IRQ0	TYPE 8. TIMER COUNTER CHANNEL 0

NOTE: TO GET ACTUAL TABLE VALUE, USE 'DEBUG' AND DISPLAY THIS AREA OF MEMORY

Fig. 9-5. The 8259A interrupt controller vector table.

address pointers for the eight interrupt levels that are supported by the 8259A interrupt controller.

The PC BIOS initializes the A9 through A5 value to 00001. Thus, the vector table of the 8259A controller is located in low PC RAM at hex address 00020 (Fig. 9-5). The interrupt vector pointer of Level 0 is located at hex address 00020 and Level 4 vector pointer is located at hex address 00030. Fig. 9-5 shows the memory map for the interrupt vector table, as initialized by BIOS. Note that the four-byte pointer in the table is stored with the IP value in the two lowest addresses and the CS is stored in the two highest addresses. In addition, the least-significant byte of the addresses of the IP and CS are stored in the least-significant byte of their two-byte fields.

It is possible to move the vector table location of the 8259A controller by changing the A9 through A5 field in ICW2, but the consequences of doing this should be carefully considered, since the PC BIOS expects the table to be at hex address 00020.

INITIALIZING THE 8259A INTERRUPT CONTROLLER

Now that we know how to initialize the interrupt vector table so that it will point interrupts to the desired service routine, we must now consider the initialization and operation of the 8259A interrupt controller.

The controller can be addressed through I/O port addresses hex 0020 and 0021. A quick look at the register set that needs to be initialized will reveal that there are more registers than the two I/O address ports can support. The 8259A controller overcomes this problem by first using the I/O port addresses in an *initialization mode* and, then, by reusing the addresses in an *operation command mode* that is automatically entered after the initialization mode is completed. The initialization mode can be entered at any time by writing to port address hex 0020 with data bit 4 set to a one. This byte of data contains other information to be defined later and is called *initialization command word one* (ICW1). Up to three additional initialization command words must follow ICW1 before the operation command mode is entered. The three additional ICWs are written to I/O port address hex 0021 and are pushed on an internal register stack in the 8259A interrupt controller. They must be written in sequence. After the last ICW is written to the 8259A controller, it enters the operation control mode. Writing to I/O port address hex 0021 sets operation control word one (OCW1). OCW2 is addressed by writing to I/O port hex address 0020 with data bits 3 and 4 set to zero. OCW3 is addressed by writing to I/O port address hex 0020 with data bit 3 set to a one and data bit 4 set to zero. There are only three OCWs and their bit definitions will be covered later.

Table 9-2 summarizes the addressing structure of the 8259A interrupt controller.

Table 9-2. ICWS and OCWS Addresses of the 8259A Interrupt Controller

Port Address	Register
HEX 0020	ICW1
HEX 0021	ICW2
HEX 0021	ICW3*
HEX 0021	ICW4
HEX 0021	OCW1
HEX 0020	OCW2
HEX 0020	OCW3

*Skipped in PC initialization.
**Note: These addresses are only valid if executed in the order shown.

INITIALIZATION COMMAND WORDS

When initialization command word one (ICW1) is written to the 8259A, an initialization sequence starts during which the following steps occur.

1. The edge-sensitive mode is reset, which means that following initialization, an interrupt input request must make a low-to-high transition to generate an interrupt.
2. The interrupt mask register is cleared.
3. Interrupt input 7 is assigned the lowest priority.
4. The slave mode address is set to 7.
5. Special mask mode is cleared and the Status Read is set to IRR.
6. If IC4 = 0, all functions selected in ICW4 are set to zero.

ICW1 Bit Definitions

D0 (IC4): This bit is set to a one if the initialization sequences are to include an ICW4. For the first initialization sequences in the PC, ICW4 must be set.

D1 (SNGL): This bit indicates that there is more than one 8259A interrupt controller in the system. The PC will initialize this bit to a one, indicating that there is only one 8259A controller in the system.

D2 (ADI): This bit is not used in the 8088 mode and the PC sets it to zero.

D3 (LTIM): This bit indicates that interrupt requests are to be generated on either an input level or on an input edge. A one indicates the level-triggered mode is set and a zero indicates that the level-sensitive mode is set. The PC sets this bit to a zero for an edge-triggered mode.

D4: This bit MUST be set to a one, since it indicates that this byte is in ICW1.

D5–D7: These bits are not used in the 8088 mode and are set to zero by the PC.

In summary, the PC BIOS sets the ICW1 to a hex value of 13.

ICW2 Bit Definitions

D0–D2: These bits are not used when the 8259A controller is in the 8088 mode; they are set to zero by the PC.

D3–D7: These bits are the high-order bits of the 8-bit pointer that are sent on the second INTA bus cycle and which are used to locate the interrupt vector pointer table in low PC memory.

In summary, the PC BIOS sets the ICW2 to a hex value of 08.

ICW3 Definition

ICW3 is not used in the PC system since it does not allow multiple 8259A interrupt controllers in the system. Since bit 1 in ICW1 is set to a one, indicating only one 8259A controller in the system, the third I/O port *write* does not go to ICW3 but to ICW4. Thus, only three ICWs are written to an 8259A interrupt controller in the PC system.

ICW4 Bit Definitions

D0 (uPM): This bit indicates that the 8259A controller is either in the 8085 or the 8088 mode. It is set to a one in the PC to indicate that it is in the 8088 mode.

D1 (AEIO): This bit enables the automatic resetting of the interrupt request in the in-service register (ISR) as soon as the 8088 MPU honors the interrupt request. This happens on the second INTA pulse sent by the 8088 processor. As soon as the ISR bit is reset, the controller can send another higher-level request to the 8088 microprocessor. This may or may not be desirable depending on the function of the first interrupt service routine. Normally, the service routine would perform its function and then issue an EOI command allowing further interrupts. The PC BIOS sets this bit to zero indicating that the service routine must send an EOI command to clear the ISR bit and enable additional interrupts.

D2 (M/S): This bit indicates to the controller that it is either a master controller or a slave controller in a multiple controller system. The PC design only supports a single controller. The PC BIOS sets this bit to a one, indicating master mode.

D3 (BUF): This bit indicates to the controller that it is in a buffered data bus system and that it should generate a control signal to enable the bus buffer during interrupts. The PC is a buffered data bus system, thus, this bit is set to a one.

D4 (SFNM): This bit indicates to the controller that it is in a multiple controller system and it must use a special fully nested mode of interrupt prioritization that will establish a priority between controllers. Since the PC is a single controller system, this function is not used in the PC and this bit is set to zero.

D5–D7: These bits are not used and are set to zero.

In summary, the PC BIOS sets ICW4 to a hex value of 09.

Now, the 8259A controller is initialized and is ready to accept interrupt requests at its inputs. During the operation of the controller, it may be necessary to change its mode of operation or obtain the status of interrupts pending in the controller. To enable these functions, the controller goes into a new mode after initialization, where it accepts commands called *Operation Control Words* (OCWs). Fig. 9-6 is a summary of the ICWs with the 8259A interrupt controller.

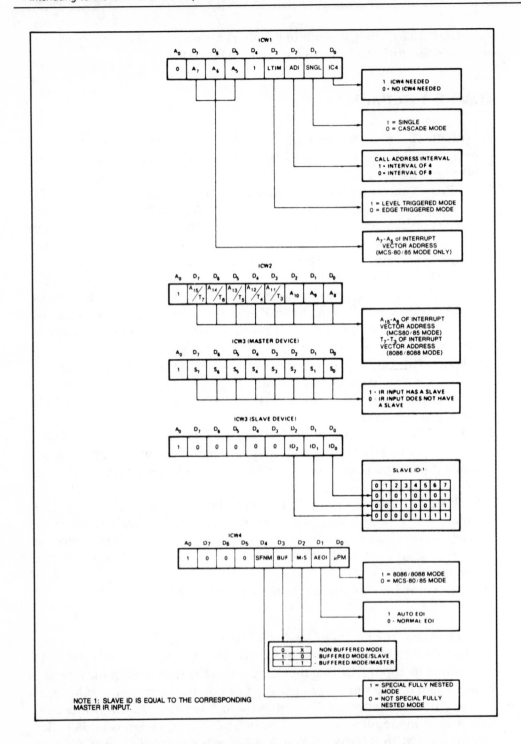

Fig. 9-6. Summary of the ICW format (Courtesy Intel Corp.).

OPERATION CONTROL MODE WORD

In the operation mode, the I/O addresses and the register bit values change meaning and writing to I/O port addresses hex 0020 and 0021 is now changed to write to operation control word registers. There are three OCW registers which are written to as follows:

OCW1—Port address hex 0021.
OCW2—Port address hex 0020 with data bits 3 and 4 set to zero.
OCW3—Port address hex 0020 with data bit 4 set to zero and data bit 3 set to one.

OCW1 Bit Definitions

The bits in OCW1 are used to set and clear the masking of interrupts at the input to the controller. Thus, an interrupt source can be enabled or disabled by writing data to this register. Bit 0 masks (enables or disables) level 0 and bit 1 controls level 1, and so on in order, so that all eight bits will control all eight interrupt levels. A zero written to a bit in the OCW1 mask register resets the mask and enables the corresponding interrupt level. Thus, 1 bit sets the mask and disables the corresponding interrupt level. The present value of this register can be obtained by reading the I/O port register address, hex 0021, while in the operation mode.

OCW2 Bit Definitions

This register is used to rotate and change the priority of the interrupt requests and to select the end of the interrupt mode to be used.

D0–D2: These bits are used to indicate to the controller the specific level that is to be acted upon by the other commands specified in OCW2. This field is an encoded value where the binary value 000 indicates level 0 and 001 indicates level 1, and so on through binary value 111, which indicates level 7.

D3 and D4: These bits are not used and are set to zero.

D5–D7: These three bits are also encoded and they represent eight possible commands to the controller. D5, the EOI bit, indicates that the command is an end-of-interrupt mode command. D6, the SL bit, indicates that the command uses the encoded-level select field specified in bits D0–D2. D7, the R bit, indicates that a level-priority rotate function is to be set.

The following is a description of all the combinations of commands that are defined by this 3-bit field.

001—A hex value of 1 in this field defines a nonspecific end-of-interrupt command. If the automatic end-of-interrupt mode is not set in ICW4 during initialization, as is the case in the PC, the interrupt request set that is in the in-service register (ISR) must be reset using an end-of-interrupt (EOI) command. This command is issued in the interrupt service routine and resets the highest level in the IS register.

011—A hex value of 3 in this field specifies a specific EOI command. In this case, the level specified in the D0–D2 field is reset in the IS register.

101—A hex value of 5 in this field will cause a nonspecific EOI command, which resets the highest IS register request, and sets it to the lowest priority and moves all other levels up one position in priority.

100—A hex value of 4 in this field will cause an automatic priority rotation mode to be set, such that each time an automatic EOI occurs, the priorities are rotated. The PC is initialized in the nonautomatic EOI mode so this command is not normally used.

000—A hex value of 0 in this field clears the automatic priority rotation mode in automatic EOI mode.

111—A hex value of 7 in this field will cause a rotation of the priority, and a specific EOI command, where the level reset in the IS register is specified in the D0–D2 field.

110—A hex value of 6 in this field causes a set priority command. The D0–D2 field contains the level that is to have the lowest priority; thus, fixing all other priorities. Therefore, if the lowest priority is set to level 5, level 6 will have the highest.

OCW3 Bit Definitions

DO and **D1:** These bits, RIS and RR, are encoded and are used to select a *status read* mode. A hex value of 0 or 1 in this field causes no action. A hex value of 2 allows the reading of the value that is in the controller's interrupt request register (IR), on the next read command issued to the controller. The read command may be issued to either I/O port address hex 0020 or 0021. A hex value of 3 in this field allows the reading of the contents of the in-service (IS) register on the next read command issued to the controller.

D2 (P): This bit issues a special command to the controller, which is similar in function to the first INTA pulse issued on a hardware interrupt response. (It sets the highest requesting level in the IS register.) On the next read command issued to the controller, the data returned have the encoded value in D0–D2 of the interrupt request. This mode is not used in the PC BIOS.

D3: This bit is not used but must be set to one.

D4: This bit is not used but must be set to zero.

D5 (SMM) and **D6 (ESMM):** These bits allow the mask register to be used in a special way. When an interrupt is set in the in-service register and is not reset with an EOI, all levels both higher and lower, that are not masked, can still be serviced while interrupts on the original level are inhibited. This mode is selected by setting bits D5 and D6 to 1s and is reset by setting bit D5 to 0 and bit D6 to 1. This mode is not used in the PC BIOS.

Fig. 9-7 is a summary of the bit definition in the OCWs.

IMPACT OF CHANGING ICWS AND OCWS

As can be seen from the multitude of initialization and operation modes available in the 8259A interrupt controller, it is a complex device that has significant control over the operation of the Personal Computer. A change in these modes can, if care is not taken, impact the operation of the PC and its software to the extent that much of the BIOS and application software will not function properly. It is thus recommended that your applications, using the interrupt facility, use the initialization modes and operation modes selected by BIOS.

INTERRUPT PERFORMANCE

In many applications, the amount of time it takes for the processor to begin servicing an interrupt request, from the initial interrupt request on the I/O bus, is critical. This time, typically called the interrupt latency time, is made up of several items. The following is a list of the items that should be considered.

1. The 8088 MPU hardware processing time. This is the time that it takes the 8088 microprocessor to receive the interrupt from the 8259A interrupt controller, get the level and pointer value from the 8259A controller, push the flags and present program address onto the stack, and branch to the interrupt service routine. This time is 61 processor clocks. At 210 nanoseconds per clock in the PC, the 8088 MPU processing time is 12.81 microseconds.

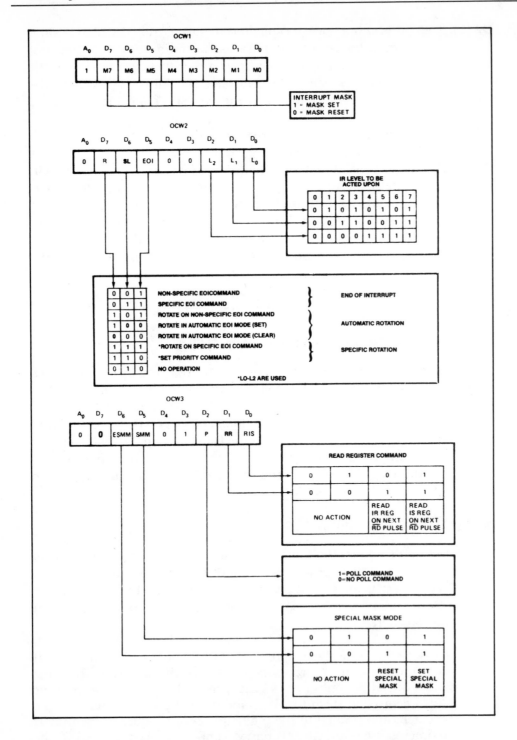

Fig. 9-7. Summary of the OCW format (Courtesy Intel Corp.).

2. Interrupts are only serviced at the end of each 8088 instruction. Thus, if an interrupt request occurs at the beginning of an instruction, it will not be serviced until the end of that instruction. Since most instructions are not very long, this time is typically in the range of 1 to 5 microseconds. But, in the 8088's instruction set, the multiply and divide instructions are quite long and may require analysis if your application is very time dependent. Some 8088 instructions will not allow an interrupt until the execution of the next instruction. The repeat, lock, and segment override prefixes are considered part of the instruction that they prefix and no interrupts are allowed between the prefix and the instruction. The move to a segment register and POP segment registers instructions does not allow interrupts to be recognized until after the following instruction.

3. If your application is on a low level, it must wait for interrupt service routines on a higher level to complete. Thus, the execution time of active interrupt-service routines must be added to your interrupt latency time. A simple solution to this problem is to go to a higher level or mask off interrupts on higher levels. However, don't mask off an interrupt source that BIOS needs to operate, particularly if you are using BIOS functions requiring interrupts.

4. Any 8088 registers that will be used by your interrupt service routine must be saved at the beginning of the service routine. If a large number or all of the processor's registers must be saved, it can amount to a significant amount of time. A technique that is sometimes helpful is to save only those registers that are needed to perform the critical task in the beginning of the routine. Then, later, save the remaining registers that are used in the routine.

Due to the variables in any interrupt latency calculation, no specific

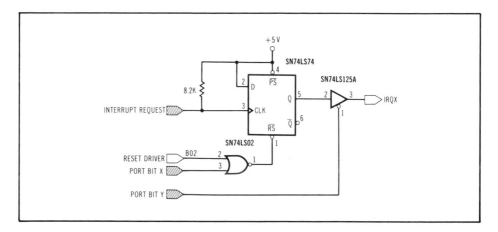

Fig. 9-8. Interrupt request circuit for the PC bus interface.

value can be used as a general rule of thumb. Each application will require analysis in order to arrive at a latency value.

CIRCUIT FOR INTERFACING TO AN I/O BUS INTERRUPT-REQUEST LINE

Fig. 9-8 illustrates a circuit that can be used to interface to the system's I/O bus interrupt-request lines. In this circuit, a positive-going edge from your application sets the SN74LS74 "D" latch. The output of the latch is then fed to the input of an SN74LS125 tri-state buffer and its output is attached to the system-bus interrupt-request line. Both the clear on the D latch and the enable on the tri-state buffer are controlled through programmable I/O port bits. The D latch holds the request active so that it is seen by the second INTA pulse from the 8088 microprocessor. The latch can then be reset by an OUT instruction in the interrupt service routine. The programmable I/O port bit on the D latch "clear" can also be used to inhibit an interrupt request from occurring without using the mask register in the 8259A interrupt controller. The tri-state buffer and its I/O port bit allow the source to be enabled or disabled from the bus interface. Thus, the interrupt-request line on the bus can be used by other features or applications when it is disabled from your source.

CHAPTER 10

SYSTEM DIRECT-MEMORY ACCESS

INTRODUCTION

In many interfacing applications, it becomes necessary to accept or transmit data to or from an interface, at rates higher than possible with a simple programmed I/O loop that uses IN and OUT instructions. A good example of this problem is the data transmitted and received from the Personal Computer's diskette drives. The data rate to and from the diskette drive adapter is sufficiently high enough that it would be difficult for the 8088 processor to keep up with it and still service other devices, such as the keyboard. To solve these high data-rate interface and adapter problems in the PC design, a special function called Direct-Memory Access (DMA) is provided. The DMA function allows an interface or adapter to read or write data to or from memory without using the 8088 microprocessor. This function is provided by a DMA controller device. In the PC design, this device is an Intel 8237-5 DMA controller chip.

BASIC CONCEPT OF DMA

During normal program execution, the 8088 microprocessor drives the system bus, providing address and control information, and is the source or destination of data. When an interface wants to transfer data using the DMA facility, it sends a request signal to the DMA controller. The controller will prioritize this request and send a "hold" request signal to the 8088 microprocessor. At the end of the current bus cycle, the 8088 MPU will remove itself from the system bus and will send a "hold" acknowledge signal to the DMA controller, indicating that the bus is now free. The DMA controller will then attach itself to the system bus and will drive the address bus and control bus, executing a data transfer cycle between the requesting interface (or adapter) and memory. The interface (or adapter) is notified of this action by the DMA controller sending a DMA acknowledge signal to the interface or adapter. The DMA controller can be thought of as a third party, which, when requested, will take over as the system-bus master and will direct the transfer of data between memory and the adapters or interfaces. It should be noted that during DMA operations, the DMA controller does not handle the bus; data are transmitted directly between the memory and the interface or adapter. Fig. 10-1 shows a block diagram illustrating the concept of DMA data transfer in the PC system.

DMA Usage in the Personal Computer

The 8237-5 DMA controller chip in the PC has four DMA channels. Two of these channels are presently used in the PC design. Channel 0 is used by the System Unit's dynamic memory refresh function. Channel 2 is used to transfer data between the diskette drive adapter and memory. Channels 1 and 3, at present, are not used. Channels 1, 2, and 3 are available on the system bus for use by features or interfaces installed in the bus card slots. The PC BIOS initializes the DMA controller so that Channel 0 has the highest priority and Channel 3 the lowest. The following list summarizes the priority and use of the four PC DMA channels.

Highest priority	Channel 0	Supports memory refresh.
. . .	Channel 1	Not used at present.
. . .	Channel 2	Supports diskette drive adapter.
Lowest priority	Channel 3	Not used at present.

DMA Operation

The following procedure is a step-by-step description of the actions taken by the PC during a DMA operational cycle.

1. Before a DMA operation can occur, the 8237-5 controller must be initialized to perform the proper type of cycle. The following list is a summary of the items that will require specification by initialization.

    —Select read to or write from memory function.
    —Type of transfer: burst or single byte.
    —Byte count to be transferred.
    —Priority of channels.
    —Memory address for start of transfer.
    —Enable the channel's request signal.

    This initialization is accomplished by writing control words to the 8237-5 controller using the I/O port OUT instructions of the 8088 microprocessor. Initialization will be covered later in this chapter.

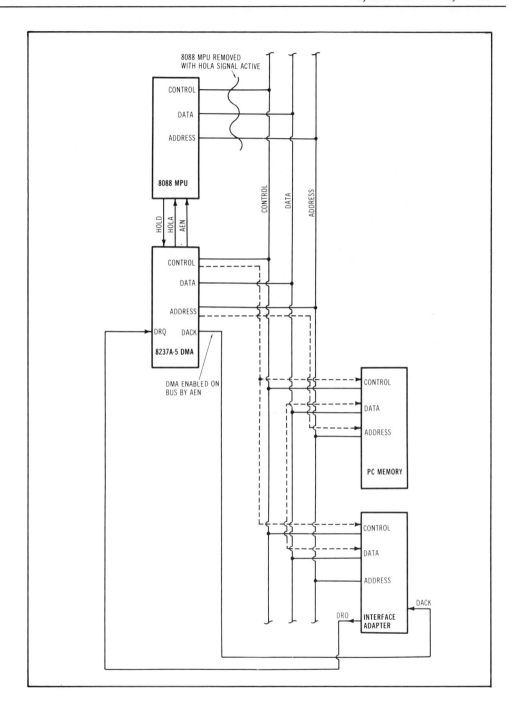

Fig. 10-1. Flow diagram of the DMA operation.

2. The interface adapter sends a DRQ signal to the 8237-5 controller, indicating that a data transfer is requested on a specified channel. There are three DRO signals on the system bus; one for each of Channels 1, 2, and 3.

3. The 8237-5 controller prioritizes this request with other requests from other channels and sends an HRQ signal to the 8088 MPU wait-state generation circuitry.

4. The wait-state circuits scan the 8088 microprocessor's status lines and look for a processor-passive state (not bus activity or a bus cycle is just about to end).

5. When a passive state is detected, the control logic sends a "not ready" signal to the 8088 processor, causing it to put the 8088 MPU in a wait state at time T3 of the next cycle. A HOLDA signal is also sent to the 8237-5 controller, indicating that at the next clock, the bus will be free and a DMA cycle can take place. Signals are also sent to the bus address, control, and data buffers, which remove the 8088 microprocessor from the system bus. It should be noted that the 8088 MPU still proceeds with the bus cycle until clock time T3 and, then, it suspends the cycle.

6. The 8237-5 controller will detect the HOLDA signal and send a DACK signal to the requesting interface adapter. This signal acts as a chip select for the adapter enabling it on the system bus.

7. The 8237-5 controller will now drive an address onto the system bus, pointing to the memory lcoation where the data transfer will take place. The 8237-5 controller will also take control of the bus control lines (MEMR, MEMW, IOR, and IOW) and will perform the actual read and write operation on the bus.

8. The interface or adapter, after receiving the DACK signal, will then drop the DRQ signal to the controller. The controller, after completing the cycle, will drop the HRQ signal to the wait-state control logic. The wait-state circuits will then drop the HOLDA signal to the controller, indicating that the 8088 microprocessor will again take over the bus. Finally, the wait-state circuits will drop the "not ready" condition to the 8088 processor and will reenable its bus buffers. The bus cycle that was suspended at clock time T3 is restarted and the 8088 MPU continues normal bus-cycle operations. Note that when the bus cycle is restarted, two extra clock times are inserted in the bus cycle to give the suspended bus cycle sufficient access time.

The above operations are done on every DMA cycle. The DMA function is done in this manner so that the 8088 microprocessor can operate in maximum mode and still support the auxiliary processor socket. In maximum mode, the 8088 processor does not support the hold/hold-acknowledge protocol; thus, the function is simulated using the wait-state control circuitry on the baseboard. This scheme seems at first to be inefficient, but it does allow overlapping of the 8088 MPU bus cycle with a DMA cycle, since the 8088 processor executes the suspended bus cycle up to clock time T3.

INITIALIZATION OF THE 8237-5 CONTROLLER

The 8237-5 DMA controller has 16 read/write I/O port register addresses that contain both initialization data and device status. Note that not all 16 port addresses can be both read and write. The PC decodes the 8237-5 device so that the port addresses will reside in the I/O port address range of hex 0000 to 000F. In the 8237-5 controller, the port addresses are divided into two groups. Addresses hex 0000 to 0007 are read/write registers that contain DMA starting memory addresses for each channel, the current memory address for the next DMA cycle on each channel, the byte count that is to be transferred for each channel, and the current byte count of each channel. The second group of I/O port addresses, hex addresses 0008 to 000F, contain control and status registers that define the operation of each channel.

Control and Status Register Definitions

Table 10-1 defines the functions of each of the addresses in the range hex 0008 to 000F. Note that the functions are different on a "read" than they are on a "write." Thus, it is typically not possible to read the contents of write-only registers. The definitions of the write registers will be covered first.

Table 10-1. Control and Status Register Addresses

I/O PORT (READ) ADDRESS (Hex)	FUNCTION
0008	Read Status Register
0009	Not used
000A	Not used
000B	Not used
000C	Not used
000D	Read temporary register
000E	Not used
000F	Not used

I/O PORT (WRITE) ADDRESS (Hex)	FUNCTION
0008	Write Command Register
0009	Write Request Register
000A	Write single-mask bit register
000B	Write Mode Register
000C	Clear byte pointer flip-flop
000D	Master Clear
000E	Clear mask register
000F	Write all mask registers

Command Register

The command register is loaded by writing to I/O port address hex 0008. The definitions of the register bits are summarized next and are defined in Fig. 10-2.

Bit 0 enables or disables the memory-to-memory move function of the controller. When this function is selected, Channels 0 and 1 are used to point to two different blocks of memory and can be used to transfer data

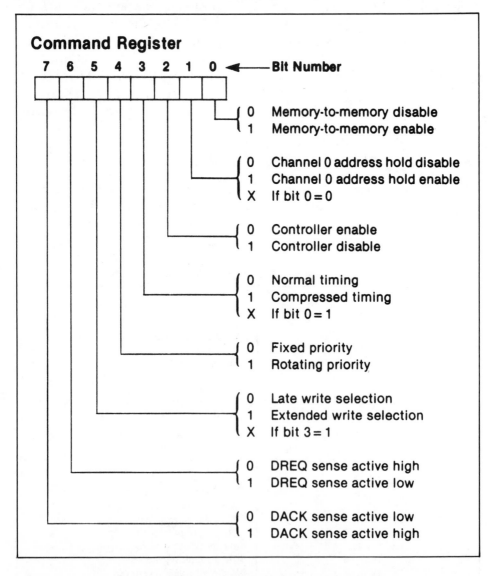

Command Register

Bit Number	7 6 5 4 3 2 1 0

| 0 | Memory-to-memory disable |
| 1 | Memory-to-memory enable |

0	Channel 0 address hold disable
1	Channel 0 address hold enable
X	If bit 0 = 0

| 0 | Controller enable |
| 1 | Controller disable |

0	Normal timing
1	Compressed timing
X	If bit 0 = 1

| 0 | Fixed priority |
| 1 | Rotating priority |

0	Late write selection
1	Extended write selection
X	If bit 3 = 1

| 0 | DREQ sense active high |
| 1 | DREQ sense active low |

| 0 | DACK sense active low |
| 1 | DACK sense active high |

Fig. 10-2. Command register bit definitions (Courtesy Intel Corp.).

between the two blocks. This function cannot be used in the PC since Channel 0 is dedicated to the memory refresh function.

Bit 1 is only valid when the memory-to-memory move function is selected. It will disable the address incrementing or decrementing function on Channel 0, allowing a fixed pattern to be written into a block of memory. Again, this function is not used in the PC.

Bit 2 is used to enable or disable the DMA controller.

Bit 3 is used to select a special compressed DMA bus cycle. In this mode, only three clocks are used to generate the DMA bus cycle. This mode should not be selected in the PC since it would reduce the memory and I/O port addresses' access time below their specified limits and would cause an invalid operation.

Bit 4 is used to select a special rotating priority mode. This function should not be selected in the PC since the memory refresh on Channel 0 must always have the highest priority.

Bit 5 is used to select the timing of the bus cycle's write signal. The PC selects a late-write mode. This should not be changed since the system's dynamic memory cycles are triggered from off the leading edge of the write signal and, if it comes earlier on a DMA cycle, the data would not be valid, resulting in an invalid data-write operation.

Bit 6 will select the active level of the DRQ signals coming to the controller. The PC selects the high level as active.

Bit 7 will select the active level of the DACK signals sent by the controller. The PC selects the low level as active.

The PC BIOS initializes the command register with a hex value of 00.

Write Request Register

The write request register can be loaded by writing to I/O port address hex 0009. This register can be used to generate a DMA request under software control. The bit definitions of the write request register are defined in Fig. 10-3.

Write Single-Mask Bit Register

Writing to this register, hex address 000A, allows individual DMA channels to be masked off or on. Fig. 10-4 defines the bit's functions in this register.

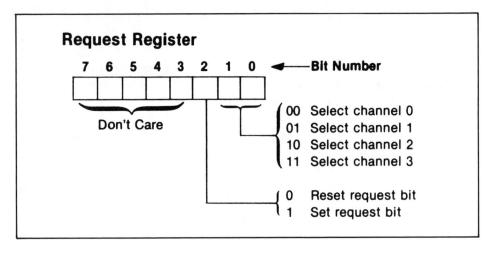

Fig. 10-3. Write request register bit definitions
(Courtesy Intel Corp.).

Mode Register

This write-only register defines several modes of operation for each of the four DMA channels. It is loaded by writing to I/O port address hex 000B. Fig. 10-5 defines the functions of each bit in the mode register.

Bits 0 and 1 are used to select the DMA channel that the mode command is to be applied to.

Bits 2 and 3 define the type of cycle that is to be performed on the specified channel. There are three operations available: (1) a verify operation

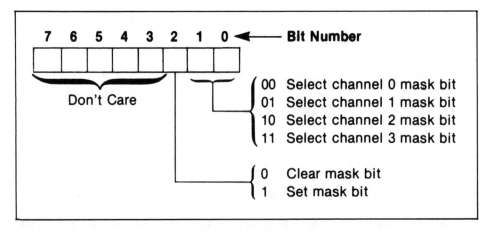

Fig. 10-4. Write single-mask bit register definitions
(Courtesy Intel Corp.).

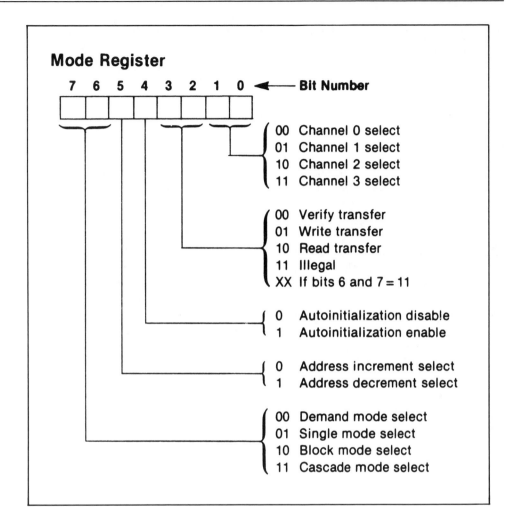

Fig. 10-5. Mode register bit definitions (Courtesy Intel Corp.).

that performs a bus cycle without a write or write operation, (2) a write operation that takes data from an interface or adapter and writes them into memory, and (3) a read operation that takes data from memory and writes them into the interface or adapter.

Bit 4 is used to enable or disable a special autoinitialization mode on a specified channel. This mode, when selected, will reinitialize the DMA channel's current address register and current count register with the values in the base address and the count register. This happens when the current count register reaches zero and a terminal count signal is issued from the controller. This function allows the controller to be automatically set up to accept more DMA requests after an earlier DMA function has been completed.

Bit 5 is used to select an increment or decrement function on the current DMA address register.

Bits 6 and 7 are used to select the type of DMA operations permitted on the selected channel. There are four basic modes of operation available.

1. In the *Single Transfer Mode*, the DRQ signal must be raised for each and every byte transferred. If DRQ is held active, the controller will allow one 8088 MPU bus cycle after each DMA cycle, thus ensuring that the processor is never completely locked off from the bus due to a hung DMA request.
2. In the *Block Transfer Mode*, only one DRQ signal request will initiate the transfer of an entire block of data. The block transfer is stopped when the terminal count is reached. The 8088 MPU is blocked from the bus during the block transfer. This mode of operation should not be selected in the PC since it could block DMA cycles that are required to support the memory refresh function and the diskette-drive data transfers, thus causing overrun conditions. In addition, the memory precharge timing specification is violated when back-to-back DMA cycles are allowed.
3. In the *Demand Transfer Mode*, data are transferred as long as the terminal count has not been reached and the DRQ signal is active. This mode of operation can be used if the DRQ signal is dropped after each DMA cycle; otherwise, the same problems are present as for the block transfer mode.
4. The *Cascade Mode* is the fourth method of operation. The PC programs all of the DMA channel for Single Transfer Mode operation.

For the two channels not used by the PC (Channels 1 and 3), the PC BIOS initializes them with the hex values of 41 and 43, respectively.

Clear Byte Pointer Flip-Flop

There are no data associated with the write operation to this PC I/O port address. A write-to-port hex address 000C will clear an internal flip-flop that is being used to point to the high or low byte of the 16-bit word values, which are loaded and read from the port addresses hex 0000 to 0007. When the flip-flop is cleared, the next read or write operation, at the port address, loads or reads the low-order bits of the 16-bit value. The read or write operation toggles the flip-flop so that the next read or write operation points to the high-order 8 bits of the 16-bit value. This technique is used to conserve the register decodes in the controller. This function is used to read and write the contents of the current address register for each channel, the base address register for each channel, the current count register for each channel, and the base count register for each channel. Each of these registers is 16 bits in length but has only one 8-bit port address.

Master Clear

This I/O port address (hex 000D), when written to, will cause a clear function to be performed on the controller. The controller will require initialization after a master clear command is sent. Note that there are no data associated with this command.

Clear Mask Register

Writing to the PC I/O port address hex 000E will cause all of the DMA channel mask-register bits to be reset, thus enabling all four channels.

Write All Mask-Register Bits

This register is written to by addressing PC port address hex 000F. It is used to both individually and simultaneously control the DMA channel's mask-register bits. Fig. 10-6 defines the bits in this register.

Status Register

The controller's status can be obtained by reading PC I/O port address hex 0008. This register contains status bits that indicate if a channel has reached its terminal count and, thus, has completed the DMA transfer. The register also contains status bits that indicate if a channel has a DMA request pending. Fig. 10-7 defines the bits in the status register.

Temporary Register

After a memory-to-memory transfer operation, the value of the last byte transferred can be obtained by reading this register. The PC I/O port address is hex 000D. Since the memory-to-memory transfer cannot be used in the PC design, this register is not used.

Address and Counter Registers

Each DMA channel has four 16-bit registers that are used to point to the memory location for the transfer and count, and to terminate the length of the transfer.

The starting address of a DMA operation is loaded into a base register in the controller by writing to a PC I/O port address. A second address register, called the current address register, contains the next address to be

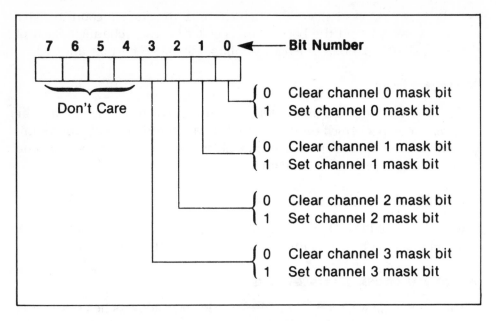

**Fig. 10-6. Write all mask-register bit definitions
(Courtesy Intel Corp.).**

used on the next DMA cycle. It should be noted that when data are written to the base address for a specific channel, the current address register is also automatically loaded with the same value. There is a base and current address register-pair for each of the four DMA channels.

The number of bytes that are to be transferred, before the operation is terminated or reinitialized by the autoinitialization function, is controlled by the contents of the base and current word-count registers. Each of these registers is 16 bits in length, and there is a set for each of the four DMA channels. The base-count register is loaded with the number of bytes that are to be transferred. The current count register contains the count value that is left to be transferred before the operation is terminated or reinitialized. Note again that loading the base-count register will automatically load the same value into the current count register.

All of these registers are read and written using the PC port addresses in the hex range of 0000 to 0007 and the function of the byte-pointer flip-flop that was described earlier. Table 10-2 describes the PC I/O port addressing for the address and count registers in the 8237-5 controller.

DMA PAGE REGISTERS

The 8237-5 DMA controller chip will support only 16 bits of addressing and will only transfer lengths of 65,536 bytes. The PC's 8088 microproces-

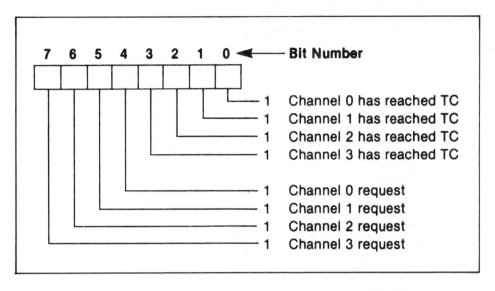

Fig. 10-7. Status register bit definitions (Courtesy Intel Corp.).

sor supports a full one megabyte of system memory. Thus, the controller cannot perform DMA operations using the full one-megabyte address space of the system. To overcome this problem, the System Unit's base logic board provides a set of 4-bit page registers. There is a 4-bit page register for Channels 1, 2, and 3. The contents of these registers can be loaded and read using the I/O port addresses of the PC. When a DMA cycle takes place, the contents of the appropriate page register is gated onto the system's address bus and becomes the high-order 4 bits of the DMA address used to access memory. Thus, a unique 20-bit address is generated for each transfer on each DMA channel. This allows a DMA operation to take place in every 64K-byte block of the one-megabyte space of the system. This page register scheme does not allow a DMA operation to cross a 64K-byte boundary. Fig. 10-8 illustrates how the DMA transfer address is formed using the page registers.

The page registers can be loaded and read using the following PC I/O port addresses.

DMA channel	PC I/O port address
1	hex 0083
2	hex 0081
3	hex 0082

Table 10-2. Port Addresses for the PC Word-Count and Address Registers

Channel	Register	Operation	CS	IOR	IOW	A3	A2	A1	A0	Internal Flip-Flop	Data Bus DB0-DB7
						Signals					
0	Base and Current Address	Write	0	1	0	0	0	0	0	0	A0-A7
			0	1	0	0	0	0	0	1	A8-A15
	Current Address	Read	0	0	1	0	0	0	0	0	A0-A7
			0	0	1	0	0	0	0	1	A8-A15
	Base and Current Word Count	Write	0	1	0	0	0	0	1	0	W0-W7
			0	1	0	0	0	0	1	1	W8-W15
	Current Word Count	Read	0	0	1	0	0	0	1	0	W0-W7
			0	0	1	0	0	0	1	1	W8-W15
1	Base and Current Address	Write	0	1	0	0	0	1	0	0	A0-A7
			0	1	0	0	0	1	0	1	A8-A15
	Current Address	Read	0	0	1	0	0	1	0	0	A0-A7
			0	0	1	0	0	1	0	1	A8-A15
	Base and Current Word Count	Write	0	1	0	0	0	1	1	0	W0-W7
			0	1	0	0	0	1	1	1	W8-W15
	Current Word Count	Read	0	0	1	0	0	1	1	0	W0-W7
			0	0	1	0	0	1	1	1	W8-W15
2	Base and Current Address	Write	0	1	0	0	1	0	0	0	A0-A7
			0	1	0	0	1	0	0	1	A8-A15
	Current Address	Read	0	0	1	0	1	0	0	0	A0-A7
			0	0	1	0	1	0	0	1	A8-A15
	Base and Current Word Count	Write	0	1	0	0	1	0	1	0	W0-W7
			0	1	0	0	1	0	1	1	W8-W15
	Current Word Count	Read	0	0	1	0	1	0	1	0	W0-W7
			0	0	1	0	1	0	1	1	W8-W15
3	Base and Current Address	Write	0	1	0	0	1	1	0	0	A0-A7
			0	1	0	0	1	1	0	1	A8-A15
	Current Address	Read	0	0	1	0	1	1	0	0	A0-A7
			0	0	1	0	1	1	0	1	A8-A15
	Base and Current Word Count	Write	0	1	0	0	1	1	1	0	W0-W7
			0	1	0	0	1	1	1	1	W8-W15
	Current Word Count	Read	0	0	1	0	1	1	1	0	W0-W7
			0	0	1	0	1	1	1	1	W8-W15

(Courtesy Intel Corp.)

"0" = READ CMD
"0" = WRITE CMD
HEX PC PORT ADDRESS 000 X

DMA PERFORMANCE

If your interfacing design uses DMA and requires a high data rate or a very low latency time to the first byte transferred, this section will be of interest.

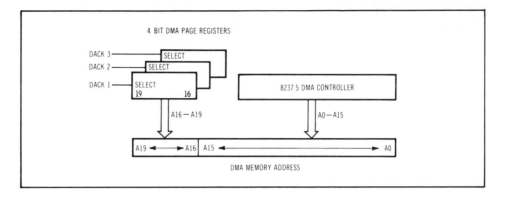

Fig. 10-8. DMA memory address generation.

Maximum DMA Transfer Rate

Each DMA cycle takes five processor clock times, but in the PC design, the baseboard logic automatically inserts one extra clock as a *wait state.* This is done to ensure a long enough access time from memory and I/O ports. Thus, in the PC, each DMA transfer takes six clocks. Since each clock is approximately 210 nanoseconds long, the total cycle time is 1.26 microseconds. The PC design also requires that the DMA controller be run in the single-byte transfer mode. This means that there must be an 8088 MPU bus cycle between each DMA cycle. Since 8088 processor bus cycles are four clocks long, or 840 nanoseconds, this time must be added to the DMA cycle time. Thus, the minimum time between DMA cycles is 2.1 microseconds. This gives the PC a maximum DMA data rate of 476 kilobytes per second.

Note that if any other devices or memory inserts a wait state in other 8088 MPU bus cycles, this will further reduce the maximum data rate.

DMA Latency

Often an important requirement of a design is not the data rate but how quickly the first byte can be transferred. This will often determine if a byte buffer is required between the interface and the PC bus.

In the PC design, after a DMA request is raised, it may take up to seven processor clocks before the cycle actually begins. This time can also be extended if 8088 processor bus cycles have some wait states inserted.

REUSE OF A DMA CHANNEL

The use of a specific DMA channel by an interface or an adapter does not preclude it from being used again on a different interface design. Obvi-

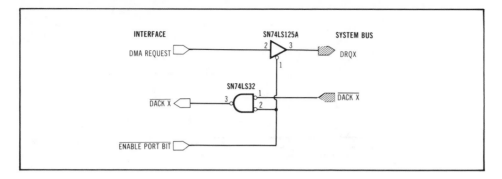

Fig. 10-9. Circuit for enable/disable programming of a DMA channel.

ously, both interfaces cannot use the same channel at once, but if there is no requirement to run both interfaces at the same time, it is possible to share the DMA channels.

A good example of how this can be accomplished is in the PC's diskette adapter design. Here a programmable I/O port bit is used to enable and disable the DMA DRQ2 request signal and the DRQ2 signal. In this case, if a 0 is written to bit 3 of the PC I/O port hex address 03F2, the diskette adapter disconnects from the bus signals and they are free to be used by a different interface adapter. Fig. 10-9 illustrates how this can be accomplished in an interface design.

TERMINAL COUNT SIGNAL

The 8237-5 controller generates an output control signal that is activated each time any of the four DMA channels reaches a terminal count condition. That is, the transfer byte counter decrements to zero. This signal is typically used by the interface to terminate further DMA requests on a specific channel. Since the terminal count signal is activated on any channel's terminal count condition, it must be conditioned, or "ANDed," with each DACK signal so that a specific channel's ending condition can be detected. The terminal count signal is available on the system bus.

CHAPTER 11

SYSTEM TIMERS AND COUNTERS

INTRODUCTION

A facility that is often required in an interface design is a timing or counting function. To support these types of functions, the PC has three independent timer counters designed into the base system board. The timer counter functions are implemented using an Intel 8253-5 timer counter chip. In general, these timer counter channels are used to support the basic I/O functions of the PC and are not available for general use by an interface design.

Each timer counter channel has a clock input signal and a gate input signal, where the gate controls the clock input to the timer counter. Each timer counter has an output signal whose function is set by programming the mode of operation of the channel. In the PC design, the clock input to all channels is the same, a 1.19318-MHz square-wave signal. Thus, each tick of the timer counter channels is approximately 838.1 nanoseconds in duration. Each timer counter channel is 16 bits in length.

SYSTEM USE OF THE TIMER COUNTER CHANNELS

Channel 0

Channel 0 is used as a general system timer. Its gate signal is tied high, or "on," all of the time and the clock input signal is a 1.19318-MHz square-wave signal. The output of the Channel 0 timer is tied to interrupt level 0, the highest maskable interrupt level. This channel is set up by the PC BIOS to generate an interrupt request on level 0 every 54.936 milliseconds, or 18.206 times a second. These interrupt requests are counted by a BIOS routine, which generates a time-of-day clock count that can be read or written. This routine also uses the interrupt count to generate the motor-off delay after a "seek" operation on the diskette drives. At each interrupt request, the routine updates the time-of-day clock, checks to see if the motor on the diskette drive needs to be shut off, and attempts to invoke a user-defined routine. It is this last function of the BIOS timer Channel 0 routine that may be of interest to an interfacing application. On each interrupt, or every 54.936 milliseconds, the BIOS routine will issue a software interrupt to interrupt level hex 1C. This interrupt-vector table value is set with an offset and code segment value that simply returns control to BIOS. An applications program can go in and alter the interrupt-vector value and direct the periodic interrupt to a user routine. As an example of where this may be useful, consider an interface design that must scan for activity on a periodic basis, yet has other tasks that it must perform. In this case, it would not be practical to devote the entire capability of the PC to simply looping and waiting for an interface event. A simple solution to this problem would be to write a sensing routine that is invoked on each, or a multiple of, timer Channel 0 interrupts. The address of this routine is then entered into the interrupt vector table for the hex 1C interrupt.

The time-of-day count routine can also be used to time between events, since the count can easily be read at any time. It can also be set at any time, but care should be taken when doing this because the time-of-day clock function of DOS will be affected. It is also possible to affect the operation of the diskette drive. To read the count value, first set the AH register to 0; this indicates a read operation. Next, issue a software interrupt to interrupt hex 1A. Upon return from the interrupt, the CX register contains the high value of the count and the DX register contains the low portion of the count. If the counter has not passed 24 hours since it was last read, the AL register will be zero. To initialize the time-of-day count, first set the AH register to one, and then set the high count value in the CX register and the low portion of the count in the DX register. Next, issue a software interrupt on level hex 1A. Upon return from this interrupt, the time-of-day count will be initialized. Remember that the values in the CD and DX registers are a binary count of time, in increments of 54.936 milliseconds, or 0.054936 second.

Channel 1

This timer counter channel is used in a dedicated manner to support the memory refresh function of the system. The clock input is tied to the 1.19318-MHz square-wave signal and the gate is tied high, or always on. The output of the time channel is used to generate a direct-memory access (DMA) cycle request on DMA Channel 0. This DMA channel is used to refresh the system's dynamic memory by creating dummy memory-read cycles every 72 processor clock cycles (210 nanoseconds), or every 15.12 microseconds.

The PC's BIOS initializes the time counter channel in a mode that allows the output to generate an 838-nanosecond output pulse every 18 ticks of the input clock. Because the input clock is approximately 838 nanoseconds in duration, the timer counter output is generated approximately every 15 microseconds.

Since the system's dynamic memory refresh function is critical to the proper operation of the system, it is highly recommended that this timer counter channel not be modified or used in any manner.

Channel 2

This timer counter channel serves a dual purpose in the PC. First, it is used to output serial data written to the audio cassette port of the system. Secondly, it is used to drive the audio speaker of the System Unit. The clock input is the same 1.19318-MHz signal that is attached to the other channel's clock inputs. The gate signal is tied to an I/O port bit such that it can be controlled by the system's software. The gate to timer counter Channel 2 is controlled by writing to I/O port address hex 0061, bit 0. A 1 written to this bit will "enable" the clock input to the timer counter channel. A 0 will "disable" the clock input.

The output of timer counter Channel 2 is used in two places. First, it is used to write serial data to the audio cassette port of the System Unit. In this mode, the timer counter channel is programmed to write pulses on the audio cassette's tape, either a 250- or a 500-microsecond pulse, depending on the data bit to be written. A 0 bit is a 250-microsecond pulse with 250 microseconds of blank space, and a 1 bit is a 500-microsecond pulse with a 500-microsecond blank space. If a specific interface application design requires access to a programmable timing signal, it is possible to pick up the output of timer counter Channel 2 in the 5-pin DIN connector that is used to attach an audio cassette. The signal is available at pin 5 of the connector. Note that the signal level is not a TTL level. Depending on the position of the cassette microphone auxiliary select jumper, the signal will be either 75 millivolts or 0.7 volt in amplitude. The auxiliary select is 0.7 volt.

The second place that the output of timer counter Channel 2 is used is as an input to the System Unit's audio speaker. The output is ORed with an I/O port bit such that both can be used to drive the speaker. The I/O port bit is addressed as bit 1 of hex address 0061. Note that the speaker and the cassette write functions cannot be run simultaneously.

Fig. 11-1 shows a block diagram of the timer counter function of the System Unit.

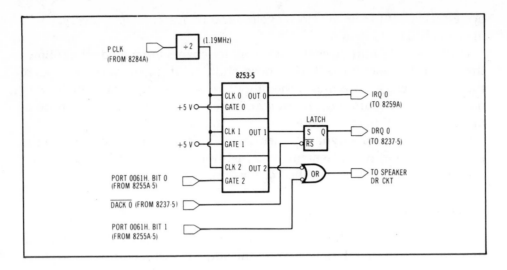

Fig. 11-1. A block diagram of the timer counter.

PROGRAMMING THE TIMER COUNTERS

Timer Counter I/O Address

The System Unit's timer counters in the 8253-5 chip can be addressed by using IN and OUT instructions at addresses hex 0040 through 0043. The decoding of the timer counter is not unique, since some of the bits in the address field are not included in the decode circuits. The following arrangement shows the bits used and the bits not used.

Address bits   9 8 7 6 5 4 3 2 1 0   (Bits 10–15 are never used in I/O port decodes)

8253-5 decode   0 0 0 1 0 Z Z Z A A

     Z = not in decode
     A = addresses bits decoded in the 8253-5

The following comments give a brief description of the functions of the addresses of the 8253-5 timer counter chip when they are read and written.

Write Operations
hex address 0040—load count value into Counter 0
hex address 0041—load count value into Counter 1
hex address 0042—load count value into Counter 2
hex address 0043—set channels mode of operation

Read Operations

hex address 0040—read count value in Counter 0
hex address 0041—read count value in Counter 1
hex address 0042—read count value in Counter 2
hex address 0044—invalid operation, cannot
read mode registers

Mode Control Registers

Since each channel of the 8253-5 timer counter has a variety of operational modes and there is no reset going to this chip, it must be initialized before use. The PC's BIOS does this for the modes of operation that it requires.

The mode of operation for each of the channels is set by writing a mode control word to each channel. This is done by writing an 8-bit value to each of the channels using I/O port address hex 0043. The definitions of the bits in the mode control word are defined In Fig. 11-2 and are summarized below.

Bit D0 is used to select the counting mode of the counter with binary or binary-coded decimal.

Bits D1–D3 are used to select the mode of operation of the channel.

Bits D4 and D5 are used to select the number of bytes and the sequence to be used when reading and loading the timer counter channels.

Bits D6 and D7 are used to select the timer counter channel that the mode control word is directed to.

Reading and Writing the Counters

When reading and writing to the counters in the 8253-5 timer counter, care should be taken to read and write in the order and the number of bytes that were programmed into each channel mode control register. If this is not done, invalid operation and results will occur.

Another feature of the 8253-5 counter that may cause some confusion is the requirement that it must have a positive- and a negative-edge transition of a channel clock input before the channel's value can be read. This means that you cannot load a channel counter and simply ''read back'' its value. The clock input must make both a positive and a negative transition first.

Reading a counter on the fly can also create a problem. It is possible to read the contents of any of the timer counter channels at any time but if the counter is in the process of decrementing, you may get invalid results. One way to avoid this is to degate the clock input before reading so that the counter will not decrement as you are reading it. The 8253-5 timer counter also has a special mode control command that will latch the current value of the counter into a read register so that the counter can be read correctly without stopping it. This command is defined in Fig. 11-2.

It should be noted that all of the timer counter channels are countdown counters.

TIMER COUNTER MODES OF OPERATION

As defined in the mode control word for each channel, there are six program-selectable modes of operation for each channel of the 8253-5 timer counter. The following explanation is a description of each of these modes.

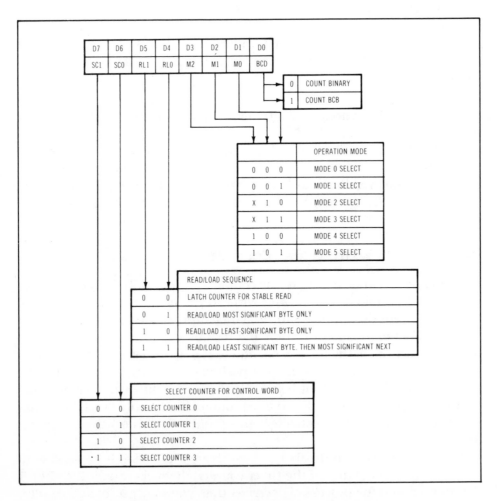

Fig. 11-2. The mode control word format.

Mode 0: Interrupt-On Terminal Count

The output of the channel will be set low after the mode control word is written. After the count value is loaded into the selected channel, the output will remain high and the counter will begin to count. When the terminal count value has been reached, the output will go high and will remain high until the counter is reloaded. If a counter channel is rewritten while it is still decrementing, writing of the first byte of the count value will stop the counter and writing of the second byte will restart the counter with the new count.

Mode 1: Programmable One-Shot

The output will initially be high after the mode and count are loaded. The output will be set low on the count following the rising edge of that channel's gate signal. The output will remain low for the value of the count loaded in the counter. Thus, a one-shot pulse, of a programmable duration, is triggered by the rising edge of the channel's gate signal. This function is retriggerable and is, thus, repeated on each rising edge of the gate signal.

Mode 2: Rate Generator

In this mode, the count value is used to divide the input clock by the counter value. After the input clock has counted to the counter value, the output of the channel will go low for one period of the input clock. If a new count value is loaded between output pulses, the present period will not be affected but the next period will reflect the new period value. The gate, if low, will force the channel's output high. When the gate input goes high, the counter will start from the initialized value. Thus, it is possible to use the gate signal to synchronize the counter's divide function. When this mode is selected, the channel's output will go high and will remain high until the count is loaded and, then, it will go low after the count has been reached. Thus, the counter can also be synchronized by software.

Mode 3: Square-Wave Rate Generator

This mode is similar to mode 2, except that the output will remain high until one-half of the count has been completed (for even numbers) and will go low for the other half of the count. This is accomplished by decrementing the counter by two on the falling edge of each clock input pulse. When the counter reaches terminal count, the state of the output is changed and the counter is reloaded with the full count and the whole process is repeated. If the count is odd, the output will be high for $(N+1)/2$ counts and low for $(N-1)/2$ counts. N = the counter value programmed.

Mode 4: Software-Triggered Strobe

After the mode is set, the output will be high. When the count is loaded, the counter will begin counting. On terminal count, the output will go low for one input clock period; then, it will go high again. If the count register is reloaded between output pulses, the present period will not be affected, but the next period will reflect the new value. Reloading the counter register will restart the counting, beginning with the new number.

Table 11-1. Gate Input Control Summary of the 8253-5 Counter

Modes	Signal Status		
	Low or Going Low	Rising	High
0	Disables counting	—	Enables counting
1	—	1. Initiates counting 2. Resets output after next clock	—
2	1. Disables counting 2. Sets output immediately high	1. Reloads counter 2. Initiates counting	Enables counting
3	1. Disables counting 2. Sets output immediately high	Initiates counting	Enables counting
4	Disables counting	—	Enables counting
5	—	Initiates counting	—

(Courtesy Intel Corp.)

Mode 5: Hardware-Triggered Strobe

In this mode, the counter will start counting after the rising edge of the gate input and the output will go low for one clock period when the terminal count is reached.

The control of the channel's gate signal is important and is different for some of the modes of operation. The gate signal operations for each mode are summarized in Table 11-1.

Many of the modes of operation are not practical to use with the System Unit's 8253-5 timer counter, since its functions are more or less dedicated to supporting the base function of the PC. This device can easily be used in an interface design, since it easily attaches to the system bus. Thus, it is treated in fair detail here, with the intention that this knowledge will be useful in incorporating timing and counting functions when using the 8253-5 timer counter device.

CHAPTER 12

SYSTEM MEMORY, I/O MAP, AND DECODING TECHNIQUES

INTRODUCTION

This chapter provides information relative to the use of the I/O and memory address spaces of the PC. Maps of the present usage of both the I/O and memory space are presented. In addition, decoding techniques are presented which can be used in your interface designs. Also covered in this chapter are the various aspects of bus buffering, transceiver control, and system memory refresh.

I/O PORT ADDRESSING AND USAGE MAP

Port Addressing

Most of the support devices and the I/O adapter in the PC are controlled and sensed using the digital input and output ports. These ports are addressed using the I/O port address space of the 8088 microprocessor. Data can be sent to these ports using the OUT instruction of the 8088 MPU. Data can be sensed or read from these ports using the 8088 IN instruction. The 8088 processor architecture supports an I/O port address space of 65,536 unique port addresses. The PC design does not use the full address space. Only the lower 10 bits of the address field are used in the PC. Thus, bus bits 0 through 9 are used to decode device or port addresses.

It is important to note that the 8088 OUT and IN instructions can still be used to specify port addresses with the high-order bits active, but the presently designed devices will only look at, decode, and respond to bits 0 through 9.

Bit 9 of the I/O port address field has special meaning in the PC design. When this bit is inactive, data cannot be received on the system bus from the five card slots on the system board. When inactive, this bit enables data only from the devices and the I/O port addresses on the system board. When this bit is active, it enables data from the five card slots. This means that for input ports, the 1024 port addresses supported in the PC are equally divided into 512 port addresses that must exist only on the system board and 512 port addresses that must exist only on the card slot bus.

It is important to note that this restriction does not apply to output ports. Any of the 1024 port addresses can be used as output port addresses in the card slots. However, output port addresses that are used on the system board should not be replicated in the card slot system bus, since writing to the port address would write to both ports.

Fig. 12-1 illustrates the PC's usage of the I/O address field. Fig. 12-2 illustrates how the 8088 address space is allocated in the PC design.

I/O Port Address Map

The I/O port address map can be divided into two parts. The first part is the address space hex 0000 through 01FF, or that part which resides on the base system board. These port addresses are used to address the 8088 MPU support devices and the integrated I/O on the base system board. Fig. 12-3 defines the address port's functions on the base system board. For detailed information on the functions of these ports, the *IBM Technical Reference Manual* should be consulted.

It should be noted that the hex addresses 00C0 through 01FF are not used as either input or output ports on the baseboard. As previously

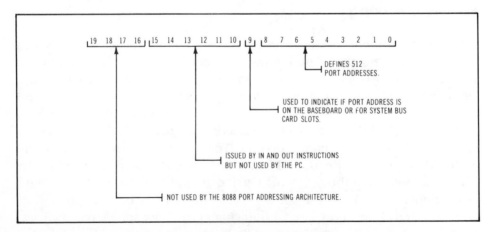

Fig. 12-1. I/O port addresses of the 8088 MPU.

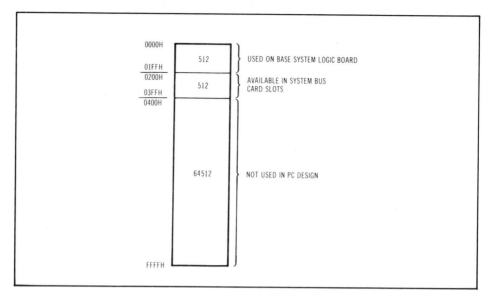

Fig. 12-2. Usage of the I/O port address space.

stated, these addresses cannot be used as input ports but it is possible to decode these addresses as output ports on the system bus for use in an interface design.

Fig. 12-4 defines the present usage of the second part of the PC I/O port address space, hex addresses 0200 through 02FF. This address space is used for port addresses decoded on the system bus and available in the five card slots on the system board. It should be pointed out that as IBM and other manufacturers provide new feature cards for the PC, more of these address decodes will be used. Since this is occurring at a rapid rate, an accurate map of the usage of these decodes is impossible to maintain. If your system configuration does not use some of these devices or feature cards and has no plans to do so, you may use those address decodes in your interface designs.

I/O PORT ADDRESS DECODING TECHNIQUES

Fixed Address Decode

The simplest way to decode an I/O port address or group of addresses for an interface design is to inspect the address space and find a block of unused addresses and, then, construct the proper decode circuitry. Most of the present IBM feature cards use this technique. Fig. 12-5 is an example of a fixed I/O port decode design. In this example, four port addresses are decodes that begin at hex address 02F0. These decodes can be further

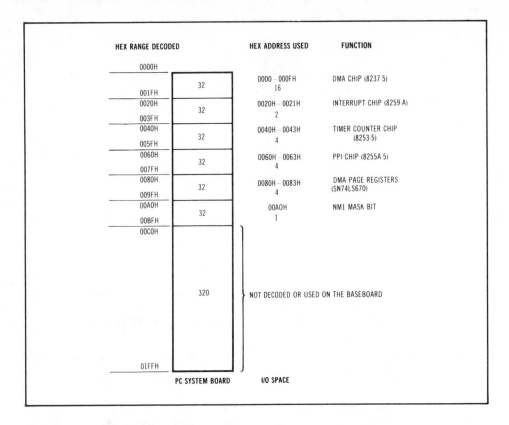

Fig. 12-3. Baseboard I/O port address usage.

ANDed with the bus signals IOR and IOW to generate output and input strobe signals for digital output and input registers. The back edge of the write register signals can be used to clock data from the data bus into the digital output registers. The read register signal can be used to gate data from an input register onto the system bus. The group select signal is generated such that it can be used to enable a bus transceiver when any of the four register decodes are detected. Note that address bit 9 has to be active for the decode, indicating that the port address is in the address space supported in the system-bus card slots. The bus signal AEN is used to degate the decode. This is necessary to prevent an invalid port address decode during DMA cycles.

There are two timing concerns when decoding a port address. The first is at the beginning of an I/O port bus cycle. If the port address decode has a lot of delay, it may occur after the bus control signals IOR and IOW become valid. Since the address bits from the system are skewed, the decode may momentarily decode some other port address. If these invalid decodes are late and are ANDed with the bus control signals, data may be written to the

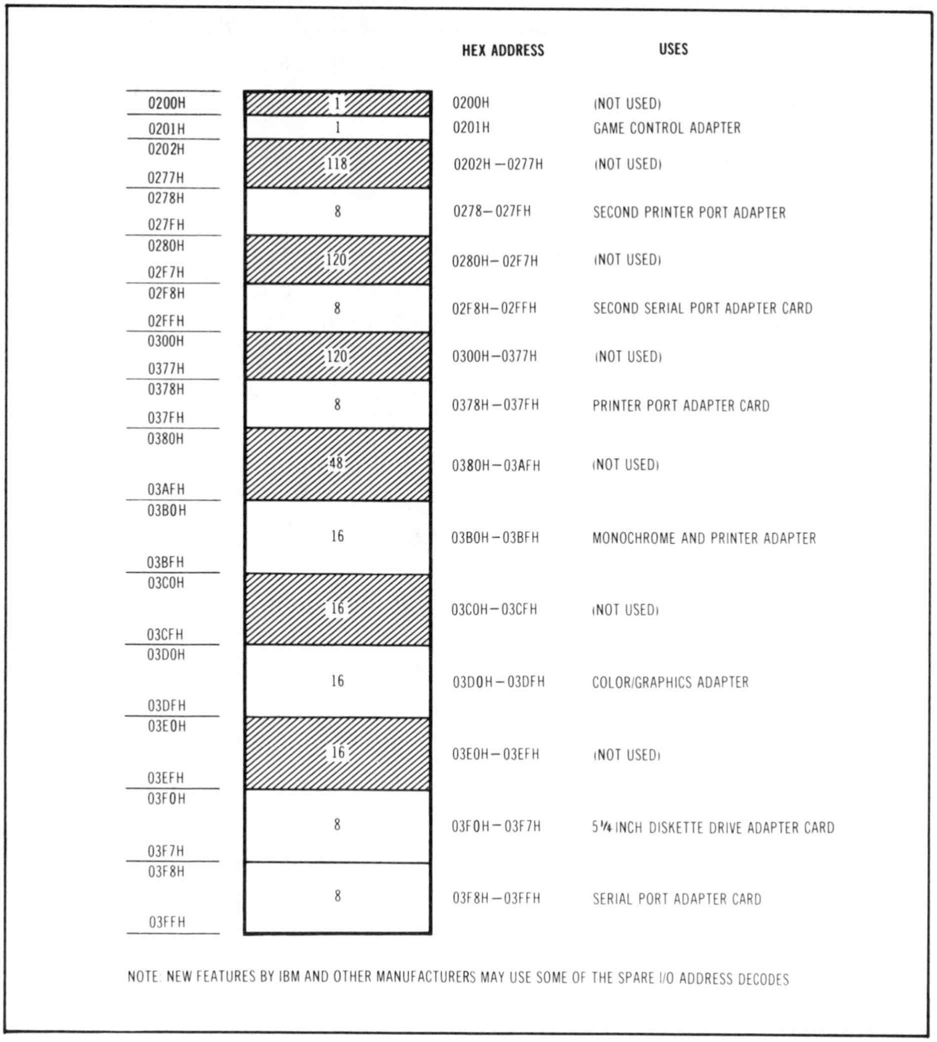

	HEX ADDRESS	USES
0200H — 1	0200H	(NOT USED)
0201H — 1	0201H	GAME CONTROL ADAPTER
0202H / 0277H — 118	0202H—0277H	(NOT USED)
0278H / 027FH — 8	0278—027FH	SECOND PRINTER PORT ADAPTER
0280H / 02F7H — 120	0280H—02F7H	(NOT USED)
02F8H / 02FFH — 8	02F8H—02FFH	SECOND SERIAL PORT ADAPTER CARD
0300H / 0377H — 120	0300H—0377H	(NOT USED)
0378H / 037FH — 8	0378H—037FH	PRINTER PORT ADAPTER CARD
0380H / 03AFH — 48	0380H—03AFH	(NOT USED)
03B0H / 03BFH — 16	03B0H—03BFH	MONOCHROME AND PRINTER ADAPTER
03C0H / 03CFH — 16	03C0H—03CFH	(NOT USED)
03D0H / 03DFH — 16	03D0H—03DFH	COLOR/GRAPHICS ADAPTER
03E0H / 03EFH — 16	03E0H—03EFH	(NOT USED)
03F0H / 03F7H — 8	03F0H—03F7H	5¼ INCH DISKETTE DRIVE ADAPTER CARD
03F8H / 03FFH — 8	03F8H—03FFH	SERIAL PORT ADAPTER CARD

NOTE: NEW FEATURES BY IBM AND OTHER MANUFACTURERS MAY USE SOME OF THE SPARE I/O ADDRESS DECODES

Fig. 12-4. Card slot I/O port address usage.

wrong port address. The PC is designed such that the worst-case delay permitted in the decode is 92 nanoseconds.

The second timing concern is at the end of the I/O port bus cycle. Here, if the bus control signal IOW is delayed sufficiently and the decode is very fast, the back edge of the write signal may write data to an address that is decoded from the next bus cycle. In the PC design, the IOW signal delay should be less than 200 nanoseconds. The tightest timing, however, is the relationship of the back edge of the IOW signal to valid data on the data bus. If the IOW signal is delayed more than 120 nanoseconds, the port address may be written with invalid data. Similarly, if the IOR signal is delayed, it will reduce the read access time available to the I/O port. The timing charts in Chapter 6 should be consulted to ensure sufficient margin in your designs.

Switch-Selectable Decode

The problem with a fixed decode design is that it may overlap that of a future feature card that you may want to add to your system. Fig. 12-6 illustrates a decode design that allows the address of a block of eight port addresses to be moved in the address space by simply setting a new value

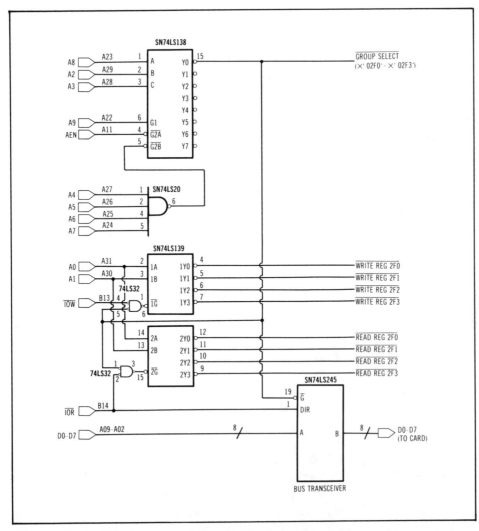

Fig. 12-5. Example of a fixed I/O port address decode.

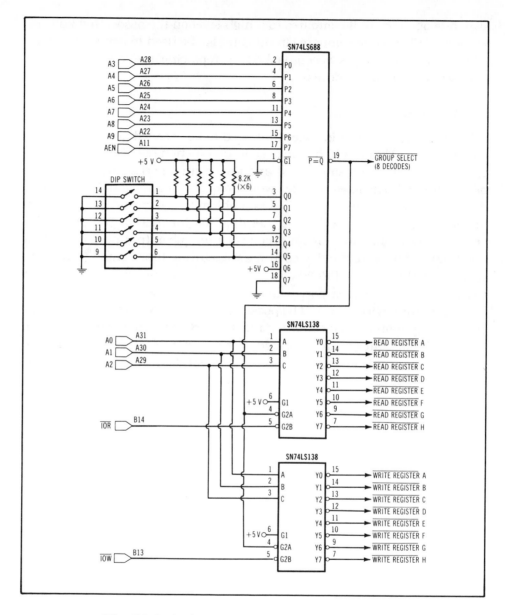

Fig. 12-6. Switch-selectable I/O port decode.

in a bank of dip switches. In this design, an SN74LS688 octal compare circuit is used. On one side of the compare circuit, the address bus bits A3 through A9, and the bus signal AEN, are attached. On the other side, the output of the dip switches is attached. When the value set in the dip switches equals the value on the address bus, the compare equal output is activated and can be used as the group select control signal. When a switch is open or off, it compares to a high level on the associated address bus signal. The same compare circuit can also be used to generate a fixed address decode. This is accomplished by replacing the switches with a hard-wired pattern or address.

PROM Select Decode

Sometimes, the port addresses that need to be decoded are widely different on a card. This would be the case if the function of several cards were to be combined onto a single card and the original port addresses were to be maintained. The fixed decodes would require a large amount of logic to decode. An often-used solution to this problem is to use a PROM (programmable read-only memory) for generation of the decode outputs. The address input signal to a PROM decode is a unique output bit pattern that has been written into the device at manufacturing time. Thus, if the data that was written into a PROM corresponded to the output conditions that were required to select a port, when the port address was applied as an address to the device, it would be possible to select any decode as active by simply programming that condition into the PROM when it was addressed.

Fig 12-7 illustrates a circuit design that uses a 512 x 8 PROM to decode eight different port addresses. Fig. 12-8 illustrates the data that would

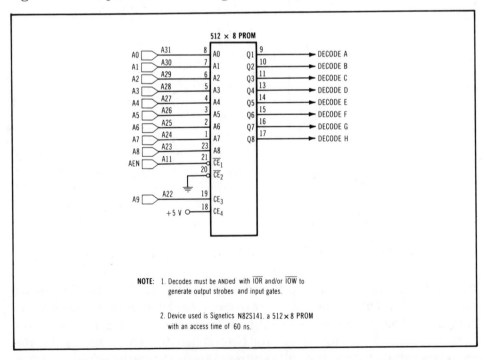

NOTE: 1. Decodes must be ANDed with $\overline{IOR}$ and/or $\overline{IOW}$ to generate output strobes and input gates.

2. Device used is Signetics N82S141. a 512 × 8 PROM with an access time of 60 ns.

Fig. 12-7. PROM I/O port address decoding.

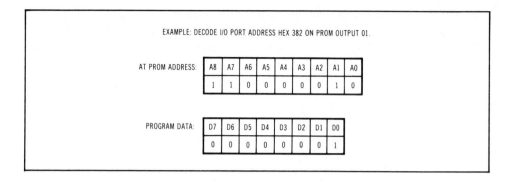

Fig. 12-8. PROM decode programming example.

have to exist at the PROM addresses to decode the port select signals for the different port addresses. All other PROM addresses would be programmed to the zero state. Note that the PROM access time must be faster than the minimum decode time of 92 nanoseconds that was specified earlier. This technique is most often used in high production designs where a unique PROM can be justified.

EXPANDING PORT ADDRESSING ON THE PC

With the PC design supporting only 512 port addresses on the system bus and with a large number of them being used, interfacing designs with requirements for large numbers of I/O ports will be difficult to implement. This section describes some techniques that can be used to increase the maximum number of port addresses available on the PC.

High-Order Address Bit Usage

As pointed out earlier, the PC design does not use address bits 10 through 15 when decoding port addresses. It is possible to still use these bits and remain compatible with the cards that do not use them. To use the additional bits, we must first satisfy the requirements of the other cards that will be attached to the bus. This means that they must not be read or written when the additional bits are used. To do this, we must find a single unused address in the normal 512 address field. This address then becomes the group-select decode for the addresses decoded from the bits 10 through 15. Thus, we have used one normal address to enable the decode of bits 10 through 15 and have expanded the decode by 64 addresses. Using this technique, it is possible to expand each unused address in the normal 512 address space to an additional 64 addresses. Thus, if a block of 8 unused addresses is decoded and used as the group select, an additional 512 addresses can be supported. Since 8 addresses were used to generate the group select decode, a net of 504 new addresses was generated. Fig. 12-9 is an example of how 8 addresses are expanded to 512 addresses. In this design, the block of 8 unused addresses is selectable by a dip switch.

Indirect Port Addressing

Another scheme that is often used to expand I/O port addressing is to use indirect port addressing. In this scheme, the contents of a port are used

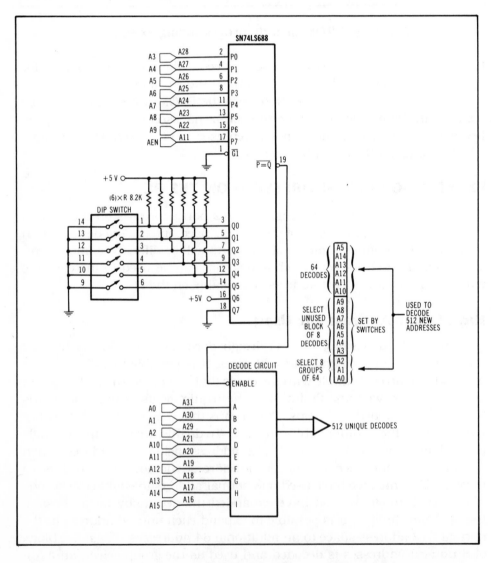

Fig. 12-9. Extending the port addressing by using high-order bits.

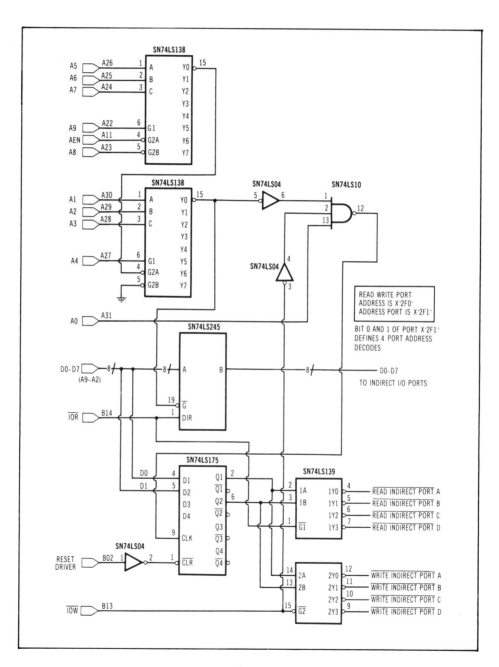

Fig. 12-10. Example of indirect port addressing decode.

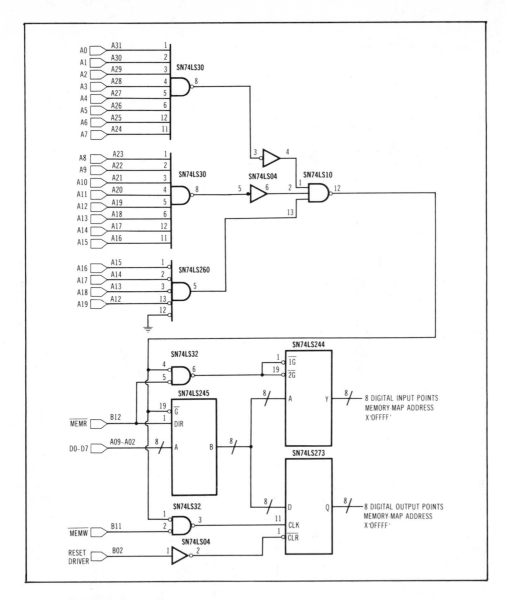

Fig. 12-11. Memory-mapped I/O port input and output registers.

to address other ports. Thus, if 8 bit ports are used, a single port address
can be used to specify an additional 256 port addresses. This scheme actually requires 2 port addresses to implement indirect addressing. The first
port address is a digital output port that, when written to, contains the
indirect port address. The second port address is the data port. When data
are written to this port address, the data actually are written into the port
address specified in the other digital output register. Similarly, when this

port is read, the data comes from the indirectly addressed port. Fig. 12-10 is an example of a circuit schematic that indirectly addresses 4 ports using the indirect addressing technique. It should be noted that to address an indirect port, an additional OUT instruction must be used. Thus, there is a small performance loss using this scheme.

Memory-Mapped I/O Port Addressing

The PC normally uses I/O-mapped addressing, but there is nothing in the design that precludes using memory-mapped I/O port addressing. This scheme simply uses memory addresses as I/O port addresses. This scheme is commonly used to expand I/O port addressing and, in many microprocessor architectures, is the only means of addressing I/O ports. Since the 8088 MPU has a 1-megabyte address space, limitations of port addresses are normally not a concern. A design that uses memory-mapped I/O also has the advantage of having no conflicts with other I/O port mapped addresses. Fig. 12-11 is an example of a circuit that decodes and implements a digital input and output port using memory-mapped I/O port addressing. Aside from removing the I/O port addressing conflicts and expanding the number of available port addresses, memory-mapped I/O has an additional advantage. Since ports are addressed as memory locations, the full power of the 8088 microprocessor instruction set can be used to manipulate the data associated with a port. There are also some disadvantages to memory-mapped I/O addressing that you should be aware of. First, all 20 bits of the system-bus address must be used in the decode of a port address. This increases the amount of circuitry used in a decode. Secondly, a define-segment register instruction may be needed before each port access in order to set the proper segment portion of the memory address. This may result in a performance loss in those cases where the segment value is different than that which is normally used by the program. Last, memory bus cycles are four clocks in length where the I/O port cycles are five clocks in length. Thus, the access-time requirement for a memory-mapped device is less than that for an I/O-mapped device.

MEMORY USAGE MAP

The 8088 microprocessor supports a memory address space size of 1 megabyte. The PC design specifies usage of certain portions of this space. This section will summarize the usage of this address space.

The PC design uses both the high and low ends of the 8088 MPU address space. In addition, the PC display adapters use a portion of the address space for display buffers. At the high end of the address space, the PC's ROM is decoded. A 64K-byte space is decoded at the high end of the address space and is occupied by 40K bytes of ROM. This ROM space is decoded on the base system board and cannot be decoded or used on the system bus in the card slots. The ROM contains the PC BIOS, diagnostics, bootstrap loader, cassette operating system, and the BASIC interpreter. An additional 8K of ROM may be added using the spare module socket on the system board. The remaining 16K in the 64K block that is decoded on the system board is nonusage and is lost.

RAM is added to the PC, starting from the low end of the address space. The first 64K of RAM is decoded on the base system board and any additional RAM must be added as cards in one of the 5 card slots on the system board. When DOS is in the system, it occupies approximately the first 12K bytes of the system RAM space. When DEBUG is loaded, an additional 6K bytes are used. If advance BASIC in loaded, an additional 10K bytes of space is used. Thus, in a 64K system, this would leave approximately 36K of space for a BASIC workspace. It should be noted that these numbers are approximate values and with each new release of system software, they will vary.

Each of the PC's display adapters decodes a 32K block of storage for use as a display "regen" buffer. The color graphics card actually uses only 16K bytes of the 32K that it decodes. The remaining 16K-byte block is not usable in the system. The monochrome display adapter uses 4K of the 32K bytes that it decodes. The remaining 28K bytes are not usable. It should be noted that when one of the display adapters is not in the system, the memory space that it would have used is free and can be used by the system. The PC design has reserved certain areas of the system memory for future enhancements. To ensure compatibility with future devices, you should try to avoid using these reserved areas of the memory address space. Fig. 12-12 illustrates the memory map, the usage, and the reserved area of the PC system memory.

MEMORY ADDRESS DECODING

Decoding memory addresses is very similar to that of decoding I/O port addresses. The major difference is the inclusion of the extra high-order 4 bits that are used in addressing the 1-megabyte address space. The bus signal AEN is not used to degate the decodes as was done with the port addresses. Similarly, the techniques of fixed and switch-selected decodes still apply and can be used in memory address decoding.

Fig. 12-13 is an example of a circuit that can be used to address a block of 8K bytes of static memory to the system. The circuit also includes a bus buffer and shows how it can be enabled and its directions controlled. This technique can be used to add small amounts of memory in an interface design. If larger blocks of memory are required, a more efficient method

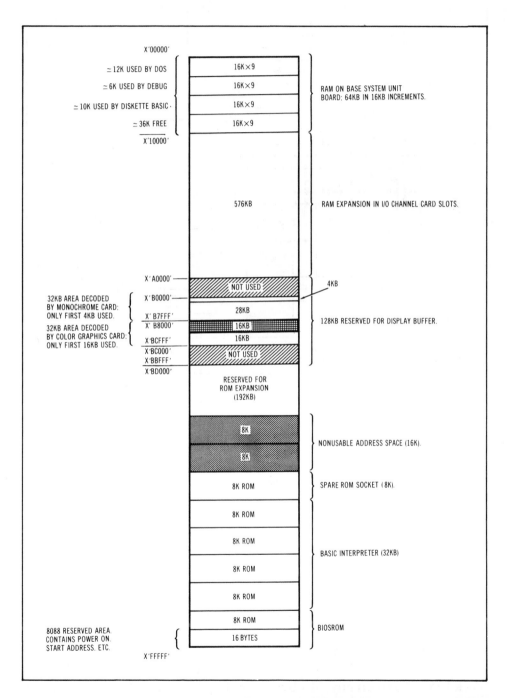

Fig. 12-12. The PC memory map.

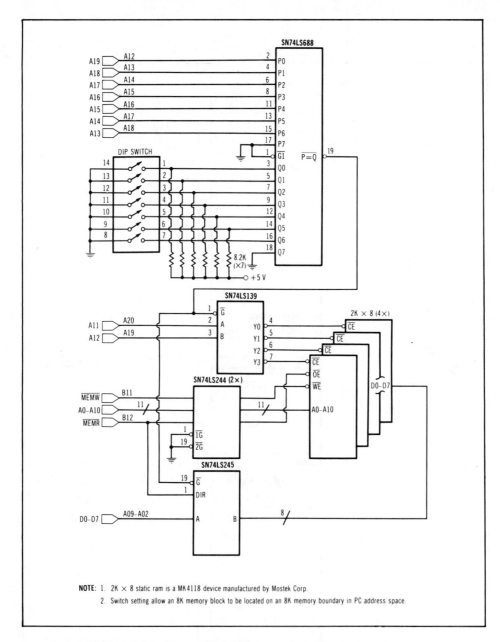

Fig. 12-13. Decoding 8K bytes of static memory.

would be to use 64K × 1 dynamic memory devices. Fig. 12-14 is a circuit diagram that decodes a block of 64K memory addresses and allows the block to be placed on any 64K-byte boundary in the system-address space by simply setting the appropriate value in a set of dip switches. This

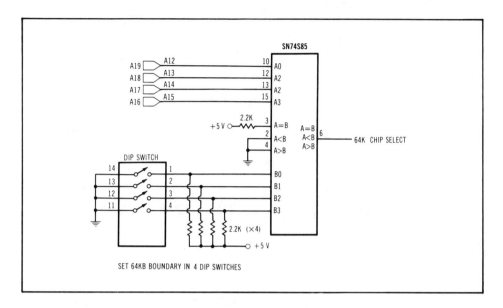

Fig. 12-14. A switch-selectable decode for a 64K-byte block of memory.

scheme allows a memory design that can skip over areas of memory that are being used by setting the desired location of each 64 block in the dip switches.

DYNAMIC MEMORY REFRESH FUNCTION

When dynamic memory devices are added to the system, they require a refresh function. Typically, the memory devices require that each of the first 128 memory locations be read at least once every 2 milliseconds. If this is not done, the memory will not maintain its data. To perform this function, two problems must be solved. First, a refresh address must be generated and applied to the memory devices. Secondly, the refresh cycle must be arbitrated with the normal system processor and the DMA cycles. The PC is designed to provide both of these functions so that a memory design using dynamic memory can easily be attached to the system bus. The system automatically generates a special refresh bus cycle every 72 processor clocks, or approximately every 15 microseconds. This bus cycle is indicated on the bus by the activation of the DACK0 bus signal. During this bus cycle, the address bus will contain a valid refresh address and will perform a memory read using this address, thus fulfilling the memory refresh requirements. The memory should be designed such that, each time a DACK0 signal is activated, the memory is attached to the bus and a refresh cycle is taken.

CHAPTER 13

WAIT-STATE GENERATION

INTRODUCTION

A common problem, when attaching interfaces to the bus of the PC, is that of matching the speed of the PC bus cycles with that of the interface design. It is not uncommon for an interface to operate at a slower data rate than what the bus cycles provide for. The PC system bus is designed such that these problems can be solved. A signal called READY on the system bus, when controlled properly by an interface, can be used to extend the length of a PC bus cycle to match that of a slower interface or to halt a bus cycle until it is synchronized with an interface cycle.

8088 WAIT-STATE GENERATION

As pointed out in earlier chapters, all 8088 microprocessor bus cycles are normally four clock times in length and are described as T1 through T4. In some bus cycles, the PC hardware automatically inserts an extra clock time, called a TW time, in the bus cycle. The READY bus signal line can be used to insert new or additional wait states. The 8088 memory read and write bus cycles and the I/O read and write bus cycles have different timing requirements and, thus, the READY signal must be controlled differently.

Wait-State Generation in the Memory Bus Cycles

The PC hardware does not insert any wait states into the 8088 memory read or write bus cycles, thus they are four clock cycles in length. It should be noted that the "regen" memory buffers on the display cards do request wait states for synchronization, but this is done using the READY signal and is generated by the adapter and not by the system card's logic. Fig. 13-1 is an illustration of the signal timings on the bus that are necessary

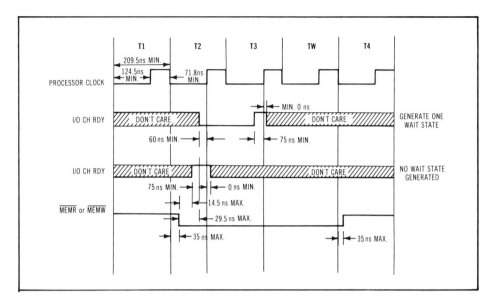

Fig. 13-1. Wait-state timing for a memory read or write bus cycle.

for the generation of a wait state for an 8088 memory read or write bus cycle. Note that the system-board circuits sample the status of the bus signal READY at the rising edge of the T2 bus clock time. Since there is a setup time requirement and the delay of a 74LS74A latch circuit, the bus signal must be valid (active high) 75 nanoseconds prior to the rising edge of the T2 bus clock in order for no wait state to be generated. If a wait state is required, the READY bus signal must be valid (inactive low) 60 nanoseconds prior to the rising edge of the T2 bus clock. If the READY signal is held low (inactive) until the rising edge of the next clock, an additional wait state will be inserted. Again, due to setup time and circuit delays, READY must go active high 75 nanoseconds before the rising edge of the next clock time or an additional wait state will be generated. These timings are based on the worst case setup and the delay timings of the circuits used in the READY circuit path.

The circuit shown in Fig. 13-2 can be used to generate from one to six wait states in an 8088 memory read or write bus cycle. The first part of the circuit decodes the block of memory that is to have a wait state generated. This is done by simply decoding the significant bits from the address bus that define the address range that is to have wait states generated. The output of the decoder is then sampled by the falling edge of either the MEMR or MEMW bus signals. Note that if only wait states are required on a read operation, the MEMW signal can be left out of the "OR." Similarly, if wait states are only required on the memory write cycles, the MEMR signal

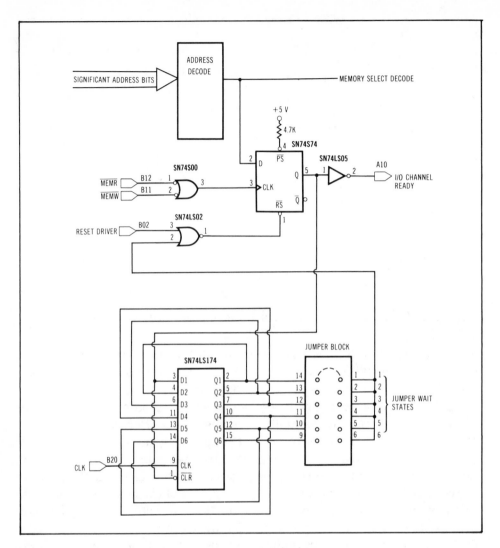

**Fig. 13-2. Wait-state generation for the memory read
and write cycles.**

is removed from the "OR." When the SN74S74 latch is set, the READY signal on the bus is deactivated. The circuit's timings are such that it will meet the setup and delay timings required to ensure that a wait state will be granted. The shift register circuit, generated using the SN74LS174 device, is used to count the number of clocks and, thus, the wait states that are to be generated before READY is activated by clearing the SN74S74 latch. The number of wait states is thus selected by jumpering the appropriate output of the SN74LS174 to clear the SN74S74 latch.

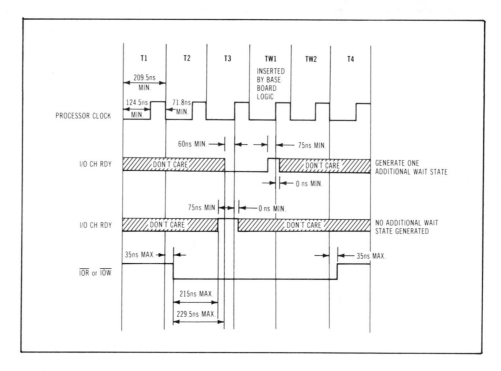

Fig. 13-3. Wait-state timing for I/O port read or write bus cycles.

Wait-State Generation for the I/O Bus Cycles

I/O read or write bus cycles for the 8088 are normally four clocks in length but, in the PC design, an extra wait state is automatically generated by the system-board circuits independent of the bus READY signal. The READY signal can still be used to generate additional wait states. Fig. 13-3 illustrates the bus signals and timings used for generation of additional wait states on the I/O read or write bus cycles. In general, the timings are the same as those used for 8088 memory read and write bus cycles except that READY is sampled with the rising edge of the T3 clock and not the T2 clock. For an additional wait state to be inserted, READY must go inactive 60 nanoseconds prior to the rising edge of the T3 clock. To ensure that an additional wait state is not inserted, READY must go active 75 nanoseconds prior to the rising edge of the T3 clock.

Fig. 13-4 illustrates a circuit that can be used to generate from one to five additional wait states in the 8088 I/O read or write bus cycles. In this circuit, the significant address bits are decoded to determine the I/O address range that is to have extra wait states generated. The falling edge of the IOR or IOW bus signals is used to sample the decoder output and set the SN74LS74 latch. This latch upon being set will deactivate the READY

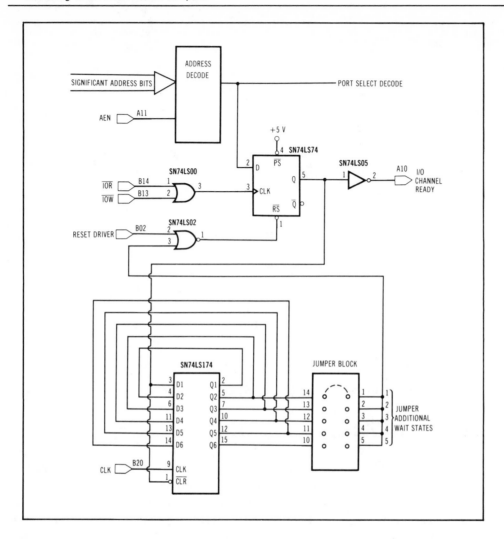

Fig. 13-4. Wait-state generation for I/O port read or write bus cycle.

signal on the bus. The SN74LS174 device, acting as a shift register, will count the clocks and, thus, the wait states generated, before its output is used to clear the SN74LS74 latch. When this latch is cleared, READY will become active and the bus cycle will end. If wait states are only required on I/O read cycles, then the IOW signal is not used to sample the decoder output. Similarly, if wait states are only required in I/O write cycles, the IOR signal is not used. Note that the first stage of the shift register output is not used to generate a wait state. This is because the system board has already generated the first wait state. This circuit just counts it but does not generate it. This circuit only generates wait states beyond that which is generated by the system board.

Wait-State Generation on DMA Bus Cycles

Wait-state generation on DMA (direct-memory access) bus cycles is different, since a DMA bus cycle contains both a read and a write operation. There are two types of DMA cycles. First, there is one which reads from memory and writes to an I/O device or adapter. Secondly, there is one which reads from an I/O device or adapter and writes into memory. The PC is designed such that, on DMA cycles, signal timings are different. This is because the DMA controller samples READY on the opposite edge of the processor clock. In addition, the PC design automatically inserts a wait state in all DMA cycles on Channels 1, 2, and 3. Channel 0 has no wait states inserted; it is only used to support memory refresh and is not available for normal DMA functions. Fig. 13-5 illustrates the timings of the bus during DMA cycles. The DMA controller uses the processor clock and the bus timing and control lines are driven from the DMA controller. Since the DMA controller drives the bus, the bus clocks are called "S" clocks rather than "T" clocks. The activation of the bus signal AEN indicates that the present bus cycle is a DMA cycle. To ensure that an additional wait state is inserted in a DMA cycle, the READY signal must be deactivated 135 nanoseconds prior to the falling edge of the bus clock SW1 state. To ensure

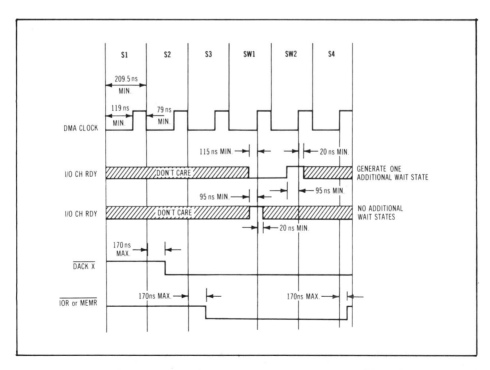

Fig. 13-5. DMA bus cycle wait-state timing.

that an additional wait state is not taken, READY must be deactivated 115 nanoseconds prior to the falling edge of the next S clock.

There are three different conditions under which additional wait states can be generated. First, when a specific channel requests a DMA cycle; secondly, when the DMA transfer is pointed to a specific block of memory; and third, when a DMA transfer takes place both on a specific channel and is pointed to a specific block of memory. Fig. 13-6 illustrates a circuit that can be used to insert up to four additional wait states in a DMA cycle when requested on a specific channel. The DACK signal is used to set a latch which drops the READY bus signal. The SN74LS174 device is used to count the bus clocks and reset the *not ready* latch when the desired number of wait states has been inserted. Note that the first and second stages of the shift register are not used. This is due to the fact that in DMA

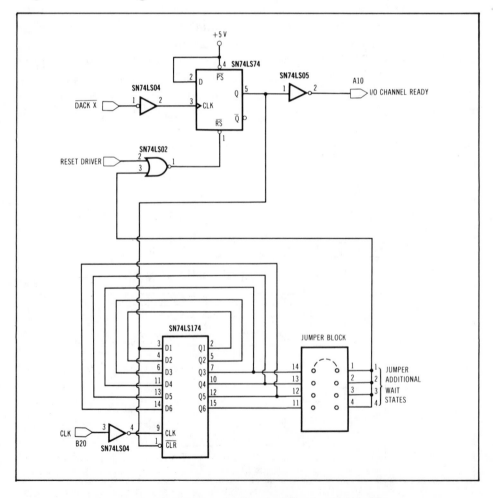

Fig. 13-6. DMA bus cycle wait-state generation.

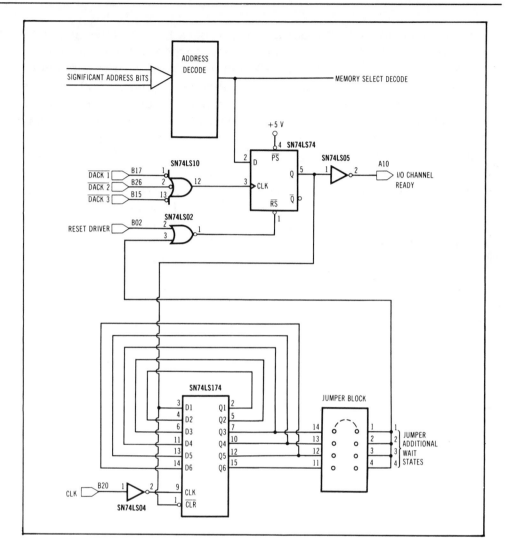

Fig. 13-7. DMA wait-state generation on a specific channel and memory block.

cycles, the READY signal is sampled one clock time later and one wait state has already been inserted by the system board.

Fig. 13-7 illustrates a circuit that will insert one to four additional wait states in a DMA bus cycle only when it is pointed to a specific memory address block. This circuit can also be used to generate wait states in DMA bus cycles that are for a specific channel and are pointed to a specific range of memory addresses. The conditioning for a specific channel is accomplished by including in the SN74LS10 ''OR'' circuit each of those channels' DACKs that require wait states.

It should be pointed out that the insertion of extra wait states in a DMA cycle may not increase the read access-time portion of the cycle. This is particularly true if the cycle is a read from the I/O and a write to dynamic system memory. Since the memory-write function is triggered off from the leading edge of the MEMW bus signal, delaying the trailing edge will have no effect on the timing requirement for data from the I/O device. This is true because insertion of wait states in DMA cycles does not change the relationship of the leading edges of the read bus signal to that of the leading edge of the write bus signal.

It should further be pointed out that if a memory or I/O device needs wait states generated, both for 8088-initiated and DMA bus cycles, it will require both circuits. The READY outputs of each circuit may be simply tied together.

CHAPTER 14

DIGITAL INPUT/OUTPUT REGISTER INTERFACING TECHNIQUES

INTRODUCTION

The most common method of interfacing a microcomputer system, such as the PC, is through the use of programmable digital input and output registers. With digital output registers, the microprocessor can write data into the register, treating the register as an I/O port or a memory location. The output of these registers can then be wired to an interface device, such as a relay. Thus, by writing data to an output register, it would be possible to activate and deactivate a relay. The relay could, in turn, control, for example, the power to a motor. Digital input registers are similar but are used to sample the status of signals attached to their inputs. For example, if a program wanted to determine if a switch was open or closed, the switch could be tied to the input of a digital input register and its state read and determined. A digital input register can be thought of as a memory location or an I/O port address that has wires attached to individual bit locations. When read, the data results reflect the state of the signals on the wires. In general, digital input and output registers allow the microprocessor to sense information about the outside world and emit control signals that cause actions to occur outside of the computer.

Fig. 14-1 illustrates the typical components of an interface design and the microprocessor functions available to implement that interface design. As illustrated in the block diagram, the three basic functions used in an interface to a microprocessor are: (1) interrupts used to signal and synchronize external events, (2) DMA used to transfer data at high speeds to or from system memory, and (3) digital input and output registers used to sense and control interfacing circuitry or the attached interface directly. Often there are functions that cannot easily be done by the system pro-

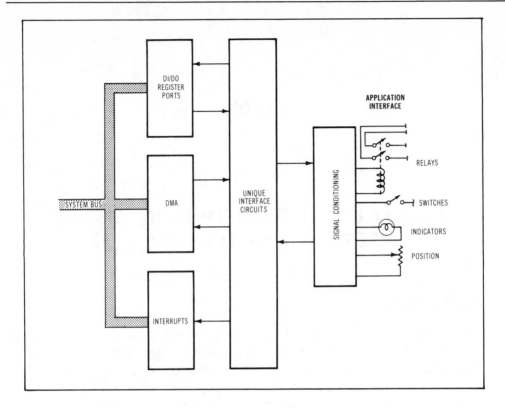

Fig. 14-1. Block diagram of an interface design.

gram using digital input/output registers directly. This is either because it is not fast enough or it requires too much software to perform efficiently. In the block diagram, this is referred to as the interface's adapter circuitry. An obvious goal in any design is to reduce or eliminate the need for the unique and custom interface adapter circuitry. This chapter discusses several different digital input and output register techniques that can help accomplish the goal of reduced custom designs in an interfacing project. The last element of an interface design is the actual attachment of the design to the real world.

Unfortunately, the real world is not digital and the signals from and to such devices or interfaces will require a conversion to other forms, such as relay drivers, switch sensors, indicator drivers, and nondigital voltage levels. In the block diagram, this is referred to as the signal-conditioning section. The functions of interrupts, DMA, and signal conditioning are covered in the specific chapters on these subjects and will not be discussed here.

In this chapter, we will discuss several general-purpose digital input (DI) and digital output (DO) register types. This discussion will provide a variety of DI/DO register approaches that can be used to implement a specific interface-attachment function. The goal is to provide a set of DI/DO registers that have sufficient functions to allow direct interfacing with a minimum of extra circuitry.

DI/DO REGISTER TYPES

Register Address Decoding

There are two basic methods used to address a DI/DO register: as a memory-mapped device or as an I/O-mapped device. The advantages of the I/O-mapped method are many. No segment register manipulation is required, a separate address space is used which does not conflict with the memory address space, fewer address bits are needed to decode a specific address, and DMA operations between I/O ports and memory are accomplished in one bus cycle. The basic limitation of this method is that only the IN and OUT instructions of the 8088 microprocessor can be used to read and write to the DI/DO registers.

One advantage of the memory-mapped method is a very large address space (i.e., lots of available addresses). Also, any 8088 MPU instruction that references memory can be used to access the registers. Thus, the full power of the instruction set can be used to manipulate data in the registers. The design discussed here will use the I/O method, but it could easily be modified to use the memory-mapped method of addressing. Fig. 14-2 is a circuit diagram that decodes eight DO register addresses. Note that only eight addresses are actually decoded. The bus signals, IOR and IOW, are used to further condition the decodes to provide the 16 possible DI/DO register read and write control signals.

Decode and Bus Buffer Circuit

The PC system bus supports nine address bits for decoding I/O port addresses. Bits A0 through A8 can be decoded to select one of 512 port addresses. Bit A9 is used as a tenth bit in the decode but its purpose is to indicate that the system bus is the source or sink for the IN or OUT instruction data. The bus signal AEN must also be used in the decode. Its purpose is to degate the decode of an I/O port address during DMA bus cycle operations. With a relatively few I/O port addresses supported on the system bus, there is a high probability that a fixed decode would overlap with that of another card on the system bus. To overcome this potential problem, the circuit is designed such that the eight decoded addresses can be placed on any eight address boundaries in the 512 address space. This is accomplished by comparing the value set in the dip switches with the address

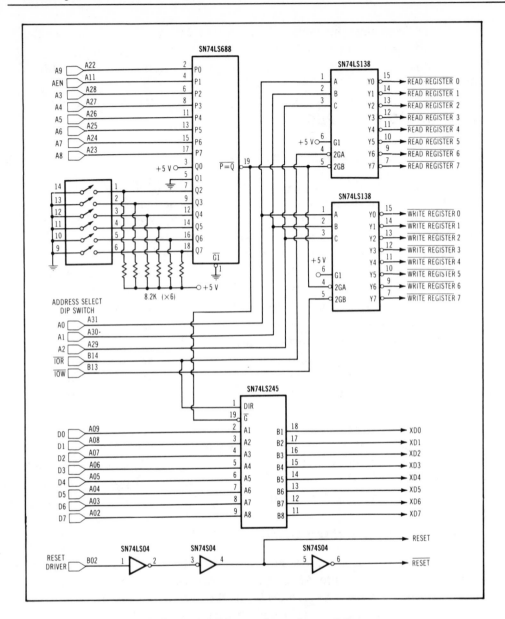

Fig. 14-2. I/O port address decode and bus repower.

value present on the bus. The comparator circuit thus compares the seven address bits (A3 through A9) with the dip-switch value and generates a card-selected signal. The card-selected signal is used to enable the SN74LS245 bus transceiver buffer and, also, to enable the further decode of the DI/DO addresses from A0, A1, A2, IOR, and IOW. This is accomplished by using the two SN74LS138 3-to-8 decode circuits. The IOR signal is also used to set the direction of the enabled SN74LS245 bus transceiver.

Digital Output Register Design

Fig. 14-3 is a circuit diagram showing the simplest form of an 8-bit DO register design. Here an octal D-type latch device, an SN74LS273 latch, is used to capture the data sent by the OUT instruction. The input to each bit of the latch is the repowered data bus from Fig. 14-2. Data from the bus are written on the back edge of the control signal WRT REG 0. This signal is activated when an OUT instruction is executed and this I/O port address is decoded. To write data to a DO register, first load the port address into the DX register. Next, load the data into the AL register and then execute an OUT variable port instruction. The data that are in the AL register will appear in the DO register. The following is a coding example, using assembly language, that will write a hex pattern AA to port hex address 0300.

```
MOV DX,0300H      LOAD DX REG WITH PORT ADDRESS
MOV AL,AAH        LOAD ACCUMULATOR WITH DATA
OUT DX,AL         WRITE DATA IN AL TO PORT IN DX
```

The same result can be obtained using BASIC. The BASIC command that can be used to write to an I/O port is also called an OUT command. The following is a coding example that performs the same function as the above assembly language program.

```
OUT &H300,&HAA
```

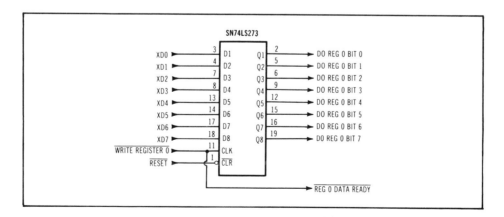

Fig. 14-3. Latched DO register.

Using these commands with the DO register, it is now possible, under program control, to manipulate the output signals of the DO register and thus control external devices. A function that is sometimes useful is to provide the WRT REG signal as an interface signal. The attaching device or circuitry can sense this signal and can use it to indicate that new data have been loaded into the DO register. The DO register should be brought to a known state when the system is powered on. This is particularly true if the DO register bits are controlling things like motors and valves. It is desirable that when the system is powered-on that these control functions are not activated accidentally. This can be accomplished using the bus signal RESET, which holds a reset condition in the register during power on and clears it to an initial state of all bits off.

With the clever selection of components for implementation of the DO registers, it is possible to construct a DO register that can also be used to perform shifting and counting functions. Consider the DO register design shown in Fig. 14-4. Here, the DO register operates as a normal output register but it has the added capability of transmitting and receiving serial data by utilizing the extra functions of the components that are selected to implement the DO register function. This design uses two 4-bit bidirectional universal shift registers (SN74LS194A devices), which can be used as serial output or input devices and which can shift either left or right. In addition to the normal output signals provided on the interface, the following additional controls are made available to the interface.

Shift Left Serial IN Data
Shift Right Serial IN Data
Select Shift Right Mode
Select Shift Left Mode
Shift Data Clock
DO Register Written

The register will operate as a DO register until either the SHIFT LEFT or SHIFT RIGHT MODE is selected. In these modes, the interface may control the register and can shift data into or out of the register using the extra interface signals. As will be demonstrated later, the output of the DO register may be attached to the input of a DI register and the shifter function can be used to transmit serial data loaded by the OUT instruction. It can also receive serial data and read it using the IN instruction. Further, DO registers of this type can be chained together to create shift registers that are greater than 8 bits in length.

Simple timing and counting functions can be added as extra functions to the DO registers by using counter devices as the latching elements in the

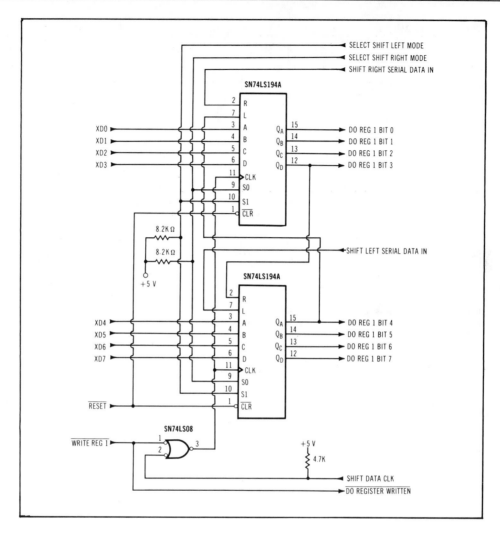

Fig. 14-4. A shifting DO register.

DO register design. Fig. 14-5 illustrates a DO register design that adds counting capability to the DO register. Here the DO register function is implemented using SN74LS193 devices, synchronous up/down counters. In addition to the normal outputs of the DO register, the following signals are also present to the interface.

    Count Up CLK Input
    Count Down CLK Input
    Counter CARRY Output
    Counter BORROW Output
    DO Register Written

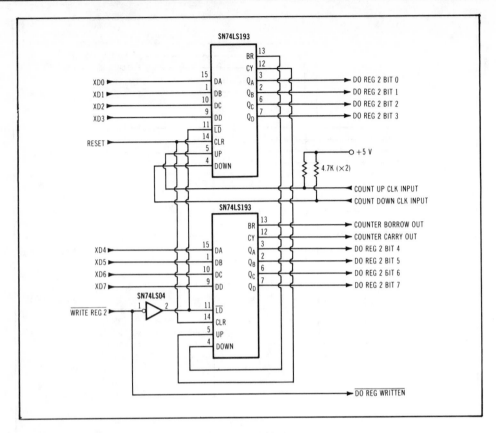

Fig. 14-5. A counting DO register.

With this design, the counter may be preset with a value, using the OUT instruction, and then decremented or incremented from the interface. The CARRY and BORROW outputs can be used to indicate a count reached or a done function. The output of this type of DO register can also be attached to the input of a DI register in such a manner that count values may be read after being incremented or decremented by the interface. Registers of this type may be chained together to give counting functions that are greater than 8 bits in length.

Digital Input Register Design

Sensing information from an interface is normally accomplished using a DI register. The simplest form of this type of register is illustrated in Fig. 14-6. In this design, data from the interface are simply gated onto the system data bus when the address is decoded and an IOR signal occurs. These conditions are generated by the execution of an 8088 microprocessor IN instruction. The IN instruction will take the data at the input of the

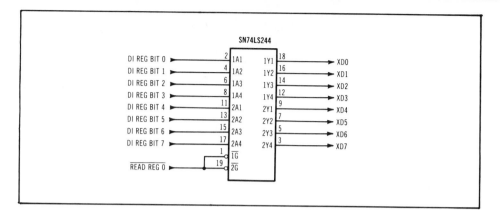

Fig. 14-6. A digital input (DI) register.

addressed DI port register and will place the data in the AL register of the 8088 MPU, where the data may be operated on by the system's software program. The following is an example of an 8088 MPU assembly language program that would read a DI register, decoded at hex address 0301.

```
MOV DX,0301H      LOAD PORT ADDRESS IN DX REGISTER
IN AL,DX          READ PORT VALUE INTO AL REGISTER
```

A DI register may also be read using the BASIC language command INP. The following is an example of the BASIC command that will read the value of a port and then place it in the variable named PORTDATA.

```
PORTDATA = INP(&H0301)
```

It is important to note that data at the input of this type of DI register are only sampled at the time of the execution of the IN command. Further, the data are actually sampled at the trailing edge of the IOW signal that is generated by the IN instruction. Thus, if an interface event is of a short duration, it is possible, when using this type of register, to miss an interface signal. A DI register design that overcomes this problem is discussed next.

Level-Latching DI Register

A common problem in an interface design occurs when the signals that need sensing are very short in duration, such as the opening and closing of a switch or the triggering of a photodetector. A program loop that is executing continuous IN instructions may not see a short-duration signal, since it only samples the register value on the back edge of the IOW signal. In addition, the 8088 MPU may have other functions to perform and cannot dedicate its time to a sampling loop. This problem even becomes more critical when BASIC is used, since its execution time is relatively slow and the sample time is very long. The level-latching DI register shown in Fig. 14-7 provides a solution to this problem. In this design, a set/reset latch is placed in front of a normal DI register and the output of the latch is used as an input to the DI register. When an interface signal goes low, even for just a few nanoseconds, the latch is set and the event is captured. When an IN instruction is later executed, the latch and the DI register will reflect the occurrence of the short-duration event. The next problem is to reset the latch such that later events can be captured and sensed. This is done by designing a special pulsed-output register function that, when written to, will reset the latch. To do this, a special timing circuit must be imple-

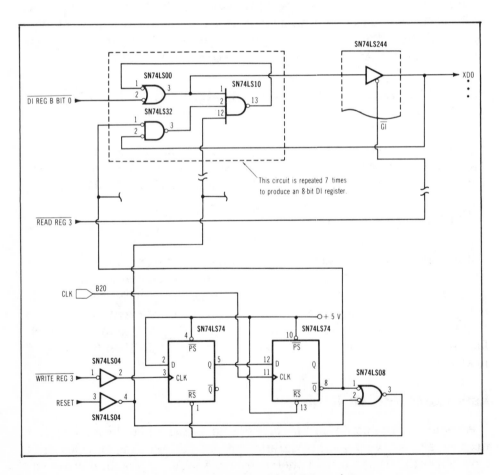

Fig. 14-7. A level-latching DI register.

mented. This is needed to generate a timing signal that, when ANDed with the data from the data bus, the IOW, and the pulsed-output register decode, can be used to generate a reset to the latch. At first, it would appear that ANDing the register write signal with the data bus would produce a reset pulse. However, the IOW signal may come before the data bus is valid, and thus result in invalid reset pulses. The timing generator circuit at the bottom of Fig. 14-7 generates a reset timing pulse that is delayed until the data bus is valid. With this design, it is possible to reset the level-sensing latches of this DI register by simply issuing an OUT instruction with the 0 bit set in the position that requires a reset on the DI latch. The circuit is also designed such that a set condition on the input of the DI register will override a reset command to the latch. This may be a useful function, since a reset can be issued and the latch read after the reset. If the latch is still set, the input has not been deactivated. It is thus possible to follow the state of the input signal by continuing to issue resets and check the reading of the latch.

The following is an example of an 8088 assembly language code that could be used to both read a level-sensitive latching DI register and reset all of the bits that may be latched. The DI register is read by issuing an IN instruction to port address hex 0302. The register latches are reset by issuing an OUT command to the same hex address.

```
MOV DX,0302H    LOAD DX REG WITH PORT ADDRESS
IN AL,DX        LOAD AL REG WITH DI DATA
MOV BL,AL       SAVE DI DATA IN BL REGISTER
MOV AL,0        SET AL REGISTER TO ALL ZEROS
OUT 0302H,AL    WRITE 0'S TO PORT AND CLEAR LATCHES
```

Transition-Sensing DI Register

Another common problem when dealing with a DI register is that of signal-transition detection on an interface. Often it is of interest to determine if an interface signal has made a transition from one state to another state. After a transition has been sensed, it would be desirable to reset the DI register bit such that it could detect the next transition. This should be possible even though the signal is still active. Fig. 14-8 illustrates the design of a DI register that can be used to detect the positive-going transition of interface signals. The design is similar to that of the level-sensing DI register. In place of the set/reset latch used as the input to the DI register, there is an edge-triggered D-type latch. Here the D input is tied high and the input is the transition-setting clock signal. Thus, any time the input signal goes from a low state to a high state, the latch is set and can be read

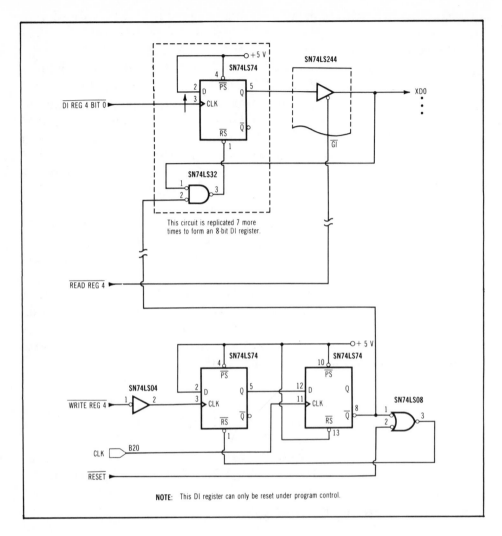

Fig. 14-8. A transition-detection DI register.

through the DI register, using an IN instruction. The transition-detection latches are reset using the same pulsed output DO register design as was used with the level-detecting DI register. The major difference is that the reset will always clear the latch regardless of the state of the input signal to the latch. As with the level-sensing DI register design, if a zero is written to a bit position in the pulsed-output register, the latch is cleared. The following is an example of 8088 processor assembly language code that can be used to sense the status of a transition-detection DI register and which can reset only bit 2 of the DI register. The DI and DO register is assumed to be at hex port address 0304.

```
MOV DX,0304H    LOAD PORT ADDRESS IN DX REG
IN AL,DX        READ PORT DATA INTO AL REG
MOV BL,AL       MOVE DATA FROM AL REG TO BL REG
MOV AL,FBH      SET DATA IN AL REG WITH BIT 2 OFF ONLY
OUT DX,AL       WRITE DATA TO PORT RESETTING BIT 2
```

Interrupts From DI Registers

The level- and transition-latching DI register designs just presented can also be used as sources of interrupts. The output of each of these types of latches, before they are fed into the DI sensing circuitry, can be wired to interrupt requests on the system bus. Thus, the latches can serve a dual function, that of detecting levels and transition for sensing using the DI function and that of interrupt sources that can be cleared under program control.

Bidirectional DI/DO Registers

It is possible to design a port register that acts as either a DI or a DO register and which can be changed under program control. Further, it is possible to program each bit so that it can be either a DI or a DO bit. Such a capability is of interest when the design is to support a variety of different interfacing functions, with each having different requirements for numbers of DI and DO bits. The register is customized by software to configure the required number of bits, either DI or DO, as needed. Fig. 14-9 illustrates a port design that has individual programmable DI or DO bits. The output portion of the port design is similar to a standard latched-output DO. Each output bit of the DO register is used to drive an open-collector device, in this design, an SN74LS05. The output of each open-collector device is pulled high through a 4.7K resister to +5 volts, which provides a load for the SN74LS05. The outputs of the SN74LS05s are now tied to the input of a standard DI register. To use a bit of this register as an output bit, simply write the desired level of the bit to the DO register using an OUT instruction. To use a bit as an input bit, first write a zero bit to the bit position in the DO register. This will turn off the open-collector driver and have the effect of removing it from the circuit. Now an input signal can drive the signal line either high or low and its state can be read in the DI portion of the circuit, using an IN instruction. It should be noted that after a power-on reset, the port is configured as an input port. In addition, when used as an output port, the output signals are the complement of the data written to the port.

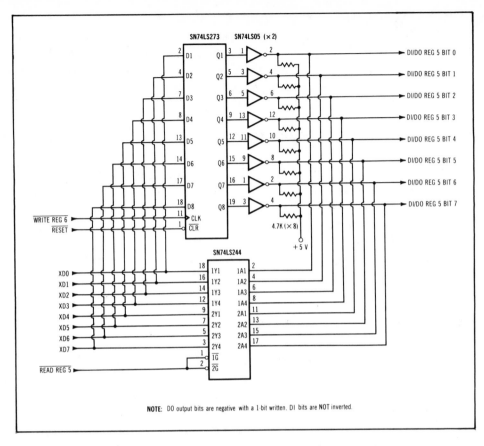

Fig. 14-9. A combination DI/DO register.

Pulsed-Output Port Design

We have used a pulsed-output port function before to reset the latches used in the level and transition DI register designs. This function is often useful by itself on an interface. This type of register can be used to strobe data into a register under program control, reset interface status latches, and generate interrupt requests to another attached system. Fig. 14-10 is a circuit diagram of an 8-bit pulsed-output register. This circuit will produce a 420-nanosecond output pulse at a port bit when a 1 bit is written to the port-bit position using an OUT instruction.

DO Register Output Drive

In the DO register designs shown here, we have used "LS"-type devices. These devices typically have a limited signal drive capability; typically, they can sink only 8 mA. To obtain additional drive capability, it is possi-

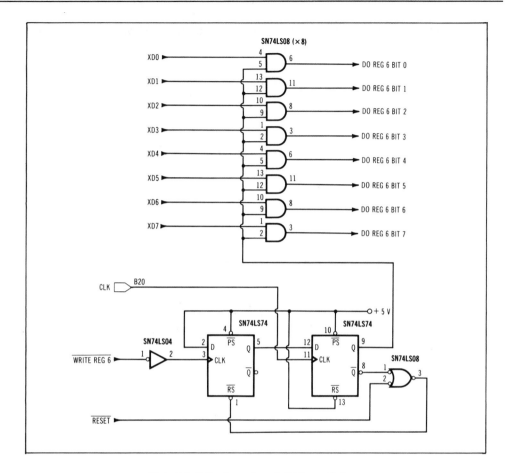

Fig. 14-10. A pulsed DO register.

ble to substitute "S"-type devices, which will support a 20 mA drive- or sink-current capability.

Setting and Resetting Bits in a DO Register

Setting and resetting bits in a DO register may at first appear to be a simple task; just load the AL register with the desired pattern and execute an OUT instruction. This technique requires that each routine that uses the DO port understand the proper setting of all the bits in the port, even though it is only interested in one of just a few of the bits in the register. The following code can be used to manipulate a bit or bits in a DO register without disturbing the other bits. For this technique to work, it is necessary to maintain an image of the current state of the DO register in memory, or be able to read the current state of the DO register through a DI register. For this example, we will assume that the DO can be read and written at port address hex 0305 and we wish to turn on bit 3 without changing the state of the other bits in the DO register.

```
MOV DX,0305H     LOAD DX REG WITH PORT ADDRESS
IN AL,DX         READ DO REG INTO AL REGISTER
OR AL,08H        OR ON BIT 3 IN AL REGISTER, OTHER BIT
                     NOT AFFECTED
OUT 0305H,AL     WRITE AL REG TO PORT, ONLY BIT 3 IS
                     AFFECTED
```

Similarly the following code can be used to reset only bit 3 in a DO register.

```
MOV DX,0305H     LOAD DX REG WITH PORT ADDRESS
IN AL,DX         READ DO PORT INTO AL REGISTER
AND AL,F7H       AND OFF BIT 3 IN AL REG
OUT 0305H,AL     WRITE DATA IN AL REG TO DO PORT WITH
                     ONLY BIT 3 MODIFIED OFF
```

Testing Bits in a DI Register

The following are some 8088 assembly language coding techniques that can be used to test the state of a DI register bit or an interface signal state. The following example will assume that the DI port is at hex address 0307 and will test bit 6.

```
MOV DX,0307H     LOAD DX REG WITH PORT ADDRESS
IN AL,DX         READ DI PORT INTO AL REG
AND AL,40H       AND OFF ALL BITS IN AL REG EXCEPT BIT 6
JZ BITOFF        JUMP TO BIT OFF ROUTINE
JMP BITON        JUMP TO BIT ON ROUTINE
```

If a signal is tested often or has a tight timing requirement, both code and time can be saved if it is assigned to bit 7 in a DI register. In this bit position, no logical operations need to be performed on the data since the data can be tested using the jump on sign instruction. The following coding example illustrates the savings.

```
MOV DX,0307      LOAD DX REG WITH PORT ADDRESS
IN AL,DX         READ DI PORT INTO AL REG
JS BIT7ON        JUMP TO BIT 7 ON ROUTINE
JMP BIT7OFF      JUMP TO BIT 7 OFF ROUTINE
```

Other DI/DO Devices

There are several devices manufactured that provide DI/DO functions in single chips and which can easily be attached to the system bus of the PC. The following is a short list of such devices that may be of use in an interface design. The operations and characteristics of these devices are specified in their data sheets and will not be covered here.

Intel 8255A-5	24 bits of DI/DO
Zilog Z80-P10	24 bits of DI/DO
Motorola 6820	16 bits of DI/DO

Summary

The DI/DO register designs presented here are a general-purpose set and can be used in a large number of interfacing applications. It should be noted that parts and pieces of these designs can be incorporated in one specific interface design, thus achieving an optimal solution for a specific project.

CHAPTER 15

EXPANDING INTERRUPTS ON THE PC

INTRODUCTION

The PC system bus only provides for six interrupt sources. Many of these interrupt levels are used to support the basic I/O functions and adapters of the system. Thus, if an interface design requires a large number of interrupt levels, it may be difficult to implement this on the PC. This chapter describes a solution to this problem. The method described will allow each of the six interrupt levels on the system bus to be expanded to eight fully prioritized sublevels. Thus, for each system-bus interrupt level that is not used, it will be possible to provide eight additional interrupts. If, for example, all six levels were not used, they could be expanded to a total of 48 interrupt levels.

INTERRUPT EXPANSION CONCEPT

As pointed out in Chapter 9, on the PC interrupts, the cascade function of the 8259A interrupt controller on the system board is not supported. This is because the bus does not provide signal lines that are required to support this function. The 8259A interrupt controller can still be used in an interface design to expand the number of interrupt sources and levels. In a specific design, the 8259A interrupt controller would be attached to the system bus and given an I/O port address. Further, it can be initialized similar to that of the controller on the System Unit baseboard. After initialization, the 8259A controller will accept and prioritize interrupts that it receives and will activate the INT output signal. The INT signal is then used to request an interrupt, using one of the system-bus interrupt-request signals. In the interrupt service routine for that level, the 8259A controller in the interface design is issued an operation control-word three command (OCW3), with bit 2 active, indicating a poll mode. After this

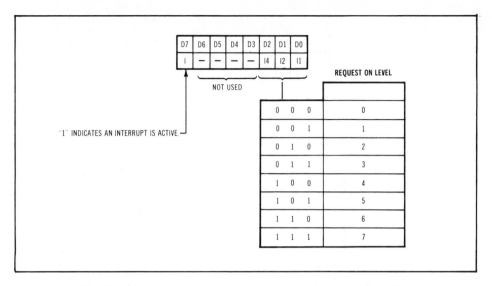

Fig. 15-1. Format of the interrupt-level status byte.

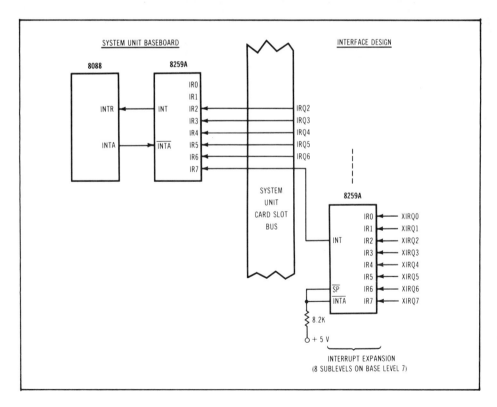

Fig. 15-2. Block diagram of an interrupt expansion circuit.

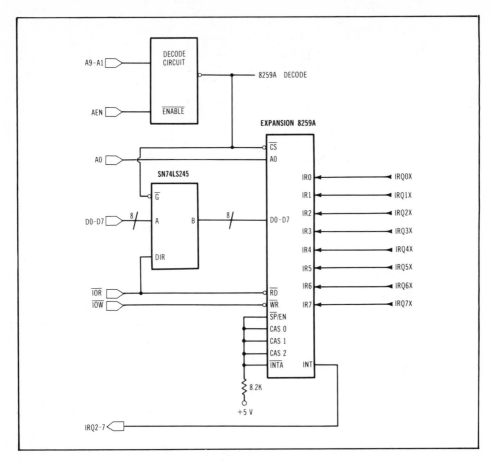

Fig. 15-3. The bus connections for an 8259A controller expansion device.

mode is set, the 8259A controller does not expect to get an INTA response signal from the 8088 microprocessor. It obviously cannot, since this signal is not available on the system bus. The 8259A controller treats the next read command to it as an interrupt acknowledge. The value that is read with this read command will contain the encoded value of the level that generated the request. Fig. 15-1 illustrates the format of the read data. The interrupt service routine for the baseboard's 8259A controller interrupt level can now use this data to branch to the service routine for the specified sublevel. In the 8259A controller of the interface designs, the interrupts are frozen between the issuing of the poll mode and the reading of the interrupt level. Fig. 15-2 is a block diagram of how the 8259A controller is connected in the system. Fig. 15-3 is an illustration of the exact connections required on the system bus for an 8259A interrupt controller that is acting as an interrupt expansion device.

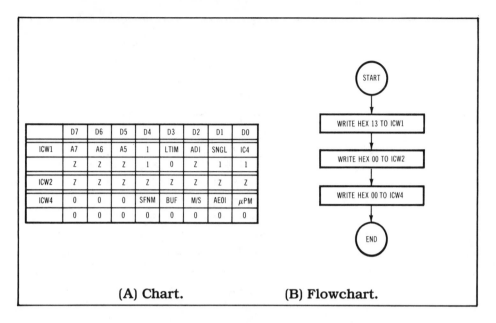

	D7	D6	D5	D4	D3	D2	D1	D0
ICW1	A7	A6	A5	1	LTIM	ADI	SNGL	IC4
	Z	Z	Z	1	0	Z	1	1
ICW2	Z	Z	Z	Z	Z	Z	Z	Z
ICW4	0	0	0	SFNM	BUF	M/S	AEOI	μPM
	0	0	0	0	0	0	0	0

(A) Chart.   (B) Flowchart.

Fig. 15-4. Initialization of the expansion 8259A device.

INITIALIZATION OF THE EXPANSION 8259A DEVICE

Another advantage of the expansion 8259A device is that it is not required to operate using the same modes as that of the controller on the baseboard. This gives the interface designer greater freedom to select the modes of operation that are best suited for the application. There are some modes that must be selected for the scheme to operate properly. During initialization, the expansion 8259A must be selected to operate in master mode and 8085 mode. Fig. 15-4 shows a flowchart and a chart that will initialize the expansion 8259A such that it will operate in a fully nested mode with edge-triggered interrupt-request inputs and a normal end of interrupt mode. For a description of the modes of operation of the 8259A controller, refer to Chapter 9.

SOFTWARE SERVICE ROUTINE FOR EXPANSION INTERRUPTS

The interrupts that are generated as inputs to the expansion 8259A controller cause interrupt requests on the base system board's 8259A controller. Thus, a special interrupt-service routine must be written to handle the expansion interrupts. Fig. 15-5 is a flowchart of one possible service routine for handling and directing the expansion interrupts to the proper software support program.

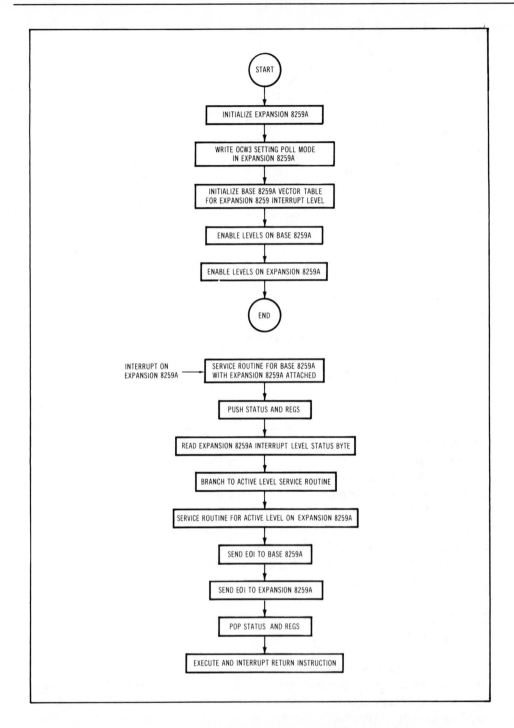

**Fig. 15-5. Initialization and service routine for the expansion
8259A device.**

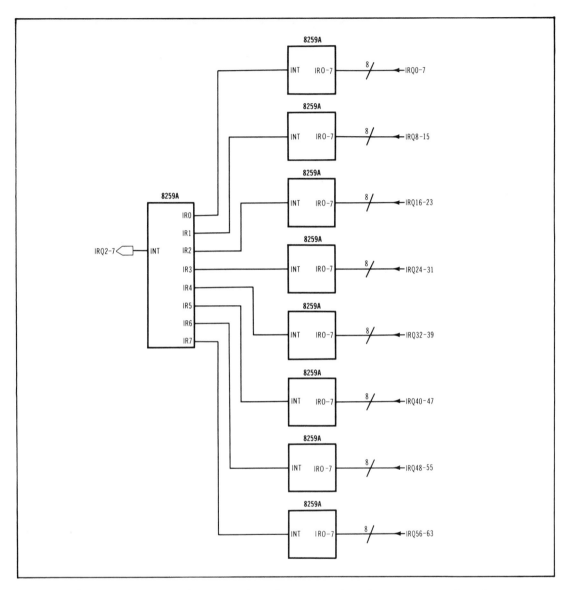

Fig. 15-6. Block diagram of 64 interrupt levels on one system-bus request level.

FURTHER INTERRUPT-LEVEL EXPANSION

This concept can be further expanded upon by adding additional 8259A devices to the first expansion 8259A device. It is possible to add up to eight additional 8259A controllers to an 8259A controller that is attached to one of the bus interrupt levels. This would allow eight 8259A devices of 64 interrupt-level expansions on a single bus-input interrupt-level request input. This would require that the software first poll the expansion 8259A device to determine which of the additional eight devices requested service. Secondly, that device could be polled to determine which of the eight inputs generated the interrupt request. Fig 15-6 is a block diagram of this two tiered 8259A implementation.

CHAPTER 16

ADDING EXTENDED TIMING AND COUNTING FUNCTIONS

INTRODUCTION

Many interfacing applications will require that extensive timing and counting functions be performed. Although the baseboard of the Personal Computer has a built-in timer counter, its functions are typically tied up in supporting the base functions of the system. Further, none of the interesting control or input signals of the timer counter are available on the system bus. As previously discussed in Chapter 11, the timing and counting functions of the baseboard are implemented using an Intel 8253-5 timer counter. This device has three 16-bit timer counters with five independent modes of operation. Each timer counter has a clock input signal that is used to decrement the counters, a gate input signal that is used to start and stop the counter, and an output signal that can be programmed to perform several functions depending on the mode of operation selected. As previously pointed out, the modes of operation and the input/output signals of the system board's 8253-5 counter are fixed and not available. Since the 8253-5 timer counter is a bus-attached device, it is possible to add another timer counter as part of the interface design and, thus, have it dedicated to a specific application. This chapter will demonstrate how an 8253-5 timer counter, when combined with a little extra circuitry, can be used to create a very versatile and capable timing and counting function.

TIMER COUNTER DESIGN

Since the system bus is available in the card slots, it is not a difficult task to attach an 8253-5 device. Fig. 16-1 shows a circuit diagram of the

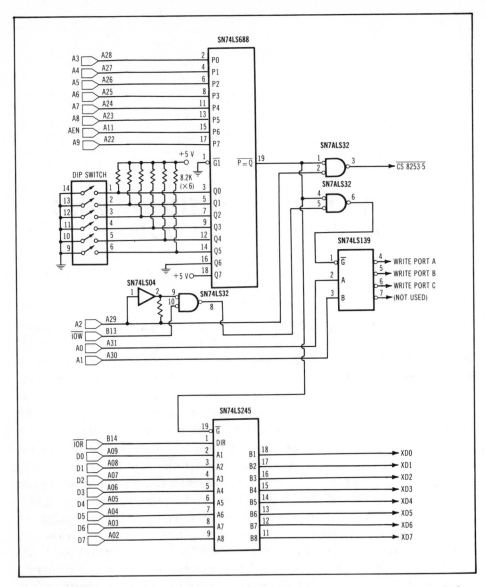

Fig. 16-1. Address decode and bus buffer for the I/O ports and the 8253-5 timer counter.

system-bus interface circuitry needed to decode a set of I/O port addresses and buffer the system bus. In this design, several port addresses are decoded; a group or "Chip Select" for the four port addresses of the 8253-5 timer counter and three port addresses that will be used to address three output ports. These three output ports will provide 24 programmable signal lines which will be used to control the support circuitry necessary to

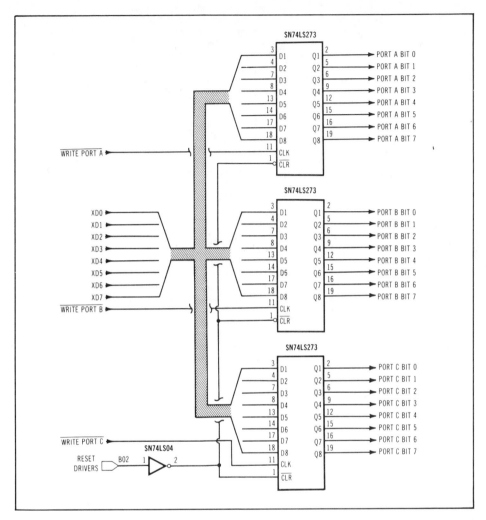

Fig. 16-2. Control I/O ports.

extend the functions of the 8253-5 counter. The decode circuitry is designed such that the location of the decoded addresses can be set in the I/O-port address space by simply setting a value in the DIP switches. The complement of the value set in the DIP switches is compared with the address on the bus, and when a match is detected, the card and bus buffer is enabled. This technique allows the addresses to be moved such that an I/O-port address overlap can easily be avoided.

Fig. 16-2 is a circuit diagram of the three output I/O port registers that provide the control function for the timer-counter extension circuitry. Each

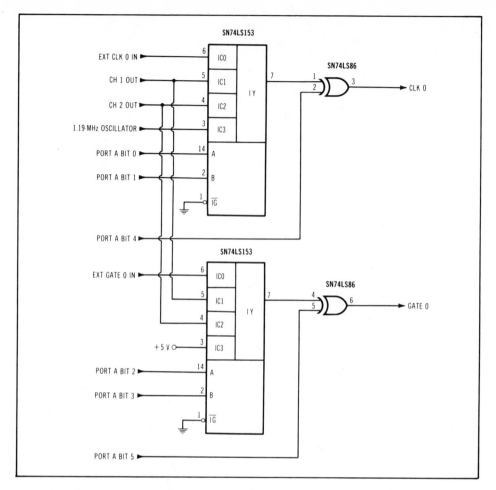

Fig. 16-3. Control gating for timer-counter Channel 0.

8-bit output register controls extended function circuits of an 8253-5 timer counter channel.

Figs. 16-3 through 16-6 are circuit diagrams of an 8253-5 timer counter with extended gating and control circuits added. The extra circuitry greatly extends the timing and counting function. The capabilities added include:

1. Allows channels to be chained together under program control and, thus, providing timing and counting functions up to 48 bits in length.
2. Allows the gate on a timer-counter channel to be controlled by the output of another channel or by an external condition.

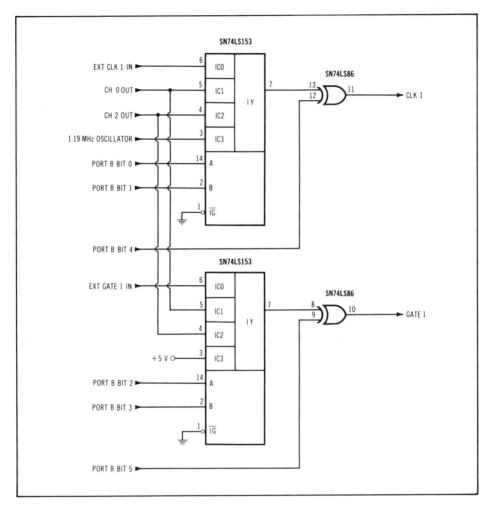

Fig. 16-4. Control gating for timer-counter Channel 1.

3. Allows the clock input on a channel to be selected from an external source, an internal source, or another channel's output.
4. Allows the active level of the gate or clock input, to a channel, to be selected as either high or low active under program control.
5. Allows the output of a timer counter to be program-selected as either active high or low.
6. Allows the output of each timer counter to generate a system-bus interrupt request.

When the combinations of control, through the use of the port bits, are combined with the modes of operation of each of the timer counters, the operational modes of this circuit are nearly limitless.

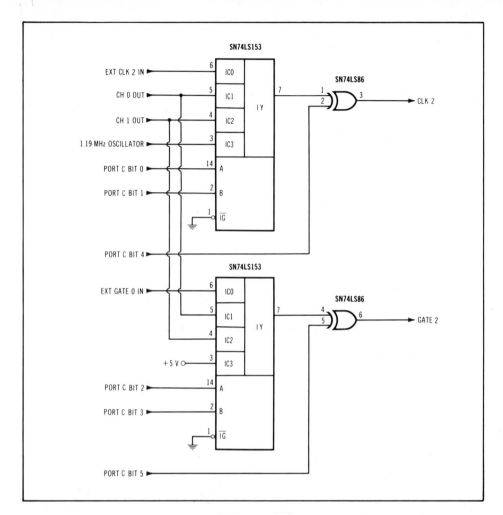

Fig. 16-5. Control gating for timer-counter Channel 2.

Circuit Description

As can be seen from the circuit diagram, each clock-output signal is attached to the input of an Exclusive-OR gate. The inputs to these gates are the output of a 4-to-1 selector and a programmable port bit. By programming the active level of the port bit, it is possible to change the active level of the signal from the selector before it is fed into the clock input of the timer counter channel. An active low level from the port bit will pass the output of the selector noninverted. An active high level from the port bit will invert the signal. The selector inputs are attached to four different sources: the outputs of the other two timer-counter channels, a 1.19-

megahertz clock, and an external source. Two bits from the I/O-output port registers are used to select which source, from the selector, will be used to drive the clock input. The selector circuit is an SN74LS153, a dual 4-to-1 selector. In this design, only one-half of the circuit is used.

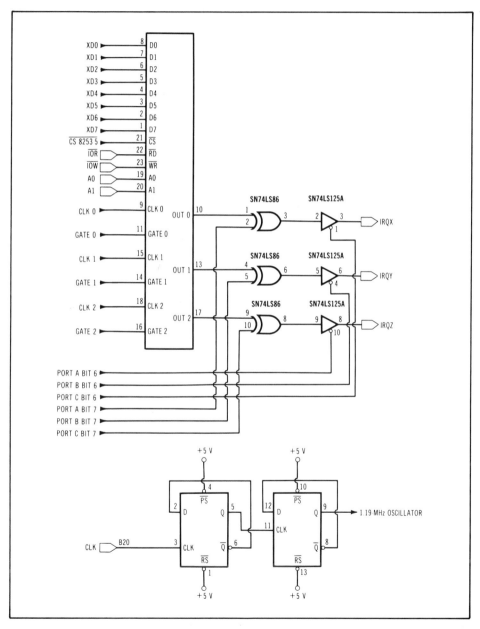

Fig. 16-6. An 8253-5 timer counter.

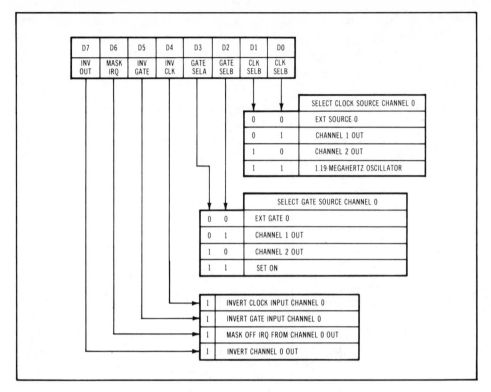

Fig. 16-7. Port A control-bit definitions.

The gate input to each channel has a similar circuit. Here again, the active level of the gate input is controlled through the programming of the state of an I/O-port output register bit. The selector circuit is also controlled by two port bits such that any of four different gate signals can be used. The four inputs to the gate-selector circuit are: the outputs of the two other timer-counter channels, an external gate source, and a tied high-level condition. By selecting the tied high condition, it is possible, under program control, to force a gate active.

The active level of the output of each timer-counter channel can also be controlled through the setting of a port bit. Again, the port bit controls an Exclusive-OR circuit which will either pass the output or invert the output. An active low signal on the port bit will not invert the channel's output. An active high port bit will invert the channel's output. The output of the Exclusive-OR circuit can be used to drive an interface or create an interrupt on the system bus. The output of each channel is attached through a tri-state buffer to an interrupt-request signal input on the system bus. Under

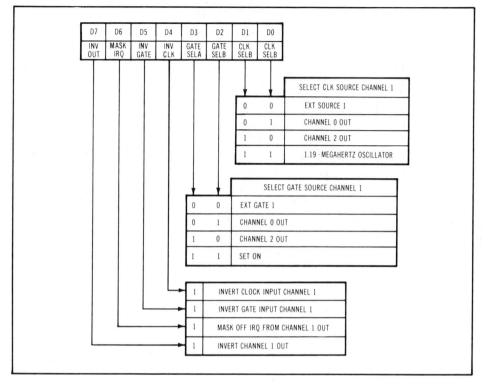

Fig. 16-8. Port B control-bit definitions.

program control, a port bit may be activated that will enable the buffer and attach the channel output to the interrupt request on the system bus.

Bit Definitions of Control I/O Ports

Inspection of the circuit diagrams will reveal that eight control signals are required for each channel to control the selectors, inverter circuits, and interrupt-enable control. Figs. 16-7 through 16-9 define the functions of the three output registers and the signal definitions of the 8-bits in each register.

Expanding Timing and Counting Functions

If a specific interface design requires more timer-counter functions than are supported by a single 8253-5 timer counter, the design can be easily expanded. The circuitry can easily be replicated and additional decodes provided.

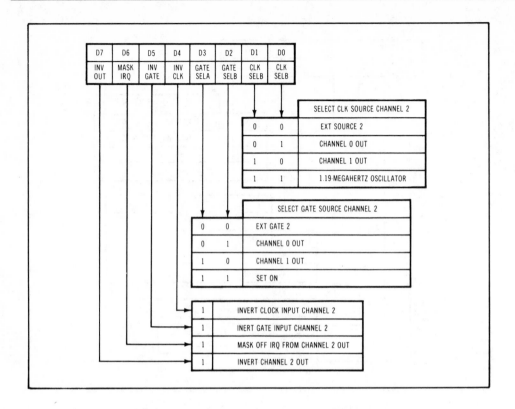

Fig. 16-9. Port C control-bit definitions.

CHAPTER 17

HIGH-SPEED DATA TRANSFER

INTRODUCTION

One of the key considerations in many types of interfacing applications is that of high-speed data transfer between the PC and an adapter or device. In this chapter, we will discuss high-speed data-transfer techniques and their performance capabilities. It is important to determine the data-transfer capabilities of the PC while using several different techniques, since your design should use the method that meets the performance requirements of your application. The techniques discussed will include programmed I/O data transfer in both BASIC and assembly language, the uses of the Personal Computer's DMA function, and the special buffering techniques needed for very-high-speed data-transfer requirements.

PROGRAMMED I/O DATA TRANSFER

The technique that is most-often used to transfer data between the PC and a device or adapter is the use of a simple programmed I/O. Using this technique, the data transfer is done entirely under program control. A typical data-transfer loop is flowcharted in Fig. 17-1. Here, the data are being transferred from a memory buffer in the PC to an I/O port address. The loop has several functions to perform beyond the simple sending of data. First, it must maintain a memory address pointing to the buffer and then increment this address on each transfer. Secondly, the loop must maintain a count of the desired number of bytes of data that are to be transferred and test the loop count for an ending condition. Third, if the I/O port cannot accept the data as fast as the loop can provide data, provisions must be added to the loop for testing for a ready signal or for date taken.

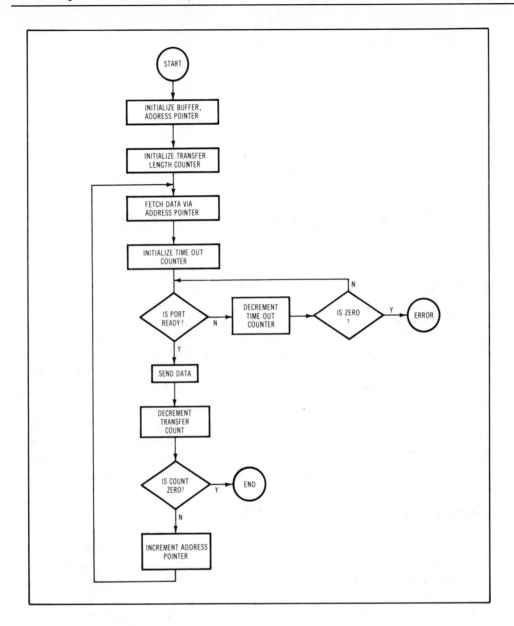

Fig. 17-1. Typical data-transfer loop program.

Programmed I/O Transfer Using BASIC

In many cases, the data-transfer function will be slow enough that it can be done in BASIC. The following is an example of a data transfer loop written in the BASIC language.

```
10 DIM BUF(1000)
20 FOR CNT=0 TO 1000
30 WAIT &H3BC,&H01
40 BUF(CNT)=INP(&H3BD)
50 OUT &H3BC,0
60 NEXT
70 END
```

This loop will transfer 1000 bytes of data from the input port address hex 03DB and will place them in the array called BUF. Statements 10 and 20 dimension the buffer and set up the loop count. Statement 30 is used to cause a wait until bit zero at input port address hex 03BC becomes active. This bit would be used to indicate that the data input port contains valid data that can now be read. Statement 40 reads the data from the port and places the data in the buffer. Statement 50 resets the data-ready bit in hex register 03BC, indicating to the adapter that the data have been read and new data can be loaded into the input I/O port. Statement 60 repeats the data-transfer function for 1000 cycles and then passes control to the next BASIC statement.

BASIC Data-Transfer Performance

The following are two BASIC language data-transfer loops that have been timed. One loop reads data from a port and puts the data in an array. The other reads data from an array and writes them to an I/O port. In both cases, it is assumed that the data are always taken and available so that no interlock control signals are needed. In both loops, the maximum data rate measured was 4.75 milliseconds per byte transfer, or approximately 210 bytes per second.

```
READ FROM PORT LOOP


10 DIM BUF(1000)
20 FOR CNT=0 TO 1000
30 BUF(CNT)=INP(&H3BD)        4.75ms/byte
40 NEXT
50 END



WRITE TO PORT LOOP


10 DIM BUF(1000)
20 FOR CNT=0 TO 1000
```

```
30 OUT &H3BC,BUF(CNT)        4.75ms/byte
40 NEXT
50 END
```

Assembly Language Data Transfer

Programmed data-transfer performance can be dramatically improved by using 8088 assembly language. The following is an example of an assembly language data-transfer loop. In this loop, data are transferred from a memory buffer to an I/O port. The loop manages the memory addresses and maintains a byte count that is tested during each transfer cycle. This loop assumes that the data will be accepted as fast as they can be sent.

```
START MOV DX,PORT      LOAD DX REG WITH PORT ADDRESS
      MOV BX,BUFFER    LOAD BX REG WITH BUFFER ADDRESS
      MOV CX,COUNT     LOAD CX REG WITH LOOP COUNT
LOOP  MOV AL [BX]      LOAD AL REG WITH DATA FROM BUFFER
      OUTB DX          WRITE AL REG DATA TO PORT
      INC BX           INCREMENT BUFFER ADDRESS
      DEC CX           DECREMENT LOOP COUNT
      JNZ LOOP         LOOP IF COUNT NOT EQUAL TO ZERO
      WAIT
```

This data-transfer loop was measured and it transferred data at a rate of 11.5 microseconds per byte, or 86.95 kilobytes per second. This is over 400 times faster than the equivalent BASIC data-transfer loop.

DMA DATA TRANSFER

The DMA function of the PC is specifically designed to aid in high-speed data transfer. This function is covered in detail in Chapter 10, but is briefly reviewed here. Using the DMA facility, it is possible to transfer data at a maximum rate of 476 kilobytes per second. At this rate, approximately one half of the system-bus bandwidth is used. This will slow the execution of any program to one-half speed when the maximum DMA data rate is in operation. The DMA facility is specifically designed such that the microprocessor cannot be locked out.

Interfacing to the DMA Facility

Fig. 17-2 is a diagram of a circuit that can be used to interface to the DMA control signals on the bus. This circuit will allow data from an 8-bit interface port to be DMA'ed into the system's memory. The interface is ena-

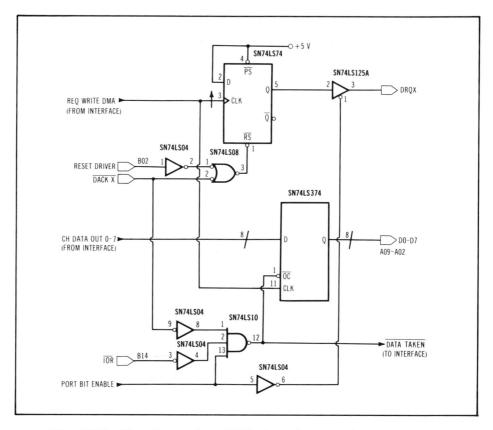

Fig. 17-2. Circuit used to DMA data from an interface port to PC memory.

bled by an I/O port bit such that the channel used can be reused by other devices when not in operation on this interface. To transfer a byte of data, assuming that the DMA devices have been previously properly initialized, the interface simply applies the data to the input port and raises the REQUEST signal. When this signal makes a positive transition, it latches the input data in the bus register and requests a DMA cycle. When the associated DACK signal goes active, the data is transferred to the system's memory and the request is reset. This action will be repeated each time the REQUEST signal makes a positive transition and the DMA's terminal count has not been reached.

Fig. 17-3 is a diagram of a circuit that can be used to transfer, under DMA control, data from the system's memory to an output port register. To request data from memory, simply raise the REQUEST signal. Data will be loaded into the port register when the associated DACK signal becomes active. This assumes that the DMA channel has been enabled by the I/O

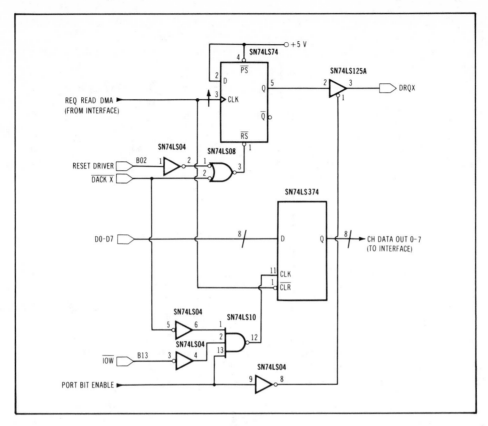

Fig. 17-3. Circuit used to DMA data from PC memory to an interface port.

port bit and the DMA device has been properly initialized. The DACK signal also resets the request. The operation is repeated each time the REQUEST signal is raised, assuming that the DMA channel has not reached its terminal count.

OTHER DATA-TRANSFER TECHNIQUES

If data must be buffered or transferred at a data rate greater than that which is available when using the DMA facility, there are still some techniques that can be used. A commonly used technique is to "dual port" a high-speed memory, so that it can be read and written by the microprocessor on one port and data transfer can take place on the other port. The display adapter "regen" buffers on the PC use this technique. The memory is time-division multiplexed with a high-speed clock. On one phase of the clock, the memory can be attached to the PC system bus. On the other phase of the clock, an interface may access the memory. This technique allows the processor to access the memory at any time, even while data are being read or written on the other port. However, this technique has two drawbacks. First, new memory must be added to the system with this capability. Secondly, the memory must be high speed, so that it can support both the microprocessor accessing and the interface data-rate requirements.

Another technique that is often used is the ping-pong buffer approach. In this scheme, two memory buffers are built, each of which is the size needed to hold the maximum burst of data required by the application. The buffers are designed such that each can be attached to either the PC system bus or to the application interface. In operation, one buffer collects or transmits data on the interface while the other is being read or written by the microprocessor. When the interface buffer is full, the buffers are swapped so that the new buffer can be used to transfer data. This technique is most useful when data comes in short high-speed bursts.

CHAPTER 18

CARDS AND PORTS FOR INTERFACING

INTRODUCTION

For many smaller interfacing projects, it may be possible to use interfaces that exist on the PC System Unit baseboard or on some of the feature cards that IBM provides for the PC. As an example, consider the cassette port on the System Unit. If your system is diskette-based, then it is likely that the cassette port on your system is not being used. This interface provides a serial input point and a serial output point for the system. In addition, the cassette port has a set of relay points that can be controlled from the system's software. Two other feature cards are also of interest. The parallel-printer port card can be used as a general-purpose digital input/output register group and the game I/O port card can be used as both a digital and an analog input interface.

CASSETTE INTERFACE

The interface to the cassette-adapter function is through a 5-pin DIN-type connector at the rear of the System Unit. It is the DIN connector that is closest to the power connectors. Fig. 18-1 defines the signals present on each of the pins in the connector.

The Channel 2 output of system 8253—5 timer counter drives the circuit shown in Fig. 18-2. The output of this circuit is then sent to the DIN connector pin. As indicated in Fig. 18-2, the output level of the signal can be selected by a jumper on the base system board. By proper programming control of the timer counter channel output 2, data may be sent out on this port. A simple modification of this circuit will allow a TTL signal to be generated at pin 5 of the DIN connector. If the 4.7K resistor is removed and

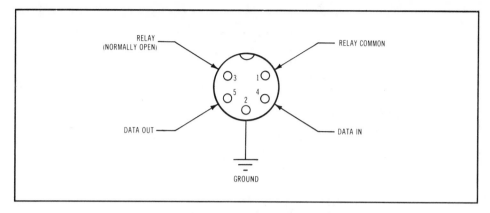

Fig. 18-1. The cassette-connector signals.

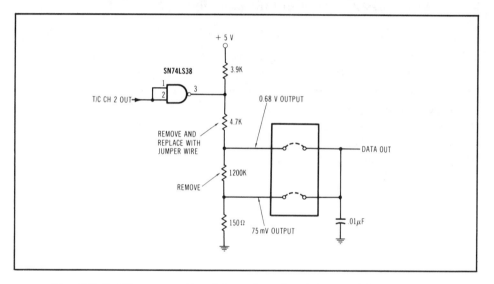

**Fig. 18-2. The cassette drive circuit with modifications for
TTL output.**

replaced with a jumper wire, and if the 1200-ohm resistor is removed, and
if the jumper is set to select the 0.68-volt output, the circuit will produce a
TTL-level output signal. Note that the output level is inverted from the output of the timer counter Channel 2.

The data from the cassette input is read as an 8255A-5 I/O digital input-
port bit. The port address is hex 0062 and the signal is on bit 4 of this port.
Fig. 18-3 illustrates the receiving circuit. Note that the input is capaci-
tively coupled to the input of the noninverting op amp. Thus, only ac signals are passed to the digital input-port bit. This circuit can also be modified to accept a TTL-level input signal. The simplest approach is to remove

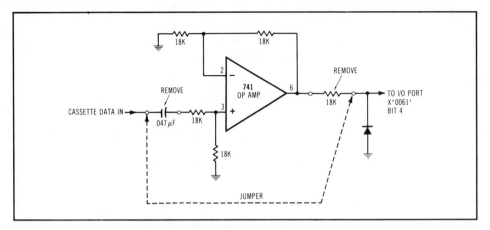

Fig. 18-3. Cassette input circuit modified to accept TTL levels.

both the 0.047 μF capacitor and the 18K resistor that are in series with the output from the op amp and place a jumper wire from the input side of the 0.047 μF capacitor to the cathode of the diode. A high level at the input of the connector will produce a 1 at the input to the port bit.

A digital output-port bit of the 8255A-5 device also controls the motor relay on the cassette interface port. Writing a zero to bit 3 of I/O port address hex 0061 will activate and close the contacts of the relay. However, the relay points are capable of handling approximately 1 ampere of current and voltages which are no higher than 50 volts. Do not use the relay to switch large dc currents, since arcing will disturb the operation of the system and cause it to fail.

INTERFACING WITH THE PARALLEL PRINTER PORT CARD

The parallel-printer adapter card can be used as a general-purpose set of digital input and output points for interfacing other devices. This card provides an 8-bit digital output register that can also be read, a 4-bit output register that can be read and changed to an input register, a 5-bit input register, and an output register bit that can be enabled to generate an interrupt on level 7. The card is designed so that its address can be modified such that it will not conflict with another printer port card in the system. All of the input/output port bits are available for interfacing on a 25-pin D-type connector at the back of the card.

Address Modification

The parallel-printer port card normally decodes the I/O port hex addresses 0378, 0379, and 037A. The card is designed to be easily modified such that the port addresses are moved to hex addresses 0278, 0279, and 027A. Inspection of the card and the circuit diagram, provided in the *IBM Technical Reference Manual*, will reveal that by deleting a single signal trace, the address modification can be implemented. There is a location for two jumper pins, called J1, that is identified on the card. When the signal trace is deleted between these two pin positions, the new addresses are decoded.

An 8-Bit Output Port

At hex address 0378, or 0278 on a modified card, there exists an 8-bit digital output register. The output of this register is connected to the connector pins, as defined in Fig. 18-4. Thus, an OUT instruction to these port addresses can write data directly to the connector pins. A 1-bit written to the port will result in a high TTL level at the connector pin. The output of the digital output register, and the state of the connector pins that it is connected to, can be read through a digital input register at the same port addresses. The purpose of the input register is to verify that the digital output register was loaded properly. A simple modification on the card can convert this output port to an input port. Removing the ground connection on the U4 component (an SN74LS373) pin 1, and tying this pin to +5 volts, will disable the output function of this port and will allow it to be used as an input port.

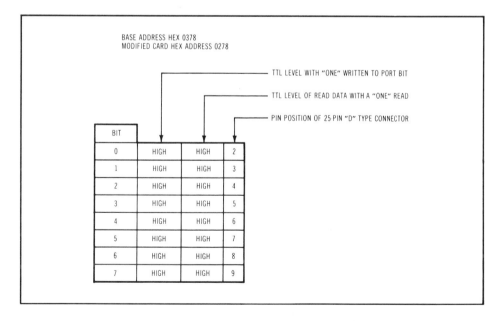

Fig. 18-4. A printer-port 8-bit output port.

A 4-Bit Input/Output Port

At hex address 037A, or 027A on a modified card, there exists a 5-bit digital output register. Four of the output bits are wired to the 25-pin D-type connector. The fifth bit is used to enable and disable interrupt requests on level 7. The output of the digital output register, and the connector pins that it is attached to, can be read by issuing an IN command to the same port address. Fig. 18-5 defines the register-bit active levels and the connector pins that they are attached to. Since the four output bits that are attached to the connector pins are driven with open-collector drivers, it is possible to use these points as input bits. If the output register is set to a value that produces a high TTL logic level at the connector pins, the outputs may be dotted low by incoming signals on these pins. Thus, an external driving circuit can control the level of these pins and, by using the input portion of this register, their states can be sensed. Thus, by programming the output bits to a high level, they can be used as input port bits.

A 5-Bit Input Port

At hex address 037B, or 027B on a modified card, there exists a 5-bit digital input register. Fig. 18-6 defines the active signal levels and the connector-pin assignments for this register. Bit 7 of this register can be used to create an interrupt on level 7, if it is enabled by the port bit in the 5-bit input/output register port.

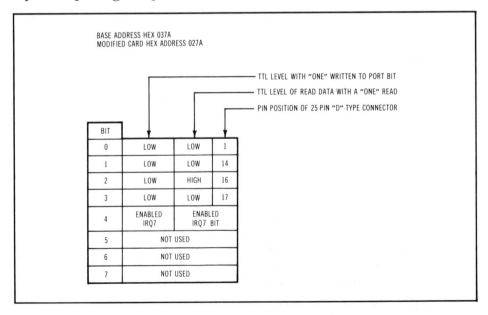

Fig. 18-5. A printer-port 4-bit input/output port.

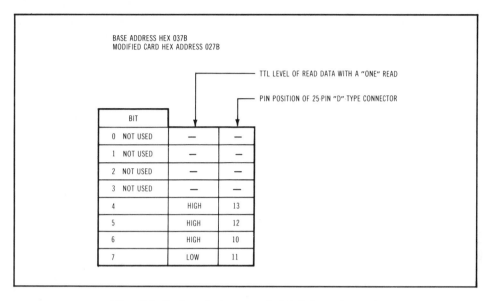

Fig. 18-6. A printer-port 4-bit input port.

INTERFACING WITH THE GAME CONTROL CARD

The game control card is designed to connect joysticks and game paddles to the PC, but there is no reason that its functions cannot be used to interface other devices to the PC. This card is an input-only device. It provides four digital input points and four resistance-sensing input points. These points are typically used to sense the trigger-buttons and joystick-potentiometer positions. This card is decoded at hex address 0201. An OUT instruction, with any data, will fire four one-shot circuit devices. The outputs of the one-shot devices can be read using an IN instruction at hex address 201. This register also contains the four trigger inputs from the connector. The outputs of the one-shot circuits are determined by an RC time-constant circuit that is attached to each one-shot device. The resistive portion of the time-constant value is added by the user's interface. Thus, by measuring the length of the one-shot output and knowing the capacitive value of the circuit, it is possible to determine the value of the resistance attached to the input. The resistive element must be attached to +5 volts for the circuit to operate properly. Thus, any external condition that can be represented as a resistive value can be sensed and read using this circuit. In the case of a joystick, the resistance represents the position of the joystick. Fig. 18-7 defines the address and bit map of the card and it shows the level and connector pin positions that correspond to each port bit.

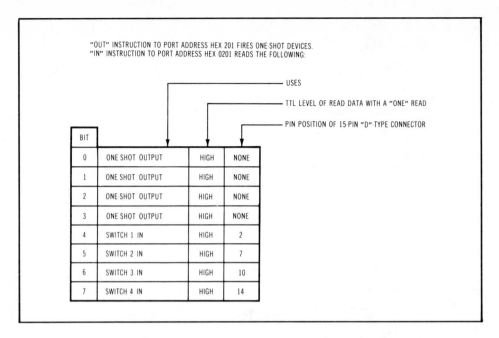

Fig. 18-7. Game control-adapter input port.

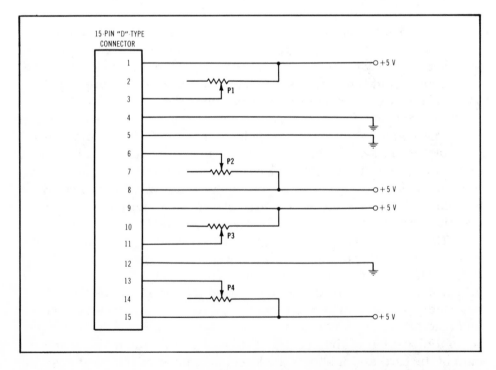

Fig. 18-8. Resistor connections to the game port card connector.

The relationship of the one-shot output pulse length and the external resistance is defined by the following equation.

$$Time = 24.2 + 0.011(Resistance)$$

This equation gives the time in microseconds. It should be noted that this will only give an approximate value in a range of resistive values from 0 to 100,000 ohms. If the cable length to the resistive value is long, extra capacitance and resistance will be added to the circuit, changing the time constant. The sample rate obtained using this circuit is dependent on the maximum resistive value being measured. The larger the resistance, the longer the time. It should also be pointed out that the one-shot circuits cannot be fired individually, but are all fired at once. Fig. 18-8 illustrates how an external resistive value should be connected to the connector pin so that the value can be measured.

CHAPTER 19

INTERFACE SIGNAL CONDITIONING

INTRODUCTION

The normal interfaces that are designed and available to control and sense information from the PC are, in general, digital in nature. For example, some typical interfaces that are generated in a design are digital input and output registers, interrupt-request inputs, timing and counting functions, and DMA data-transfer ports. All of these interfaces are digital in nature and, also, present a TTL logic-level interface. If the devices that you are interfacing with are other electronic-type equipment with digital interfaces, attachment may be straightforward. In many cases, the interface that needs to be sensed and controlled is not digital. In other cases, the signals may be digital but they are not at TTL logic levels. Sometimes the digital signals must interface at great distances, creating special problems. In this chapter, we will investigate some of the more common interfacing problems and will present some specific signal-conditioning circuits.

AN RS-232-C INTERFACE

RS-232-C refers to a very old and popular standard that is typically used to attach data-processing equipment to data communication equipment. For example, the terminals to modems. The RS-232-C standard covers the mechanical, electrical, and functional characteristics of the interface. Many intersecting devices use this interface as an attachment method. Devices such as terminals, plotters, logic analyzers, tape drives, and printers will typically have an RS-232-C interface. If your interfacing application is to attach a device to an RS-232-C interface, it will be necessary to convert the TTL logic-level signal to the nonTTL interface required by this standard. A good example of the use of this interface can be obtained by an inspection of the IBM PC serial-interface feature card. The circuit schematic and functional description is presented in the *IBM System Reference Manual.*

Interface Signal Characteristics

The RS-232-C signal lines provide for one-way data transmission on single-ended lines for distances up to 50 feet, at a maximum data rate of 20 kilobits per second. For a signal to be considered a positive "one" level, it must exceed 5 volts but not over 15 volts. A negative or zero-level signal must exceed −5 volts and not exceed −15 volts.

Level Conversion Circuit

Fig. 19-1 is an example of a circuit that can be used to convert TTL logic-level signals to RS-232-C levels and RS-232-C levels to TTL logic levels.

AN RS-423 INTERFACE

The RS-423 standard interface is an improved version of the RS-232-C interface standard. Many newer devices support this interface, particularly devices that have high data-transmission rate requirements.

Interface Signal Characteristics

The RS-423 standard provides for one-way single-ended data transmission at up to 100 kilobits per second at distances up to 40 feet. The receiver is a balanced-line receiver and, thus, permits a ground potential difference between the driver and receiver. A logical "one" state must exceed 4 volts and must not exceed 6 volts. A logic "zero" must exceed −4 volts and must not exceed −6 volts.

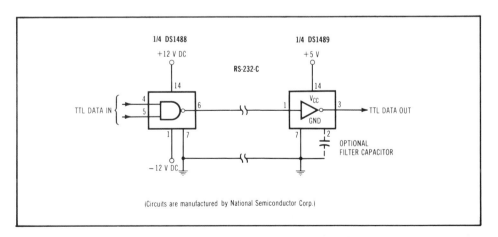

Fig. 19-1. An RS-232-C driver and receiver circuit.

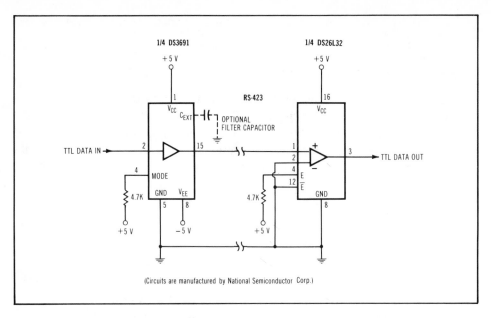

Fig. 19-2. An RS-423 driver and receiver circuit.

RS-423 Signal-Level Conversion

Fig. 19-2 is an example of a circuit that can be used to convert TTL signals to an RS-423 interface and, also, convert a RS-423 interface to TTL signals.

AN RS-422 INTERFACE

The RS-422 standard is a further improvement in the RS-423 standard, permitting even higher data rates and a much greater distance between transmitter and receiver.

Interface Signal Characteristics

The RS-422 standard provides for one-way balanced-line transmission at data rates up to 10 megabits per second at distances up to 1000 feet. Lower data rates will permit data transmission at distances of up to 4000 feet. The interface permits driver outputs of ±2 to 6 volts and the receiver will detect input signals as low as 200 millivolts.

RS-422 Signal Conversion

Fig. 19-3 is an example of a circuit that can be used to convert TTL signals to an RS-422 interface and convert an RS-422 interface to TTL

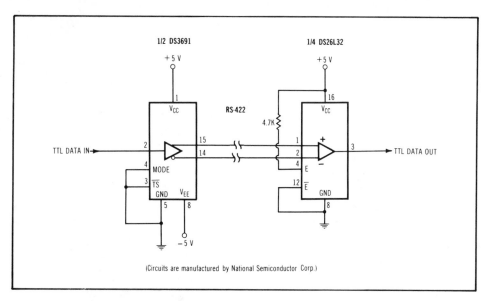

Fig. 19-3. An RS-422 driver and receiver circuit.

signals. Several manufacturers provide a tri-state control on the driver circuit that permits data to be transmitted bidirectionally on a single pair of interface lines. This facility also enables a multidrop capability, where several devices can receive and transmit data on a single pair of interface lines in a half-duplex mode.

CURRENT-LOOP DATA TRANSMISSION

Another often-used transmission scheme that will permit data to be transmitted over great distances is the current loop. With a current loop, the voltage levels are converted to currents in a closed-loop circuit. Since current-mode circuits are low-impedence circuits, they are less sensitive to noise and are often used to transmit signal in noisy environments. It is also possible to provide ground isolation between two different systems by using a current-loop scheme. Fig. 19-4 is an example of an isolated current-loop transmitter and receiver circuit. This circuit can be used to transmit data at rates of up to 50 kilobits per second for a distance of up to 3000 feet. The distance is limited by the resistance of the loop wire. In this design, the loop resistance should not exceed 30 ohms.

The use of the optical isolator is not limited to application in just this circuit. This scheme can be used at any time that it is necessary to obtain power isolation between systems or circuits that do not share the same ground or power system.

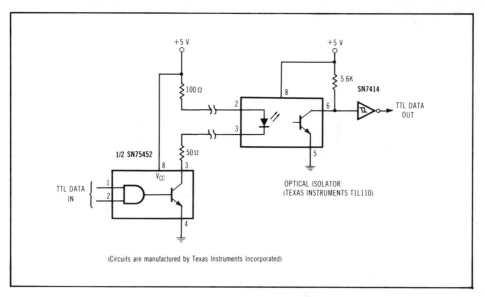

Fig. 19-4. A current-loop circuit.

SWITCH SENSING

Often an interface design requires that switches be interfaced and sensed. They could be switches used to indicate a movement, such as a limit switch, or they could operator-controlled panel switches which indicate an action should be performed by the system. A switch can be easily made to emit TTL signals for direct attachment to normal TTL-circuit input. Fig. 19-5 is an example of a switch that, when open, will provide a 5-volt level to the circuit and, when closed, will present a ground level to the TTL input.

The most common problem with switch interfacing is that of switch bounce. When a mechanical switch is opened or closed, the contacts bounce and emit a burst of noise that the sensing circuits may interpret as a rapid opening and closing of the switch. There are several solutions to this type of problem. A commonly used solution is to sample the state of a switch several times to determine that it has reached a final state. This approach will work if the system has time to dedicate to a software sampling algorithm. A simple hardware solution can be obtained if the switch presents both a normally open contact and a normally closed contact. Fig. 19-6 is an illustration of a circuit for a switch that will not exhibit switch bounce. In this circuit, when the switch is activated, the first bounce that is detected sets a latch, thus eliminating bounce on the activation. Similarly, the latch is reset on the first bounce of the deactivation, and, thus, is cleanly reset. This circuit only works with switches that have both nor-

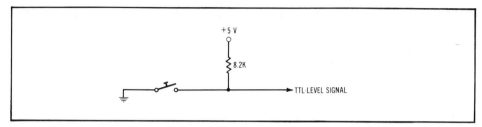

Fig. 19-5. A switch to a TTL signal levels circuit.

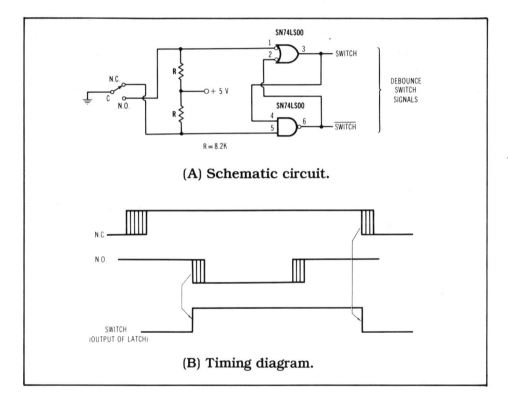

(A) Schematic circuit.

(B) Timing diagram.

Fig. 19-6. A switch debounce circuit.

mally open and normally closed contacts and which break the normally closed contact before the normally open contact is made. The timing chart in Fig. 19-6B illustrates the principle.

INDICATOR DRIVING

It is often necessary to present a visual indication of an event on an interface. It may be necessary to notify an operator that intervention is required or to simply determine the status of a process. The following are a few examples of how TTL signals can be conditioned to drive some popular indicator types.

For low-level light output, light-emitting diodes (LEDs) provide an easy to implement solution. Several manufacturers provide LEDs that can be driven directly from standard TTL or S-type (Schottky) devices. Normally, LS-type devices will not have sufficient drive to operate an LED. Also, care should be taken to not attach the LEDs to NMOS LSI devices since they normally do not have sufficient drive to operate an LED. Once an LED is tied to a TTL output, the output should not be used to drive other circuits. The LED will clamp the output at a nonvalid logic level and will cause improper circuit operation. Thus, all signals that need to be sensed with an indicator should be buffered with a driving circuit. Fig. 19-7 is an example of an LED and a circuit that can be driven from any TTL source.

When brighter indicators are required, an incandescent lamp can be used. Lamps of this type will require much higher current and a special driver circuit must be used. Fig. 19-8 illustrates a lamp and circuit that can be driven from TTL signals.

When the information that needs to be displayed is numeric data or hexadecimal characters, special display devices are needed. Several manufacturers provide dip-type display devices that can be driven directly from a TTL source and can decode and display numeric or hex data directly from encoded TTL signals.

RELAY DRIVING

When an interface design needs to operate relays or solenoids, which in turn control higher power levels, special circuits are normally required. These devices typically cannot be directly driven from TTL signals. The current required to operate a relay or a solenoid may be much more than can be provided by normal TTL circuits. In addition, the driving circuit usually requires special protection from the inductive kickback of the relay

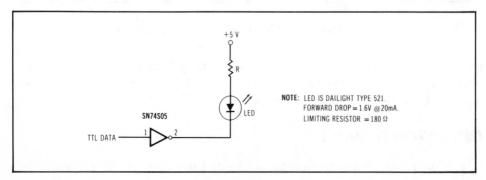

Fig. 19-7. An LED driver circuit.

or solenoid coils. The SN75475 dual peripheral-driver device manufactured by Texas Instruments Incorporated can be used to operate a wide variety of relays and solenoids. This device can provide 300 milliamperes drive from voltages as high as 100 volts. In addition, it can be driven from a standard TTL circuit and it provides an output clamp diode for transient suppression from inductive loads. Fig. 19-9 illustrates how this circuit can be used to drive a relay.

STEPPER MOTORS

Many times, an interface application will require that the PC will control motion or have the capability to move an object. A device that is often used to power or move a shaft in precise increments, direction, and speeds is a stepper motor. When a stepper motor is given the proper sequence of input commands, it is capable of very accurate repeatable movements. Depending on the cost and design of a stepper motor, it can have as many as 200 step increments per revolution and as few as 12 steps per revolution. Stepper motors are manufactured in a wide range of torque capability and physical sizes.

There are several types of stepper motors available. Each has its advantages and disadvantages.

Permanent-Magnet Stepping Motor

This motor operates by having a set of permanent magnets attached to the rotor of the motor. A set of windings can be energized on the stator

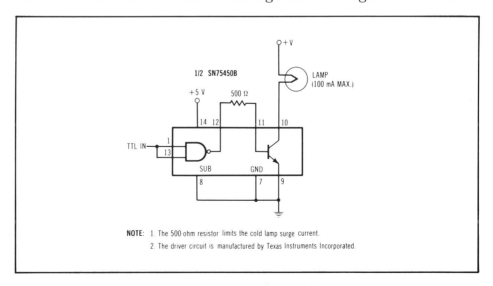

Fig. 19-8. A high-current lamp driver circuit.

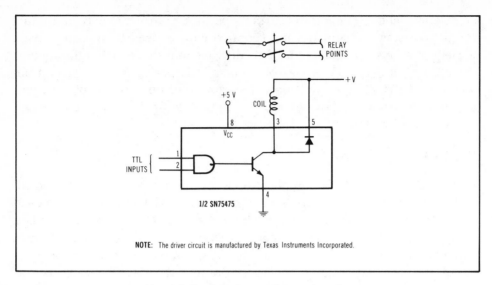

Fig. 19-9. A relay driver circuit.

portion of the motor. Thus, the north and south poles of the permanent magnet on the rotor will rotate to a position where the north and south poles of the stator and rotor line up, since unlike poles attract. Rotation is achieved by energizing adjacent sets of stator windings and by reversing the currents in other windings. The rotor will then move to the new position where the unlike poles can line up. By properly energizing and reversing the currents in the stator windings, a continuous rotation of the shaft can be obtained. The major disadvantage of this type of stepper motor is the requirement of reversing the currents in the stator windings. This, typically, will require a power supply with both a positive and a negative output, or relatively complex drive circuits. The major advantages are low cost and the fact that when power is removed the shaft is held in its last position by the permanent magnet.

Bifilar Stepping Motor

This type of motor operates similar to the permanent magnet motor. The major difference is in the design of the stator pole windings. Each stator pole position has two windings. With this design, a stator pole may be either a north or south pole depending on which winding is energized. The major advantage of this type of motor is its ability to operate from a single-output dc power supply. This motor also has a permanent magnet rotor and, thus, will stay in the last position stepped to when power is removed.

Variable-Reluctance Stepping Motor

This type of stepping motor does not use a permanent magnet in the rotor. The rotor is moved by the magnetic attraction of the rotor to the energized poles of the stator. Since there is no permanent magnet, this type of stepper motor will not hold the shaft in the last stepped position. Thus, to maintain a fixed position, the driving circuits must maintain power to the appropriate poles of the motor.

Pulse Step Motor

Some stepping motors are designed such that the stepping phase control and the winding coil drivers are part of the motor. To step the motor one position, a single TTL pulse can be sent to the motor for each step. Increasing and decreasing the pulse rate to the motor will accelerate and deaccelerate the motor.

Manufacturers of Stepper Motors

The following is a brief list of the manufacturers of stepper motors. In most cases, the manufacturers will provide data sheets on the motor describing the drivers and control sequences that are required for proper operation of the motors.

1. Portescap U. S.
   Micromotor Division
   31 Fairfield Place
   West Caldwell, NJ 07006
2. Oriental Motor U.S.A. Corp.
   2701 Toledo Street
   Torrance, CA 90503
3. Airpax North American Philips Controles Corp.
   Cheshire Division
   Chershire Industrial Park
   Cheshire, CT 06410
4. Litton Clifton Precision
   Marple at Broadway
   Clifton Heights, PA 19018
5. Superior Electric
   1200 Middle Street
   Bristol, CT 06010

ANALOG-TO-DIGITAL CONVERSION

Much of the information concerning the state of an interface is represented as a voltage that is proportional to some external condition. Most transducers convert the condition that they are sensing into a current or voltage output. This voltage or current cannot be sensed with digital signals. To perform the transformation of a voltage or current level into a digital value, a device called an analog-to-digital converter (ADC) is used. These devices have made rapid advancements in the past few years and are now highly integrated devices. Many of the ADCs now incorporate a precision voltage reference, an analog multiplexer, and a microprocessor bus port.

There are several characteristics of ADCs that should be considered when selecting one for an interfacing application.

1. *What is the input range of the device?* This specification is of concern for two reasons. First, it will determine if you can attach the input directly to your source. In general, this will not be the case since the source may produce a voltage level that is too large or small to be directly sensed. If the input level is too small, you will have to amplify the signal using a positive-gain op amp. If the input signal is too large, a simple precision resistor-divider network can be added. Secondly, to determine the minimum value that can be measured, you can divide the range by the resolution. For example, if the input you want to measure is 0 to 5 volts, and the device has 8 bits of resolution, the minimal measurable value is 5 divided by 256, or 0.0195 volt.

2. *Can it measure differential, positive, and negative voltages?* This may be important; particularly, if the transducer output is not referenced to a known ground or it outputs either negative or positive and negative voltages.

3. *Does it contain a precision voltage reference for calibration?* Most conversion techniques require a precision voltage reference. If it is not part of the device, it will have to be added as a separate component, thus adding to cost and taking up card space.

4. *What is the offset error introduced by the analog system?* If the voltage level you are trying to measure is small, the offset error will be of concern. The offset error must be much smaller than the smallest voltage to be measured. Many devices provide mechanisms for correction of the offset error.

5. *What kind of load does it present to the source that it will be sensing?* You must ensure that the device does not overload the source and alter the true value being measured. If this is the case, you can add a unity-gain operational amplifier with high-input impedance to buffer the input to the device. Note that this can introduce an additional offset error in the system.

6. *How many bits of resolution can it provide over the input range?* As pointed out in Item 1, the number of bits of resolution will determine the minimum value that can be measured by the system. An 8-

bit device, for example, will measure 256 levels while a 12-bit device will be able to measure 4096 levels over the range of the input.

7. *How is the digital data presented to the system?* This may be important for two reasons. First, if the device provides a microprocessor bus port, it will be easy to attach to the PC. Secondly, if it is difficult to obtain the data from the device, this will have an adverse effect on the minimum sample rate that can be achieved from the system. Even if the conversion rate is very fast, but it takes a complicated set of steps to retrieve the data, the total performance of the system is affected. Note that the sample rate is the sum of both steps. Thus, to maintain a high sample rate for the system, the data access method must be simple and fast.

8. *How long does it take the device to convert an analog signal to a digital value?* This specification is important since it will determine the rate at which the device can sample and convert the analog data to a digital value. If a rapidly changing input is to be sensed, the conversion rate must be fast. Typically, the faster the conversion speed, the more expensive the device. It should be pointed out that some devices have a conversion speed that is dependent on the resolution desired or the magnitude of the input signal.

DIGITAL-TO-ANALOG CONVERSION

Many times, an interface design will require that the PC generate and control a voltage or a current source. This function is typically performed by a digital-to-analog converter device (DAC). These devices will typically accept a binary value from a system such as the PC and will generate an output voltage that is proportional to the digital input value. DACs have specifications similar to those of the ADCs. In general, the output of a DAC will not provide the voltage range or power required to actually drive a device. Thus, DACs are usually interfaced with some type of amplifier that will provide the voltage gain and the output power needed in the design. DACs are now available that include a microprocessor port for control and precision voltage-reference sources.

MANUFACTURERS OF DAC AND ADC DEVICES

Most large semiconductor manufacturers provide a wide range of ADCs and DACs. These manufacturers provide detailed data sheets on their devices and, in many cases, provide application notes on how they can be attached to microprocessors and used. The following is a brief list of manufacturers of these devices and some of the more popular devices provided by each.

1. National Semiconductor Corp.
    P.O. Box 60676
    Sunnyvale, CA 94088

    National Semiconductor provides a large range of devices and tranducers. In addition, information on these devices and their application notes are available by ordering the National Semiconductor *Data Acquisition Handbook*. Its present cost is $7.00.

2. Texas Instruments Incorporated
    Literature Response Center
    P.O. Box 202129
    Dallas, TX 75220

    Texas Instruments has recently introduced a family of low-cost 8-bit analog-to-digital converters. These devices are the TL530, TL531, TL532, and TL533. They are specifically designed for attachment to a microprocessor. They incorporate an analog multiplexer and, in some parts, digital input and output ports.

3. Motorola Semiconductor Products, Inc.
    Box 20912
    Phoenix, AZ 85036

    Motorola offers a large variety of ADCs and DACs that can be attached to a microprocessor. Some devices that are of particular interest are:

    A. The MC14435 low-power analog-to-digital converter. This device is a CMOS part with a multiplex BCD output. It supports $3\frac{1}{2}$ digits of resolution.
    B. The MC14431 12-bit analog-to-digital converter subsystem. This is a CMOS device.
    C. The MC14051B 8-channel analog multiplexer. This is a CMOS low-power device.

4. Analog Devices
    Norwood, MA 02062

    This company provides a family of DACs and ADCs. Some devices that may be of interest are:

    A. The AD571, a high-speed 10-bit analog-to-digital converter. This device contains a precision voltage reference and has a tri-state microprocessor-compatible output bus. The device can be configured to support a 10-volt input range.
    B. The AD558 is a digital-to-analog converter. It supports 8 bits of resolution at a maximum output voltage of 2.56 volts. The device supports a microprocessor input bus capability for setting the output levels.

CHAPTER 20

BASIC LANGUAGE COMMANDS FOR INTERFACING

INTRODUCTION

The BASIC language for the IBM PC has several commands and functions that are specifically designed to aid in interfacing hardware designed for the system bus. Many interfacing applications can be implemented using the BASIC language of the PC, which is much easier to program in than is the 8088 assembly language. A major concern when using BASIC is performance. The interpreter BASIC, in the PC's ROM, is relatively slow when compared to the same function implemented in assembly language. Even if there is a performance requirement that BASIC cannot handle, it may be possible to still use BASIC for most of the application programming and then use assembly language subroutines for the timing of critical portions. Another alternative that still allows the use of BASIC, and which has an improved performance, is to compile the BASIC program using the IBM Basic Compiler. A compiled program will typically run from 5 to 10 times faster than an interpretive version.

In this chapter, we will briefly discuss the commands and functions that could be useful in interfacing applications. For a detailed definition of these commands and functions, including proper syntax, the *IBM Personal Computer Hardware Reference Manual* on BASIC should be consulted.

COMMANDS FOR HARDWARE INTERFACING

BLOAD Command

This command will enable you to load a binary file from an open file, such as tape or diskette. It may, for example, be an assembly language program or data for a program. It can be loaded anywhere in available system memory. Care should be taken to not overlay BASIC or BASIC workspace.

BSAVE Command

This command is the complement of the BLOAD command. This command allows you to save binary data on any device that has an open file. Data anywhere in system memory may be saved. This command could, for example, be used to save raw data, collected from an interface, on a file for later analysis.

CLEAR Command

If your system is less that 96K bytes, this command can be used to reserve memory space at the top of memory for data or assembly language programs. If your system is greater that 96K bytes, there will be space available at the top of memory, since BASIC only allows a maximum workspace size of 64K bytes. If there is still not enough space, this command can be used to reduce the size of the BASIC workspace.

CALL Command

This command allows you to call an assembly language program or subroutine from BASIC. This command also allows you to pass data, arguments, or parameters defined as BASIC variables, from BASIC to the assembly language program.

DEF SEG Command

This command allows you to define the current segment value of system memory. It is typically used to define the starting memory address-segment value for other BASIC commands and functions that reference memory directly. It would, for example, be executed prior to the use of a BLOAD, BSAVE, CALL, VARPTR, USR, POKE, or PEEK type command.

DEF USR Command

This command is similar to the DEF SEG command in that it allows you to define the starting address in memory of a specific assembly language routine that will later be called by the USR function. The address set is, however, not the segment value, but the offset value from the segment-value set using the DEF SEG command.

POKE Command

This command allows data to be written to any specific system memory location from a BASIC program. The data may be a constant or a variable. This command should be preceded with a DEF SEG command to allow setting the correct segment address. The command specifies the offset portion of the address. This command can be used to place an assembly language subroutine in system memory, which can later be called by the CALL or USR command and function. It can also be used to write data to a memory-mapped I/O port from BASIC.

WAIT Command

This command can be used to sample an I/O port address and compare its value with a mask value. If the mask and I/O port values do not compare, the BASIC program is suspended until they do compare. This command is useful when you want the BASIC program to be synchronized with some external set of conditions. The compare used is not an arithmetic compare but a logical Exclusive-OR compare. Care should be used with this command since, if no compare is ever seen, the program will hang in an infinite loop.

OUT Command

This command allows data to be written to an I/O port address from a BASIC program. The data may be a constant of the contents of a BASIC variable. A single byte of data may be written to any of the 65,536 I/O port addresses supported by the 8088 architecture. With this command, many of the ports that control the modes of operation of the PC can be modified through BASIC.

BASIC LANGUAGE FUNCTIONS FOR HARDWARE INTERFACING

INP Function

This function is the complement of the OUT command. It allows an I/O port address to be read and its value assigned to a BASIC variable. Any of the 65,536 I/O port addresses supported by the 8088 architecture can be read using this command.

PEEK Function

This function is the complement of the PEEK command. It allows any memory location in the system to be read and its value assigned to a

BASIC variable. This function should be preceded by a DEF SEG command setting the proper segment value. The offset portion of the address is specified as part of the PEEK function.

USR Function

This function allows an assembly language subroutine to be called from BASIC by specifying a single digit. The results are assigned to a BASIC variable. This function can also specify a single argument for the assembly language program. This function should be preceded by the DEF SEG and DEF USR commands which specify the segment and offset address values that identify the location in memory of the specific assembly language routine.

VARPTR Function

This function can be used to find the memory location of a BASIC variable. The value is returned in a BASIC variable and it is the offset from the current value of the segment-register set using the DEF SEG command. This function is often used to locate the address of a BASIC variable so that it can be passed to an assembly language program or subroutine. Thus, assembly language programs may get and store data from a BASIC variable. This allows easy communication and exchanging of data and parameters between assembly language and BASIC language programs.

ASSEMBLY LANGUAGE SUBROUTINES IN BASIC

The ability to call assembly language subroutines from BASIC provides a powerful method of interfacing high-performance application requirements and yet maintain the ease of BASIC language programming. There are many things to consider when using assembly language subroutines. A simple mistake in an assembly language routine can easily cause the system to crash. Worse yet, some very intermittent and difficult bugs can be created, which can require hours to fix. The subject of assembly language subroutines, using the CALL command and the USR function, are covered in great detail in Appendix C of the *IBM Basic Reference Manual*. It is suggested that this section be studied carefully before attempting to use this capability.

CHAPTER 21

BUS EXTENSION

INTRODUCTION

The PC is designed with five system-bus card slots. Even in a minimum diskette-based system, two are used: one for the display adapter and one for the diskette adapter. The remaining three slots can be used up quickly. Just by adding three commonly used features; i.e., a serial port, a printer port, and extra memory. Since PC system-bus card slots are so scarce, a good design project would be to devise a method of extending the system-bus outside the System Unit so that additional card slots could be provided. Bus extension will also be of interest if your interface design will not fit on a PC card. Bus extension will allow you to escape to another enclosure that is not as limited in space or power.

This chapter investigates two designs that can be used to extend the PC's system bus. The first design is the simplest but it has some limitations. This design can be safely used to extend the system bus approximately 3 feet and drive 4 card slots. Thus, if a modest increase in the number of system-bus card slots is required, this method is recommended. The second design is more complex but it has the advantage of driving an 8-foot interface between the System Unit and the extended card slots and it can support up to 10 additional card slots. Also included in this chapter are some techniques that could be useful in bus conversion designs, such as a PC bus to S-100 bus.

A SIMPLE BUS EXTENDER DESIGN

We will cover the simple design first and, then, alter it to the higher function design.

The Basic Concept

This design involves two parts. First, there is a card that fits in one of the System Unit's card slots and drives and receives the bus from the extended card slots. Next, there is a card that receives and drives the output of the System Unit card and contains the new card slots. Fig. 21-1 illustrates the components and the concept of the design.

Most of the signals on the PC bus can be handled quite simply. The basic concept is to repower and drive output signals from the bus onto the cable. The drive circuit's primary function is to shunt the capacitance of the cable

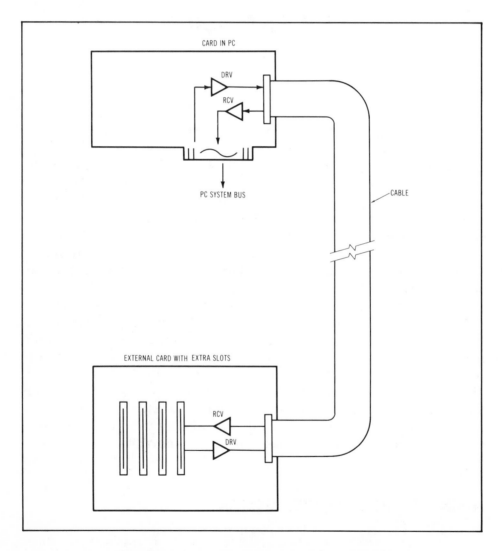

Fig. 21-1. A bus extender circuit concept.

such that it is not reflected on the system bus and, thus, add delay and signal distortion to the System Unit's bus. At the other end of the cable, on the new slot card, the signal is received and repowered again to drive the extra slots. Similarly, the receiver circuit shunts the capacitance of the cable from the new card slots providing a quiet bus for attaching feature cards in the new slots. Input signals from the extra card slots are similarly treated; that is, repowered and driven into the cable and received and repowered and driven onto the system bus. Several circuits could be used to perform the bus repower function, but suitable devices are the SN74S240 and SN74LS240 octal buffers and line drivers manufactured by Texas Instruments. Similar devices are manufactured by several other companies. These two circuits are identical except for the signal delay and power consumption.

The SN74S240 has a typical signal delay of 4.5 nanoseconds and a maximum delay of 7 nanoseconds. The SN74LS240 has a typical delay of 12 nanoseconds and a maximum delay of 18 nanoseconds. Both circuits are used, the SN74S240 on signals that cannot tolerate much delay and the SN74LS240 on signals that are less timing dependent.

Obviously, since signals are repowered twice in this design, the bus cycle appears in the extended bus card slots to be delayed. This delay is on the order of 10 to 15 nanoseconds. This means that memory and I/O port-address to data-access times are shortened by this amount. Since this delay is small, in most cases, it will have no effect. There is typically a wide margin designed into the feature cards. Fig. 21-2 is a block diagram of the signals being repowered.

The scheme shown in Fig. 21-2 works well for everything except the system data bus. These 8 signal lines are bidirectional. At first glance, it would appear that a simple solution is to insert a bus transceiver circuit, such as the octal bus transceiver SN74LS245 (manufactured by Texas Instruments). A problem arises when signals are required to control the transceiver. Both an enable and a direction signal are required. The bus

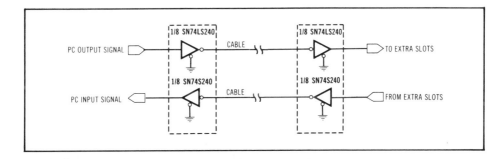

Fig. 21-2. A typical driver and receiver circuit for bus extension.

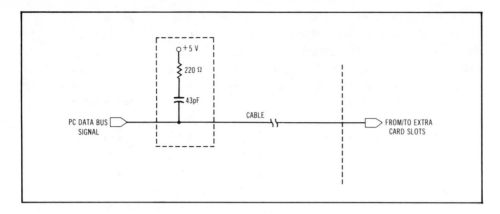

Fig. 21-3. Data bus terminator.

transceiver is normally enabled by an address decode and its direction is controlled by either the IOR or MEMR bus-control signals. Since we have no idea what memory or I/O addresses will be used in the extra bus slots, we cannot generate an enable control signal for the transceiver that will work under all conditions. Since this is a simple design, the solution to this problem is to simply not repower the data-bus lines. The system data-bus signals have sufficient drive to drive the extended card slots as long as there are just a few of them.

The major problem is the exta bus capacitance that is added by the cable and the extra card slots. This extra capacitance has several effects, none of which are good. First, it delays the data-bus signals and, secondly, it distorts the signal by creating signal undershoot. To help minimize these problems, a termination circuit can be added to the data bus. The termination circuit is illustrated in Fig. 21-3. This circuit consists of a 220-ohm resistor in series with a 43-picofarad capacitor. One end is tied to the bus line and the other end is tied to +5 volts. Since the capacitor acts as an open to the steady-state conditions of the bus line, the 220-ohm resistor is not tied to the line, except during signal transitions. When the line begins a transition from high to low, the capacitor attaches the load resistor to the circuit and, thus, lowers its impedance. Thus, the charge stored in the capacitance of the system is dissipated in the lower-impedance circuit and reduces the effect of the undershoot.

Figs. 21-4 and 21-5 are two circuit schematics of a simple bus-extender design that is capable of driving a 3-foot cable and 4 card slots.

Note that this design assumes that power for the new card slots comes from the System Unit. If the new feature cards take a reasonable amount of power, you should not have any difficulty in driving them from the System Unit's power supply. All System Unit power levels are available in the Sys-

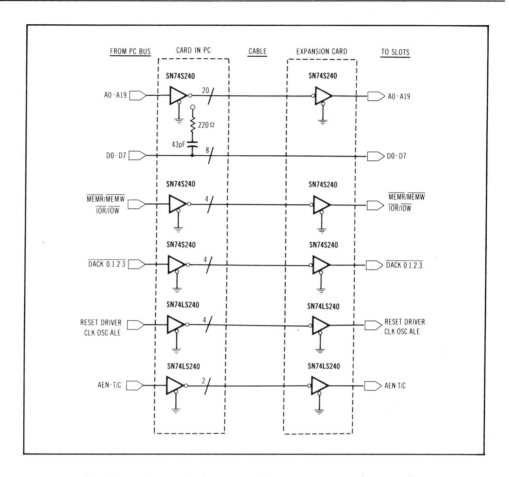

Fig. 21-4. Output signals of the bus extension design.

tem Unit's data-bus card slots and can easily be cabled to the new card slots. Care should be taken to use heavy gauge wire and/or multiple wires in cabling the power and ground signals to the extra card slots. In addition, the power levels should be decoupled as shown in the circuit diagram.

When wiring the signals through the connector and cable, it is recommended that a separate ground lead be provided for each signal. If possible, the ground lead should be placed next to each signal. An even better solution is to use a cable that has twisted-pair wire for the signals and run a signal on one of the pair and a ground on the other signal pair.

EXTENDED DESIGN

If you are not happy with the limitations of the first design, then the following modifications will be of interest. This design will enable a longer cable (up to 8 feet in length) and can drive up to 10 extra card slots.

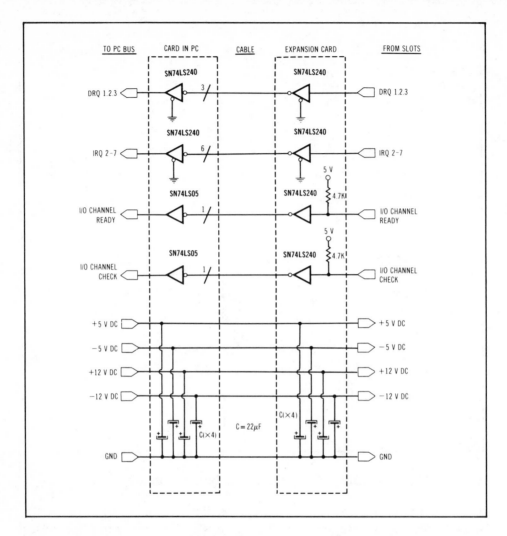

Fig. 21-5. Input signal and power bus extension design.

The major problem to solve is the capacitance and signal distortion that is created by the cable. For all of the unidirectional signals in bus, the design described earlier is sufficient when one small change is made. To reduce the effect of signal undershoot, a small series resistor can be placed in the signal lines. A value of 270 ohms will work for all lines. The 270-ohm resistor should be placed in the driving end of the signal. Fig. 21-6 illustrates how these signals are driven and received with the damping resistor. Since the maximum input low-level current of the drivers is 200 microamperes and the series resistance is 270 ohms, the low-level signal is lifted off ground by 54 millivolts. This is not sufficient to cause a problem at the receiver since it has a low-level margin of 800 millivolts before it switches.

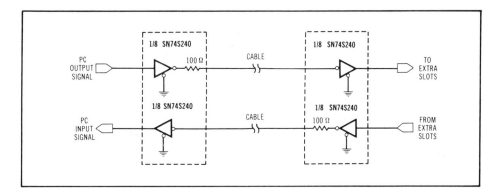

Fig. 21-6. A driver/receiver circuit modified for greater distance.

The data bus needs to be repowered in this design, since the cable and the number of extra card slots would add too much capacitance to ensure reliable operation. Fig. 21-7 illustrates the design used to repower the system data bus. Only one line is shown as all 8 signals require the same circuit. The basic principle of this circuit is to sense that data from the expansion-interface card slots are being transmitted and to allow the data to drive the bus only if the data are sensed on the other side of the circuit

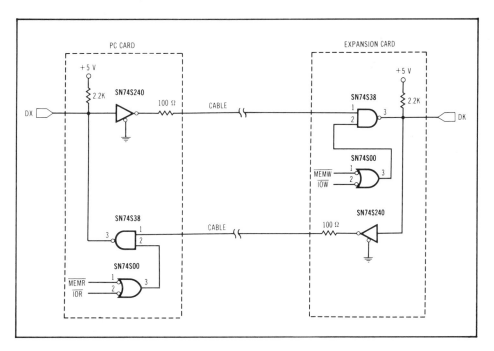

Fig. 21-7. A circuit for repowering the data bus.

and it is a read operation. Similarly, data are only transmitted if it is a write operation. The circuit does double the number of data lines from 8 to 16; thus, the cable is larger. The data-bus lines are also delayed in both directions. The maximum circuit delay is 7 nanoseconds for the SN74S240 and 10 nanoseconds for the SN74S38 open-collector buffer driver. This gives a total of 17 nanoseconds, but at least another 10 nanoseconds should be added due to the capacitance of the cable. This circuit also uses a damping resistor in series with the signal lines. In this case, the value is reduced to 100 ohms since the SN74S38 has only 400 millivolts of margin before it will switch. The only problem that you may encounter with this circuit is the tighter access-time requirements caused by the loss of approximately 27 nanoseconds due to circuit and cable delay. Most feature cards have more than sufficient margin in their design so that this should not be a problem. If this does become a problem, a simple solution is to swap the card with one in the System Unit.

Another interesting characteristic of the last data-bus repowering circuit is that it generates a split data bus. It is a circuit with a data-bus in and a separate data-bus out. This could be a useful function if one is interested in converting the PC data bus into a S-100 bus, since the S-100 bus requires a separate data bus in and out.

CHAPTER 22

HARDWARE AND SOFTWARE FOR TESTING DESIGNS

INTRODUCTION

After a design is completed and then built, it will require testing or debugging. Very rarely does a design operate correctly the first time it is tried. This is particularly true if the design has a great deal of complexity. The opportunities for errors are great, from simple wiring errors, improperly assigned component pins, and circuit loading and timing problems to a faulty design concept. In this chapter, we will discuss some hardware-support circuit designs and the software that will aid you in inspecting and verifying the proper operation of your designs.

Two subjects are covered in this chapter in support of design testing and debugging. First, a smart card-extender design is presented. This design allows detection of all types of bus cycles directed at specific port or memory locations. It displays data written or read from any specified port address or memory location and it generates an oscilloscope sync signal based on bus and external specified conditions. Secondly, the functions and capabilities of the IBM DEBUG monitor that is supplied with IBM DOS are summarized.

SMART CARD-EXTENDER DESIGN

Functional Description

Card extenders are used to extend the bus in a System Unit card slot above the rest of the cards in the unit. The card that is being debugged is then inserted into the top of the extender card so that it is now above the rest of the cards and is easy to access for inspection and signal probing.

Typically, there is no circuitry on an extender card; the bus signals are simply bused to the connector at the top of the card where the card under test is inserted. By adding a small amount of circuitry on an extender card, a powerful debug aid can be created. This is relatively simple to do, since all of the system-bus signals are already available on the extender card.

The circuitry can be used to detect the type of bus cycles being issued by the 8088 or DMA controller. Further, it can be used to determine if the bus cycle is directed to any specific port or memory location and can trap and display the data on the bus associated with the specific bus cycle. This can be done on the fly without affecting the normal performance or operation of the software or hardware being debugged. This function can be used to determine if the software is actually accessing the ports or memory locations that it should. When a specific set of conditions on the bus and the interface are detected, the circuitry will issue a sync pulse that can be used to trigger an oscilloscope. Thus, sync signals can be generated on both hardware and software conditions to aid in debugging. The sync signal will also set a latch and an indicator signaling the event has occurred. This type of circuitry is extremely useful when a circuit design will only operate correctly at full speed and cannot be easily traced or single-stepped under program control. The circuit is designed such that the compare conditions can be set either with dip switches or through programmable digital output-port bits.

Fig. 22-1 is a block diagram of the circuitry used to implement the smart extender-card function. The heart of the design is a 32-bit compare circuit. This circuit compares the state of 32 input signals against the state of either a set of 32 dip switches or the output of 32 bits of digital output registers. If the state of the two sides of the comparator are the same, an output pulse equal to the minimum duration of the compare time is issued. The following signals are fed to the signal input side of the compare circuit.

A0–A19	Bus Address Bits
IOW	Bus I/O Write Signal
IOR	Bus I/O Read Signal
MEMW	Bus Memory Write Signal
MEMR	Bus Memory Read Signal
EXT 1	External Signal 1
EXT 2	External Signal 2
EXT 3	External Signal 3
EXT 4	External Signal 4
DACK0	Bus Signal DMA Acknowledge Channel 0
DACK1	Bus Signal DMA Acknowledge Channel 1
DACK2	Bus Signal DMA Acknowledge Channel 2
DACK3	Bus Signal DMA Acknowledge Channel 3

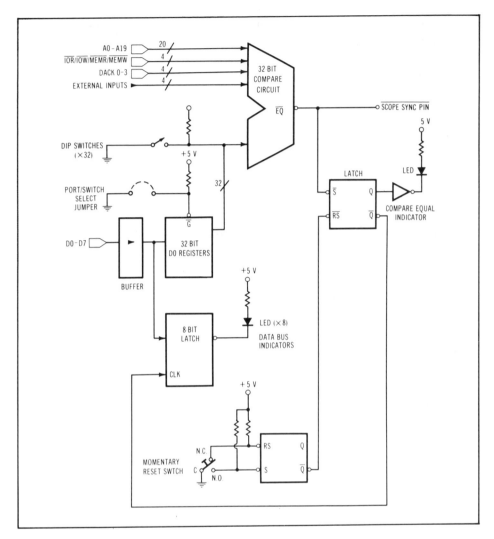

Fig. 22-1. Block diagram of the smart card-extender circuits.

Corresponding to each of the preceding signals, there is a switch or digital output-register (DO) bit fed into the other side of the compare circuit. Thus, by the proper setting of the switches or the digital output-register bits, a compare will only occur when the signals equal exactly the value in the switches or the DO bits. Thus, by setting the switches or the DO registers, it is possible to specify that a sync signal only be generated on a specific set of bus conditions and the state of four external conditions. To select between the use of the switches or the programmable DO register, a simple jumper is either removed or added. The output of the compare circuit is fed to a sync pin on the card and is also used to set a latch. The latch then drives a LED indicator. The latch and indicator can be reset by activating a momentary push-button switch. This function provides a visual indication, without the need of an oscilloscope, that a specific set of conditions did actually occur.

As an example of how this circuit may be used, let us say we wanted to examine the operation of a design, with an oscilloscope, when a DMA cycle (on Channel 3) occurred that reads data from a specific memory location and which was further conditioned, by an external signal attached to external input number 1. To do this, a sync signal is required. First, it would be necessary to set the address of the memory location of interest in the dip switches or DO port register bits. Next, the switch corresponding to DACK3 would be set to its active state. Since it is a DMA cycle with a memory read and write to I/O, the MEMR and IOW dip switches (or DO bits) are set active. To include the external signal in the sync condition, its proper level is set in the dip switch or DO bit that corresponds to external input number 1. The remaining external inputs are pulled high by the pull-up resistors. The dip switches or DO register bits corresponding to these inputs are set high. All other switches or DO bits are set inactive. The circuit will now generate a sync pulse each time the set conditions are detected. Further, the latch and indicator will be set the first time the condition appears. To determine if the condition is looping or repetitive, press the reset button. If the indicator comes on again or does not go out, the condition is being repeated.

Another feature of this circuit is the ability to capture data on the system data bus on the back edge of the sync pulse and display the bus data in the LED indicators. The back edge of the sync signal is used because the MEMR, MEMW, IOR, and IOW can be a condition of the compare and data are always valid on the back edges of these bus signals.

Smart Extender-Card Circuit Description

Fig. 22-2 is the circuit schematic of the address decode and port write signals for the eight digital output registers that are used to specify the compare condition from software. The four port addresses decoded are hex 03EO, 03E1, 03E2, and 03E3. The data bus is also buffered here with the SN74LS244 octal driver.

Figs. 22-3 and 22-4 are the circuit schematic diagrams for the digital output-port registers. The output registers are formed using SN74LS374 octal D-type latches with tri-state outputs. Note that the multiplex function between the switches and the output-port bits is accomplished using the tri-state function of the octal latches. When the switches are to be used, the output of the octal latches is disabled by removing a jumper. In this state,

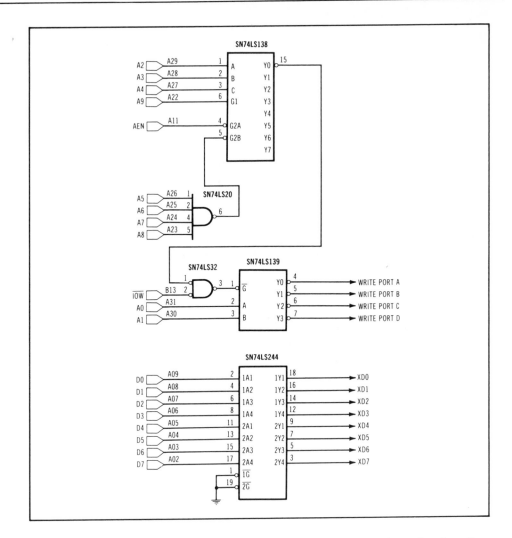

Fig. 22-2. Smart card-extender bus repower and port decode circuits.

the switches drive the input to the compare circuits and the DO outputs are removed from the circuit. Note that when a switch is on or closed, it corresponds to an active low-level compare condition. When the compare conditions are to be specified from the digital output-port bits, the jumper is added, enabling the output of the octal latches. Before the DO register bits can properly drive the compare circuits, all of the switches must be opened. With all of the switches open or off, the compare condition may now be specified under program control by writing the proper bit patterns to the DO register ports using the 8088 microprocessor OUT instruction. A "one" written to a port bit corresponds to a high-level compare condition on the associated input signal.

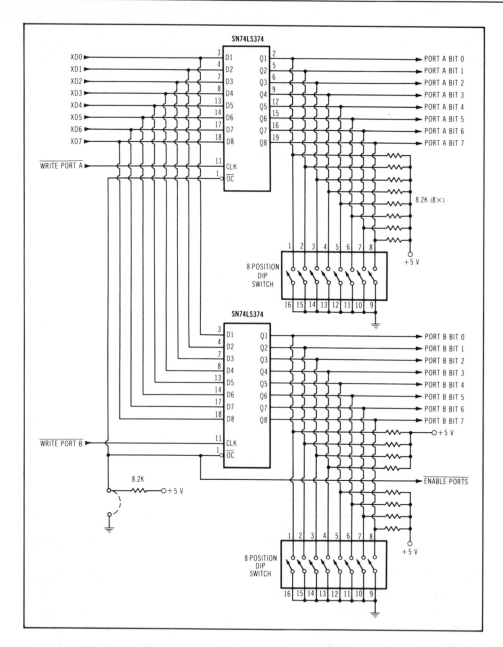

**Fig. 22-3. The port bits and switch compare selector
schematic diagram.**

Fig. 22-5 is the circuit schematic for the compare circuit. This function is
implemented using the SN74LS688 octal compare device. This device
compares the values of two 8-bit bytes and generates a compare "equal"
signal if the two bytes are equal, bit for bit. Four such devices are used to

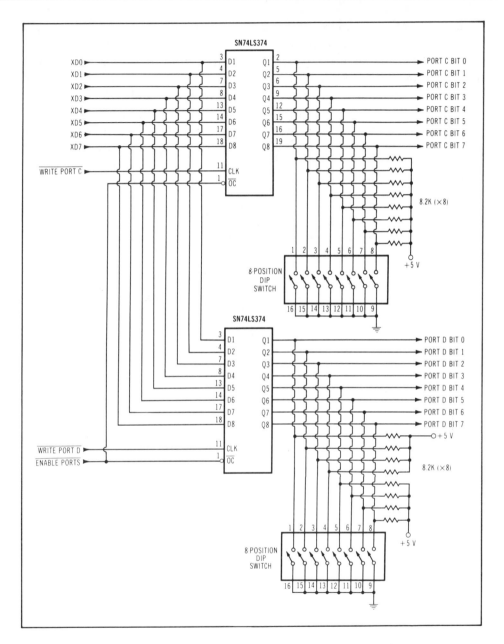

Fig. 22-4. The port bits and switch compare selector schematic diagram.

form the 32-bit compare function that is required. The outputs of each of the four SN74LS688 octal compare devices are ANDed together; thus, requiring all four of the devices to have a compare "equal" condition before a sync signal is generated.

Fig. 22-6 is the circuit schematic for the compare "equal" latch and indicator and the data bus latches and indicators. When a compare "equal" signal is generated, it is fed to three different portions of the circuitry. First, it goes to the sync pin where it can be used as a sync or a trigger for an oscilloscope. Secondly, the signal is used to set a latch which, in turn, drives an indicator, an LED. The latch and indicator may be reset from a momentary-on push-button switch on the card. This indicator allows a visual indication of a compare occurring, without using an oscilloscope. Even

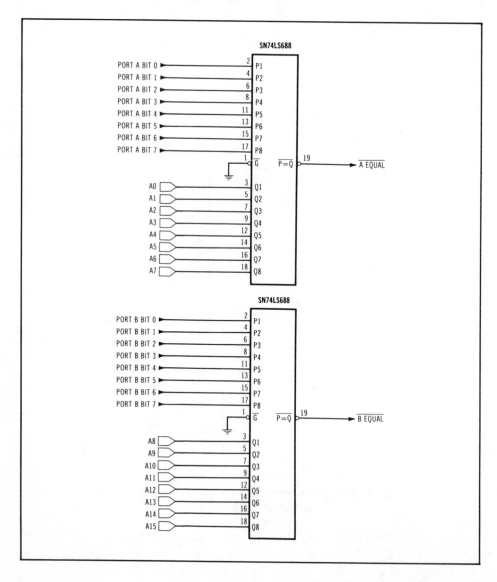

Fig. 22-5. Circuit diagram

if the compare condition is very short or only occurs once, it will be detected and indicated in the LED. The reset button allows the latched compare condition to be reset so that the next condition selected can be detected. The reset button can also be used to determine if an event is occurring repetitively. To determine this condition, simply select the condition that you want to detect. When it lights the indicator, press the reset button. If the indicator does not go out or if it comes back on, the event is looping and occurring repetitively. The last place that the compare

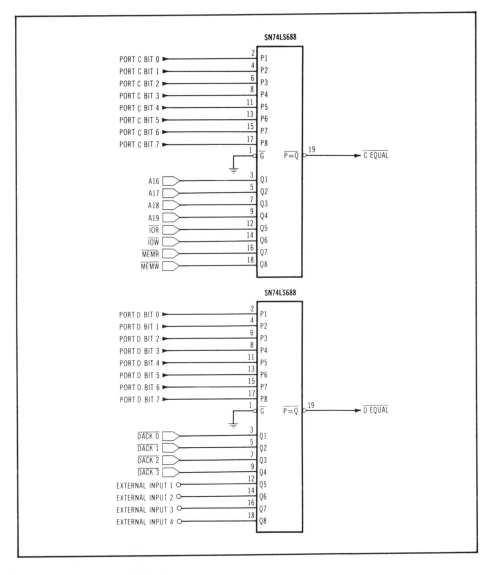

of the compare circuit.

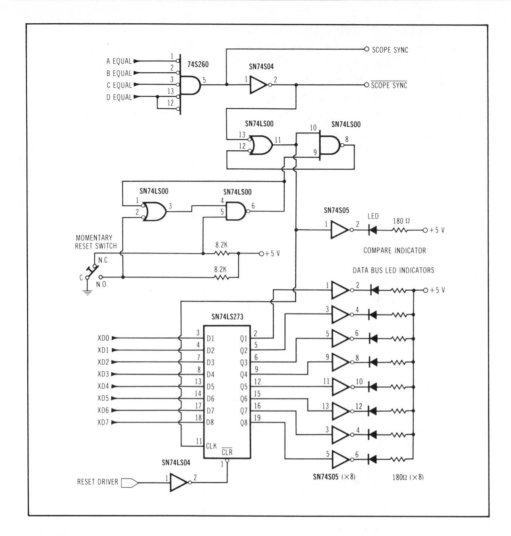

Fig. 22-6. Diagram of the compare latch and indicators circuit.

"equal" signal is used is in the data-bus capture and indicator circuits. In this circuit, the back edge of the compare "equal" or sync signal is used to latch the status of the system data bus. When the bus is captured in the latches, its value is indicated in the eight LEDs attached to the latch outputs. The back edge of the sync or compare signal is used since it can be conditioned with IOR, IOW, MEMR, or MEMW. To obtain valid data-bus status on a bus cycle, you must include one of the preceding bus command signals to ensure that the sample takes place at the time that the data bus contains valid data.

I/O Port Address and Bit Definitions

The following is a summary of the digital output port addresses and the definition of the signals that each bit controls in the compare circuit.

1. DO port A hex address 03E0
    BIT 0 Bus Address Bit 0
    BIT 1 Bus Address Bit 1
    BIT 2 Bus Address Bit 2
    BIT 3 Bus Address Bit 3
    BIT 4 Bus Address Bit 4
    BIT 5 Bus Address Bit 5
    BIT 6 Bus Address Bit 6
    BIT 7 Bus Address Bit 7
2. DO port B hex address 03E1
    BIT 0 Bus Address Bit 8
    BIT 1 Bus Address Bit 9
    BIT 2 Bus Address Bit 10
    BIT 3 Bus Address Bit 11
    BIT 4 Bus Address Bit 12
    BIT 5 Bus Address Bit 13
    BIT 6 Bus Address Bit 14
    BIT 7 Bus Address Bit 15
3. DO port C hex address 03E2
    BIT 0 Bus Address Bit 16
    BIT 1 Bus Address Bit 17
    BIT 2 Bus Address Bit 18
    BIT 3 Bus Address Bit 19
    BIT 4 Bus Signal IOR (Negative Active)
    BIT 5 Bus Signal IOW (Negative Active)
    BIT 6 Bus Signal MEMR (Negative Active)
    BIT 7 Bus Signal MEMW (Negative Active)
4. DO port D hex address 03E3
    BIT 0 Bus Signal DACKO (Negative Active)
    BIT 1 Bus Signal DACK1 (Negative Active)
    BIT 2 Bus Signal DACK2 (Negative Active)
    BIT 3 Bus Signal DACK3 (Negative Active)
    BIT 4 External Input 1
    BIT 5 External Input 2
    BIT 6 External Input 3
    BIT 7 External Input 4

DOS DEBUG PROGRAM

As part of the IBM DOS package, a special program called DEBUG is provided. This program is extremely useful in debugging both hardware and software. It provides a system debug monitor with many functions that you will find useful. You will find a full description of DEBUG and its capabilities in the *IBM Disk Operating System Manual* (see Section 6). The following is a brief summary of the commands and functions available in DEBUG.

——Compare two blocks of system memory.
——Display the contents of system memory.
——Display and modify the contents of system memory.
——Fill the memory with data or data from a string.
——Go and execute the program at a specified address.
——Specify break points in a program and display system status.
——Load data from a diskette into memory.
——Move the contents of memory from one location to another.
——Send data to an I/O port.
——Display the contents of the 8088 registers and flags.
——Search system memory for data specified in a string.
——Trace the execution of a program and display 8088 MPU status.
——Disassemble an assembly language program.
——Write a block of system memory to diskette.

BIBLIOGRAPHY

Intel Corporation, *1982 Component Data Catalog*, January 1982.

Intel Corporation, *iAPX 88 Book*, July 1981.

Intel Corporation, *iAPX 86,88 User's Manual*, August 1981.

Mostek Corporation, *Mostek 1980 Bytewyde Memory Data Book*, April 1980.

National Semiconductor Corporation, *Interface Data Book*, 1980.

Signetics Corporation, *Bipolar and MOS Memory Data Manual 1980*, 1980.

Texas Instruments Incorporated, *The TTL Data Book for Design Engineers, Second Edition*, 1981.

Texas Instruments Incorporated, *1981 Supplement to the TTL Data Book for Design Engineers, Second Edition*, 1981.

Texas Instruments Incorporated, *The Interface Circuits Data Book for Design Engineers, First Edition*, 1977.

International Business Machines Corporation, *Technical Reference, First Edition*, from the IBM Personal Computer Hardware Reference Library, August 1981.

International Business Machines Corporation, *BASIC, First Edition*, from the IBM Personal Computer Hardware Reference Library, August 1981.

International Business Machines Corporation, *Disk Operating System*, from the IBM Personal Computer Computer Language Series, 1982.

International Business Machines Corporation, *Macro Assembler, First Edition*, from the IBM Personal Computer Computer Language Series, December 1981.

INDEX

Interfacing to the IBM Personal Computer

Status register, 111
  definitions, 105
  Stepper motor(s), 207-209
  pulse, 209
  manufacturers of, 209
Stepping motors
  bifilar, 208
  permanent-magnet, 207-208
Strobe
  hardware-triggered, 124
  software-triggered, 124
Subroutines in BASIC, assembly language,
    216
Switch
  debounce, 205
  -selectable decode, 130-132, 141
  sensing, 204-205
System
  board
    bus, 22-24
    DMA, 26
    functions, 21-27
    integrated I/O adapters, 27
    interrupts, 26-27
    RAM, 25
    ROM, 24-25
    timer/counter, 25-26
  -bus
    card slots, 75-76
    drive capability, 69-70
    load presented in card slots, 70-73
    loading and driving capabilities, 69-74
    mechanical and power characteristics,
      75-80
    timings, 60-68
  direct-memory access, 101-116
  initialization for interrupts, 86-87
  interrupts, 81-100
  keyboard, 14
  memory, I/O map, and decoding techni-
      ques, 125-141
  printer, 14-15
  timers and counters, 117-124
  Unit, 11, 12, 120
    bus operations, 42-51
    card slot, 225
    power, 78-79
    processor board, 21-27

T

TC (terminal count), 58
Temporary register, 111
Terminal count
  interrupt-on, 123
  signal, 116

Terminator, data bus, 220
TEST definition, 32
Testing
  bits in a DI register, 166
  designs, hardware and software for, 225-
      236
Timer(s)
  and counters, system, 117-124
  counter(s)
    8253-5, 176
    channels, system use of the, 117-119
    control gating for, 178-181
    design, 175-184
    I/O address, 120-121
    modes of operation, 122-124
    programming the, 120-122
    system board, 25-26
Timing
  and counting functions
    adding extended, 175-184
    expanding, 183-184
    bus cycle, 60, 62-67
    diagrams and tables, 60-67
    system-bus, 60-68
Transfer rate, maximum DMA, 115
Transition-sensing DI register, 161-163

U

Usage map
  I/O port addressing and, 125-127
  memory, 137-138
  USR function, 216

V

VARPTR function, 216
Vector table
  initialization, interrupt, 88-90
  interrupt controller, 90

W

WAIT command, 215
Wait-state generation, 142-150
  8088, 142-150
  in the memory bus cycles, 142-144
  for the I/O bus cycles, 145-146
  on DMA bus cycles, 147-150
Write
  request register, 107
  single-mask bit register, 107
    definitions, 108
Writing the counters, 121-122

TO THE READER

Sams Computer books cover Fundamentals — Programming — Interfacing — Technology written to meet the needs of computer engineers, professionals, scientists, technicians, students, educators, business owners, personal computerists and home hobbyists.

Our Tradition is to meet your needs and in so doing we invite you to tell us what your needs and interests are by completing the following:

1. I need books on the following topics:

_____

_____

_____

_____

_____

_____

_____

2. I have the following Sams titles:

_____

_____

_____

_____

_____

_____

_____

3. My occupation is:

_____ Scientist, Engineer	_____ D P Professional
_____ Personal computerist	_____ Business owner
_____ Technician, Serviceman	_____ Computer store owner
_____ Educator	_____ Home hobbyist
_____ Student	Other _____
	_____

Name (print) _____

Address _____

City _____ State _____ Zip _____

Mail to: **Howard W. Sams & Co., Inc.**
Marketing Dept. #CBS1/80
4300 W. 62nd St., P.O. Box 7092
Indianapolis, Indiana 46206

22027